MW00658846

Applying the ADA

Designing for The 2010 Americans with Disabilities Act Standards for Accessible Design in Multiple Building Types

Marcela Abadi Rhoads, AIA RAS

WILEY

Cover Design: Anne Michele Abbott
Cover Illustrations: Courtesy of Marcela Abadi Rhoads

This book is printed on acid-free paper. ∞

Published by John Wiley & Sons, Inc., Hoboken, New Jersey
Published simultaneously in Canada

Library of Congress Cataloging-in-Publication Data:

Rhoads, Marcela Abadi.
Applying the ADA : Designing for The 2010 Americans with Disabilities Act Standards for Accessible Design in Multiple Building Types / Marcela Rhoads.
pages cm
Includes index.
ISBN 978-1-118-02786-8 (pbk.), ISBN 978-1-118-41588-7 (ebk.); ISBN 978-1-118-41869-7 (ebk.);
ISBN 978-1-118-43360-7 (ebk.)
1. Barrier-free design—United States. 2. United States. Americans with Disabilities Act of 1990.
3. United States. Architectural Barriers Act of 1968. I. Title.
NA2545.P5R49 2013
720.87—dc23

2012049090

Printed in the United States of America

10 9 8 7 6 5 4 3 2 1

Contents

Acknowledgments ix

Introduction xi
History xi
Summary xii

Chapter 1
GENERAL GUIDELINES 1
by Marcela Abadi Rhoads, AIA RAS
General Guidelines 1
Building Blocks 2
Accessible Routes 9
General Site 10
  Changes in Level 16
Accessible Entrances 16
  Interior Accessible Route 17
Plumbing Fixtures 18
Communication Features 23
Summary 25

Chapter 2
RETAIL AND MIXED-USE FACILITIES 27
by Marcela Abadi Rhoads, AIA RAS

Introduction 27
Shopping Malls 28
- Site Arrival Points 28
- Minimum Number of Parking Spaces Closest to the Entrances **29**
- Accessible Route to Entrances **32**
- Accessible Entrances **38**
- Interior Accessible Route to Spaces **38**
- Retail Spaces **41**
- Checkout and Sales Counters **43**
- Dressing and Fitting Rooms **44**
- Employee Areas **46**
- Common-Use Spaces **52**
- Food Court **56**
- Play Areas **60**

Strip Shopping Center 61
- Site Arrival Point **63**
- Parking **66**
- Accessible Route **66**
- Tenant Entrances **66**

Lifestyle Center 72
- Parking **72**
- Accessible Route **74**
- Residential Facilities/Offices on Upper Floors **75**

Summary 81

Chapter 3
PRIMARY EDUCATION 85
by Wally Tirado, ICC RAS

Introduction 85
Administrative Areas 86
- Employee Work Areas **87**
- Service Areas **88**
- Service Yards and Loading Docks **89**

General Application for Children Areas 89
- Reach Ranges and Operating Mechanisms **92**
- Dining and Work Surfaces **92**

Toilet Rooms and Elements 97
- Drinking Fountains **98**

Toilet Compartments 99
Water Closets and Accessories 99
Mirrors 102
Lavatories and Sinks 102
Dressing and Fitting Rooms 104
Signage 104
Ramps and Stairs 106
Assembly Areas 108
Outdoor Play Areas 111
Transportation Facilities 112
Passenger Loading Zones 112
Bus Loading Zones 112
Summary 113

Chapter 4
SECONDARY AND POSTSECONDARY EDUCATION 117
by Wally Tirado, ICC RAS
Introduction 117
Accessible Sites and Parking 118
Bus Loading Zones 118
Location and Dispersion of Parking 120
Leased/Assigned Parking 121
Playing Fields and Exterior Athletic Facilities 122
General Accessible Areas 127
Security Barriers 128
Temporary Structures and Facilities 129
Assembly Areas 129
Classrooms 130
Other Box Seating and Outdoor Seating 132
Performance Areas 135
Assistive Listening Systems (ALS) 141
Ticket Booths and Concession Stands 142
Libraries 142
Physical Education Facilities 143
Exercise Machines and Equipment 143
Dressing, Fitting, and Locker Rooms 146
Swimming Pools 148
Other Spectator Sports Areas 150
Dining Facilities 151
Administrative Areas 153
Housing at a Place of Education 158
Kitchens 159
Multi-Bedroom 159

Apartment or Townhouse Facilities 159
Summary 160

Chapter 5
HOSPITALITY 163
by Jeromy Murphy, AIA RAS
Introduction 163
New Construction 164
Existing Facilities 164
Public and Guest Areas 164
Guest Rooms with Mobility Features or Communications Features 173
Examples 177
Summary 179

Chapter 6
HEALTHCARE AND SENIOR LIVING COMMUNITIES 183
by Greg Hunteman, AIA RAS
Introduction 183
Different Types of Healthcare 183
Alterations to Existing Healthcare and Long-Term Care Facilities 184
General Guidelines 186
Accessible Routes 186
Individual Spaces 190
Patient and Resident Sleeping Rooms 191
Summary 198

Chapter 7
AMUSEMENT PARKS AND PLAY AREAS 201
by Marcela Abadi Rhoads, AIA RAS
Site Arrival 202
Play Areas 204
Ground Play Components 206
Elevated Play Components 209
Accessible Route 210
Entry Points and Seats 217
Play for Visually and Hearing Impaired 217
Amusement Rides 217
Fishing Piers 229
Summary 231

Chapter 8
HISTORIC PRESERVATION AND REMODELS 235
by Marcela Abadi Rhoads, AIA RAS

Alterations 236
Entrances 242
Accessible Route 242
Path of Travel Elements 243
Tenant Finish-Outs 244
Alterations of Medical Care Facilities' Patient Rooms 245
Alterations of Transient Lodging Sleeping Rooms 246
Alterations of Holding Cells 247
Alterations of Residential Dwelling Units 248
Alterations of Restaurants 249
Alterations of Dressing Rooms and Lockers Rooms 249
Disproportionality: The 20% Rule 249
Series of Smaller Alterations 250
Safe Harbor 251
Historic Facilities 252
Summary 254

Chapter 9
RESIDENTIAL PROJECTS 259
by Jeromy Murphy, AIA RAS

Introduction 259
- Residential versus Transient Lodging 259
- Applicability 260
- Public and Common Use Spaces 263
- Residential Dwelling Units 265

Summary 270

Chapter 10
UNIVERSAL DESIGN BEYOND THE ADA 273
by Marcela Abadi Rhoads, AIA RAS

PRINCIPLE ONE: Equitable Use 274
- Principle One Design Guidelines 274

PRINCIPLE TWO: Flexibility in Use 277
- Principle Two Design Guidelines 278

PRINCIPLE THREE: Simple and Intuitive Use 282
- Principle Three Design Guidelines 282

PRINCIPLE FOUR: Perceptible Information **285**
Principle Four Design Guidelines **286**
PRINCIPLE FIVE: Tolerance for Error **289**
Principle Five Design Guidelines **289**
PRINCIPLE SIX: Low Physical Effort **294**
Principle Six Design Guidelines **294**
PRINCIPLE SEVEN: Size and Space for Approach and Use **298**
Principle Seven Design Guidelines **298**
Summary **302**

Appendix A:
REFERENCE TABLES 303

Appendix B:
RESOURCES 317

Index 319

Acknowledgments

To be asked to write a book in one's lifetime is a great honor and achievement. But it is not often that one gets a second opportunity to write a book. I would like to thank once again my publisher John Wiley and Sons for the opportunity they gave me to write this book. I especially would like to thank Kathryn Bourgoine, her assistant, Danielle Giordano, and senior production editor Nancy Cintron for their patience and guidance. I would also like to acknowledge John Czarnecki, who had the foresight to ask me to write it.

I want to thank my wonderful husband, Dale, and my beautiful children, Linda Hannah and Jacob, for being always patient and supportive through this process.

Thank you to colleagues and contributors Wally Tirado, RAS; Jeromy Murphy, AIA, RAS; and Greg Hunteman AIA, RAS for contributing to the chapters and making this an even better book! This book also would not have been finished without the amazing assistance from Loretta Head and Janis Geleott, their hours of proofreading and editing the chapters. Lastly, I would like to thank Sara Jane Goldenberg for her clerical assistance and Celia Mendoza for her assistance with the photography and for her friendship!

To all who supported me, gave me insight, and allowed me to achieve this milestone, I'm eternally grateful.

Introduction

More than 50 million Americans have some kind of physical, sensory, cognitive, or mental disability. The building industry, including design professionals, builders, and owners, has been addressing the elimination of architectural barriers for these disabled persons for many years. In 1973, The U.S. Access Board was created. Its purpose was to develop and enforce accessibility rules and guidelines and to assist the building industry in eliminating the barriers that still exist for the disabled citizens. The Access Board helped develop guidelines that describe which buildings and facilities have to be made accessible and how to achieve that accessibility. The guidelines for federal agencies and facilities was developed and is found in The Architectural Barriers Act (ABA), which was adopted in 1968. The rules and guidelines for private and nonfederal public entities were developed after that; they are found in the Americans with Disabilities Act Accessibility Guidelines (ADAAG), which were adopted in 1991 after the passage of the Americans with Disabilities Act. After several years of receiving public comments, and internal deliberation about the contents and application, in 2004 the Access Board combined both sets of rules and reformatted them as a new version. Six years later, the Department of Justice adopted the 2004 ADAAG as the law of the land, and renamed it wthe 2010 ADA Standards for Accessible Design. This book will discuss the new guidelines and will explain how to apply these to new facilities as well as existing facilities.

This book will assist designers, contractors, and owners to apply the standards for their particular situation. Each chapter takes a different building type and explains how to design it using the 2010 ADA Standards. The reader will learn how to avoid certain pitfalls, which could create problems for access in the future.

HISTORY

During the Civil Rights movement of the 1960s, the disabled community began to have their voices heard by the government. It all started in 1961, when the American National Standard Institute (ANSI) passed the first set of guidelines to ensure that persons with disabilities would be able to enter and use public buildings. In 1968, Congress passed the first accessibility law, The Architectural Barriers Act of 1968. This was the first effort to ensure access to the built environment. The act mandated that the ANSI guidelines be followed. Subsequent guidelines began to emerge and culminated with the Americans with Disabilities Act (ADA), which was signed into law by President George H. W. Bush on July 26, 1990. It is undeniably the most comprehensive formulation for the rights of the people with disabilities in the history of the United States or of any other nation.

The ADA is divided into several parts called "Titles." Title III of the ADA established design requirements for the construction or alteration of facilities. It covers facilities in the private sector (places of public accommodation and commercial facilities) and the public sector (state and local government facilities). In 1991, the Access Board published the ADAAG, which serves as the basis for rules used to enforce the law. Along with the ADAAG, the Architectural Barriers Act (ABA) is another set of guidelines that requires that buildings and facilities that are designed, constructed, or altered with federal funds, or leased by a federal agency, comply with federal standards of construction for physical accessibility. ABA requirements were adopted in 1968 and set the path for a set of architectural standards called the Uniform Federal Accessibility Standards, in which new and altered buildings and in newly leased facilities had to be accessible. They do not address the activities conducted in those buildings and facilities. Facilities of the U.S. Postal Service are also covered by the ABA.

The Access Board has updated its guidelines for ABA facilities jointly with the new ADA guidelines so that there are higher levels of harmonization under both laws. In the revised guidelines, both the ADA and the ABA rules are included. Not only were the two accessibility guidelines combined, but they were also formatted to more closely match the American National Standard Institute's (ANSI) format, which are the standards used by the model codes.

Facilities built or altered according to earlier versions of the ADA or ABA standards will not necessarily have to meet the new adopted version, except when they are subsequently altered or renovated. Therefore, if facilities have been built prior to the new rules, they will be accepted as they are until a new construction or renovation occurs. This is called a "safe harbor." The Department of Justice (DOJ), which regulates requirements for existing facilities under the ADA, intends to address coverage of facilities built or altered according to the original ADA standards in its rule making to update the standards. It will also address facilities retrofitted under ADA provisions for existing facilities, such as the requirement for barrier removal in places of public accommodation.

SUMMARY

With the passage of the ADA civil rights law, which prohibits discrimination on the basis of disability, the disabled members of our society are able to enjoy the freedom that most other American citizens have, to hold down jobs, travel, and be more independent. Barriers in the built environment, such as stairs in front of an entrance, curbs without ramps, or lack of accessible parking, prevent citizens with disabilities from being productive members of society. The accessibility guidelines that have been put in place by the U.S. government ensures that every member of our society will have the opportunity to live and produce to the best of their abilities. This book will guide the reader to better understand how the rules to eliminate barriers in the built environment apply to everyday life and how to best implement them in the design and construction of facilities.

General Guidelines

1

by Marcela Abadi Rhoads, AIA RAS

GENERAL GUIDELINES

The Americans with Disabilities Act design standards established guidelines to provide accessibility to commercial buildings and public accommodation facilities. The guidelines are general in nature, and even though they address most conditions, each facility is different. This chapter will address the general guidelines that affect the building types that you will find in the remainder of the book. Many of the figures shown in this book were taken directly from the 2010 ADA Standards. As such, their dimensions and nomenclature are shown exactly the way they are depicted in the Standards. The following figure shows the way the ADA delineates dimension and gives measurements.

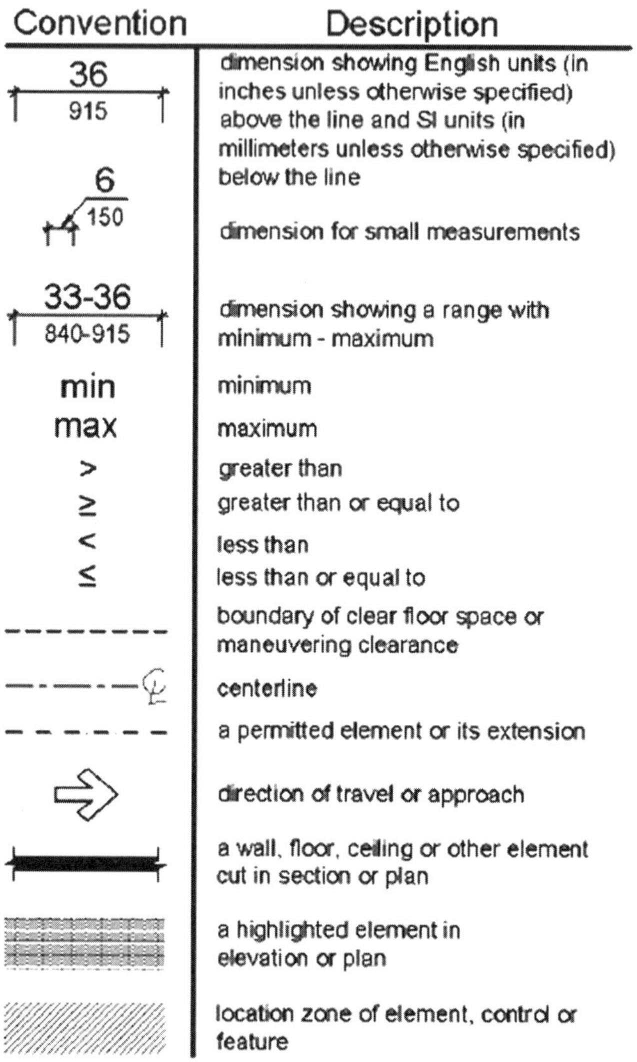

Figure 104
Graphic Convention for Figures

BUILDING BLOCKS

A person with disabilities occupies a certain amount of space. The space is measured both in plan and in section. A person with different disabilities uses certain equipment for either mobility or wayfinding. A person in a wheelchair will require a certain amount of space, typically 30 inches x 48 inches of floor space (see Figure 1.1).

If there are larger wheelchairs, such as power wheelchairs, Segways, and the like, they might even need more space. The ADA Standards are only the minimum requirements, and

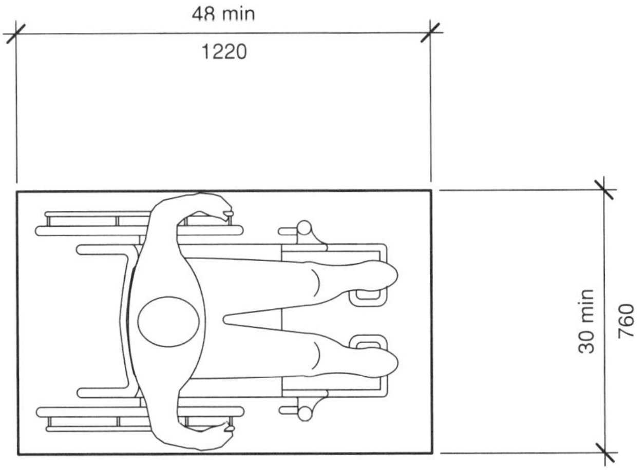

Figure 1.1: ADA Figure 305.3. Clear Floor Space Required [for wheelchairs]. The space required for a wheelchair is a minimum of 30 inches × 48 inches, and when required, it should have a slope of no greater than 2% in all directions.

whenever there is an option to have more space, one should allow for that. Vertical clearances are also required, which allow for maneuvering (see Figure 1.2).

Wheelchairs are not the only type of mobility equipment that requires certain amount of space. Persons with limited mobility who use walkers and crutches, for example, and visually impaired people who use white canes or service animals will also require a certain amount of clear floor space (see Figure 1.3).

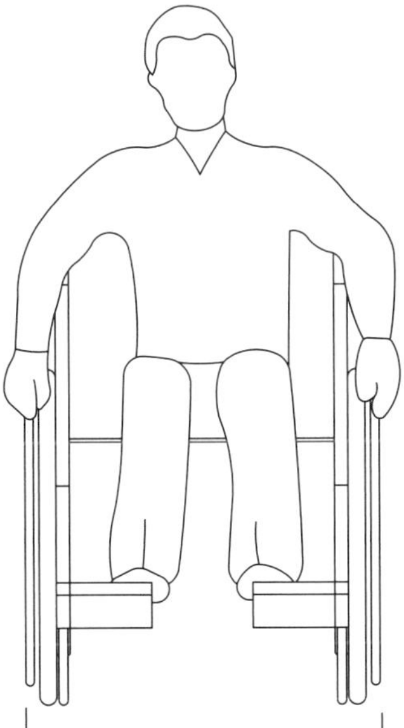

Figure 1.2a: This is a minimum width that a standard wheelchair will require.

Figure 1.2b: Vertical clearances take into consideration the wheelchair and the person using the wheelchair.

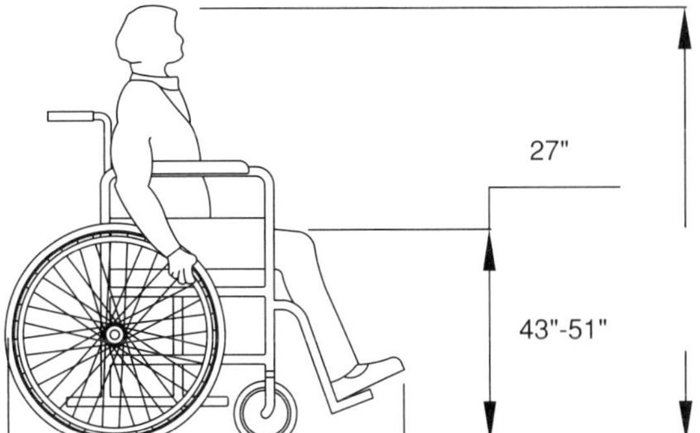

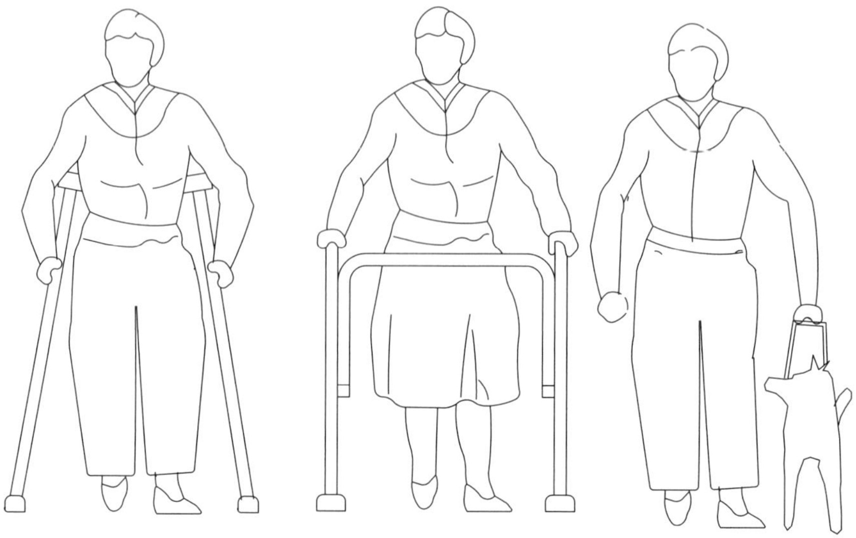

Figure 1.3: Crutches, walkers, and service animals will require different clearances. The minimum ADA requirements take into consideration these other devices.

The ADA has an entire chapter that specifically designates all the dimensions for the minimum amount of space that will be required for a person with disabilities to use and maneuver around the area. The clear floor dimensions provided in the chapter also work for the amount of space that a person with disabilities will require to turn around once he or she is inside the space. The chapter gives two types of turning clearances: a circle and a "T" (see Figures 1.4 and 1.5).

When designing a space for turning, keep in mind that a person in a wheelchair does not make a perfect circle when turning. He or she will probably need a space greater than 60 inches in diameter to turn. Also, the clearances on the floor must be clear from obstructions, as well as have a slope of 2% maximum in every direction of the space where for turning is to be completed.

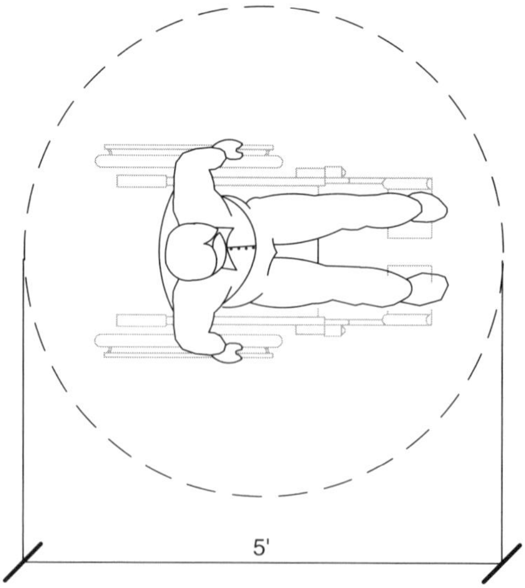

Figure 1.4: A 60-inch-diameter circle is the minimum amount of space that a wheelchair will require to make 180° turn.

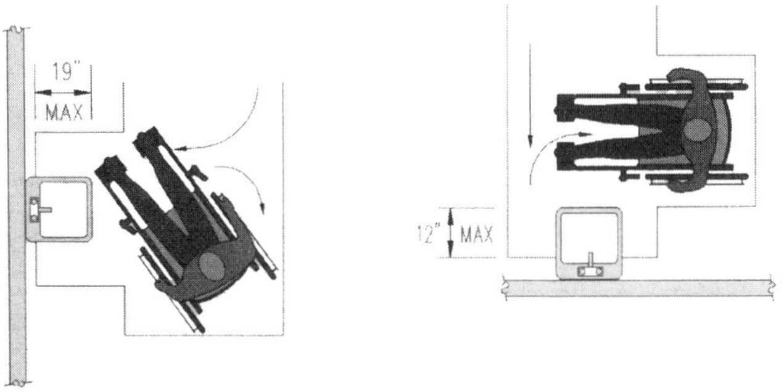

Figure 1.5: "T" turn. When there is not enough room for a 60-inch-diameter circle, space for a "T" turn is allowed.

The ADA also has guidelines for persons who are visually impaired, in order to protect them from hurting themselves with objects they cannot detect with their canes as they walk. These are called "protruding objects." A wall-mounted object is considered a "protruding object" if it is mounted higher than 27 inches from the ground, it projects more than 4 inches from the mounting surface, and it is located along a circulation path (see Figure 1.6).

There is a misconception on what constitutes a "circulation path." A circulation path is not an accessible route for a wheelchair. A circulation path is not the main hallway or corridor where

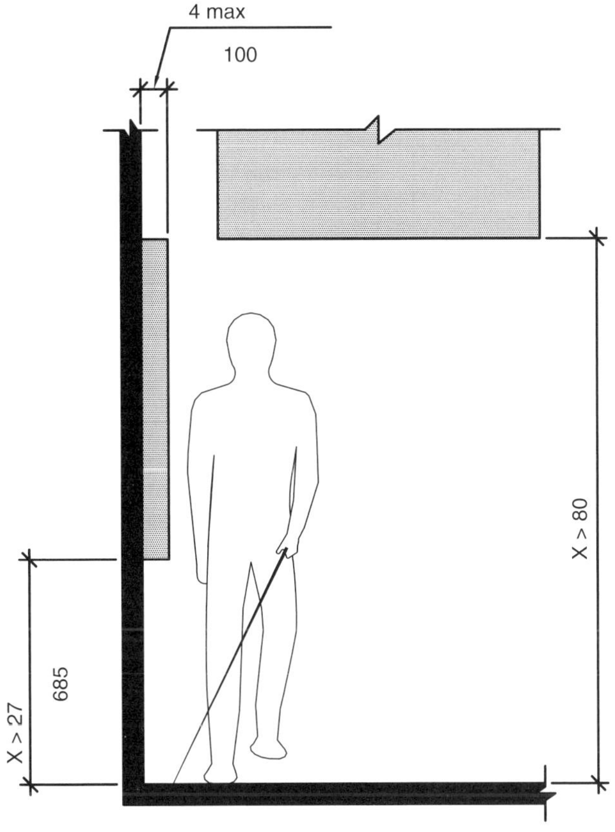

Figure 1.6: ADA figure 307.2. An object mounted higher than 27 inches from the ground or lower than 80 inches from the ground cannot be detected by a person who is visually impaired. A cane, which some visually impaired people use for wayfinding, can only detect objects mounted below 27 inches.

Figure 1.7: This drinking fountain is not located along the main path of travel, but it is a protruding object because it is along a path of travel that a blind person would use.

people walk. A circulation path is any path of travel used by a pedestrian, including the path of travel inside and around any interior space. The path of travel that a person uses inside a restroom to find the plumbing fixtures is the circulation path. Because a person who is visually impaired cannot see a sign directing him to a "designated" circulation path, we must design all walls inside an interior space or exterior space without protruding objects. If, along the path of travel, there is a permanent object mounted lower than 27 inches or even mounted on the ground, this will be detectable by a person using a cane for wayfinding (see Figure 1.7).

The ADA not only discusses the clearances for knees, toes, and floor space, but it also gives recommendations and guidelines for the way elements operate. A person with limited dexterity, arthritis, or no use of the hands will have a hard time opening or closing elements or operating any type of mechanism unless it is built in accordance with the standards. An operating mechanism should be able to be used without tight grasping, pulling, or twisting of the wrist. Also the amount of force that is required to operate it should be no more than 5 lbs. (see Figure 1.8). These requirements are universal. They help not only those who are disabled but also others who may not be able to use their hands temporarily.

The operating mechanisms will also be required to be at certain heights. There are forward approaches and side approaches that have minimum requirements according to the ADA (see Figure 1.9).

Sometimes the object that people are reaching for is over an obstruction. The obstruction could be a counter, an appliance, or even a doorway. There are reach range requirements provided for those conditions as well (see Figure 1.10).

In some instances, building owners place storage cabinets above toilets. They use them especially in single user restrooms where storage is scarce. But in doing so, they have violated

Figure 1.8: An accessible operable part should not require tight grasping or twisting of the wrist to use.

the reach ranges required over an obstruction. Since most toilets are deeper than 24", the cabinet would have to be mounted at 44" a.f.f. which would then become a hazard to the person using the water closet, since it would be so low. But if they mount it higher a person would not be able to reach the cabinet. ADA requires that at least one cabinet be accessible if it is located in a common use space (such as a restroom). This would violate that requirement. (See Figure 1.10c)

Figure 1.9a and 1.9b: ADA Figures 308.2.1 and 308.3.1. Operating mechanisms are mounted for a forward or a side approach.

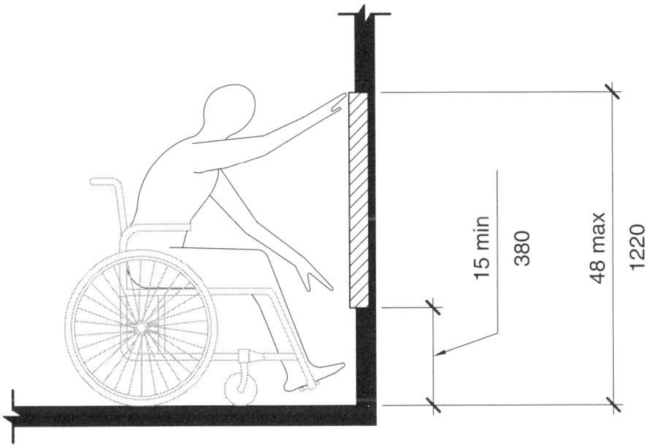

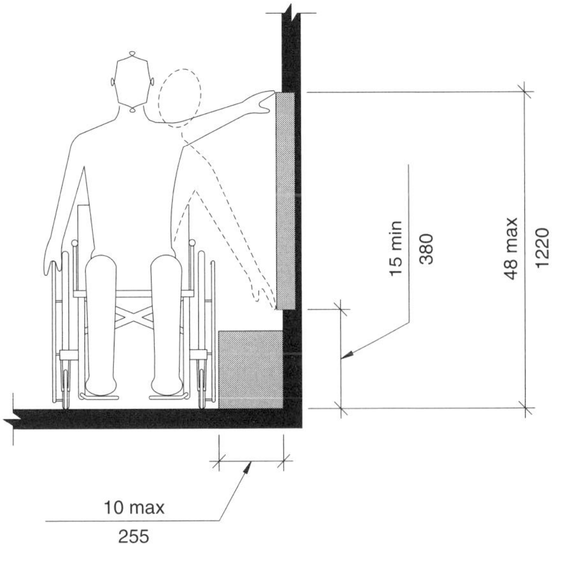

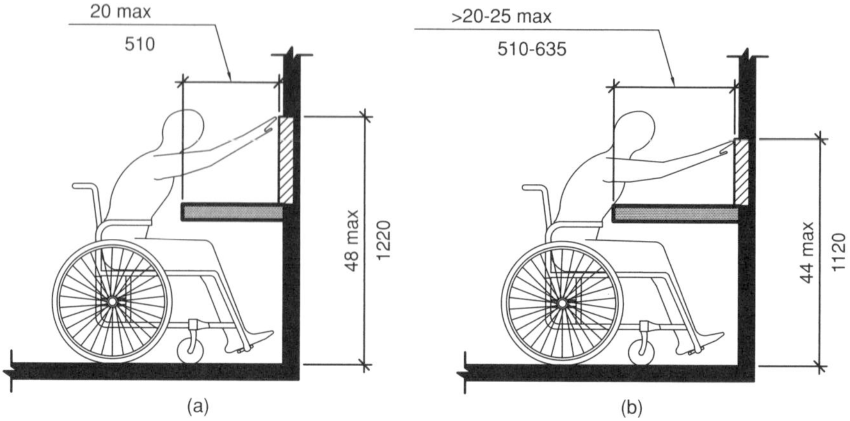

Figure 1.10a: ADA Figure 308.2.2. Objects mounted over a counter are required to be mounted lower so that a person with a disability can reach and operate them.

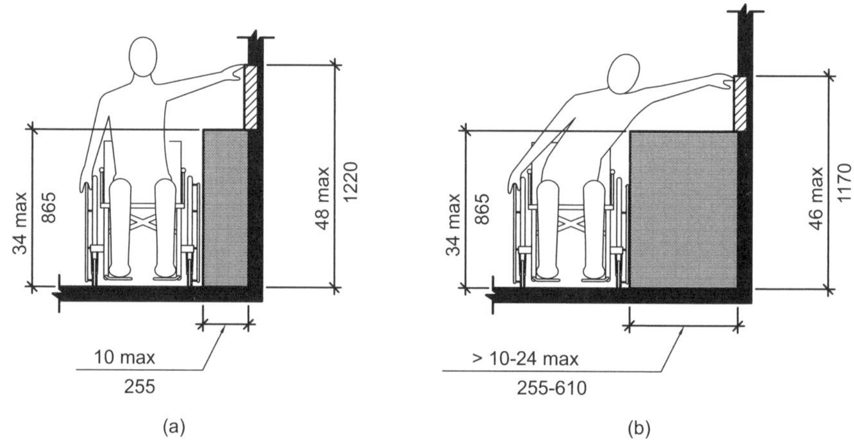

Figure 1.10b: ADA Figure 308.3.2 shows the requirements for objects located so that people must reach sideways over obstructions.

Figure 1.10c: The cabinet located above the toilet does not meet the reach ranges as directed by the ADA Standards.

ACCESSIBLE ROUTES

All routes that are used by people in wheelchairs or with mobility equipment are considered their "accessible routes." Such a route must meet the requirements in Chapter 4 of the ADA Standards. They must be 36 inches wide, but the width can be reduced to 32 inches if the path has a depth of 24 inches (see Figure 1.11).

The running slopes along the accessible route should be no greater than 5%, and the cross slope should be no greater than 2%. If slopes are greater, it becomes harder to maneuver along the path. If a slope along the accessible route is between 5% and 8.33%, that is considered a ramp and it must then have handrails on both sides, landings at the top and bottom of the ramp run, and edge protection as specified in Section 405 of the ADA Standards.

The ADA requires that at least one accessible route be provided within the site from public streets or sidewalks. An accessible route to the accessible entrances served must connect each site arrival point. The ADA advises that, if there are multiple arrival points, including multiple bus stops near the site, each one should be located along an accessible route and each must connect to the accessible entrances. It is difficult to determine which site arrival point a disabled person will be using; therefore, in order to avoid discriminating, all arrival points should be made accessible. If pedestrian access is not provided and the only means of access is vehicular, then the site arrival point will begin at the parking space.

If any part of the accessible route crosses a curb, a curb ramp must be installed. The requirements for a curb ramp are similar to those for ramps, except that they do not need to have handrails. The minimum width is 36 inches, and the maximum slope must be 1:12. A 36-inch landing at the top of the ramp must also be provided (see Figure 1.12).

Along the accessible route, doorways must be accessible. But the ADA makes a distinction between doors used for passage and those that are not used for passage. Only those manual doors used for passage must comply with the Standards. This means that a shallow closet may not be deep enough for users to enter it fully and therefore the door will not be used for passage into the closet. That door will not be required to meet the ADA guidelines.

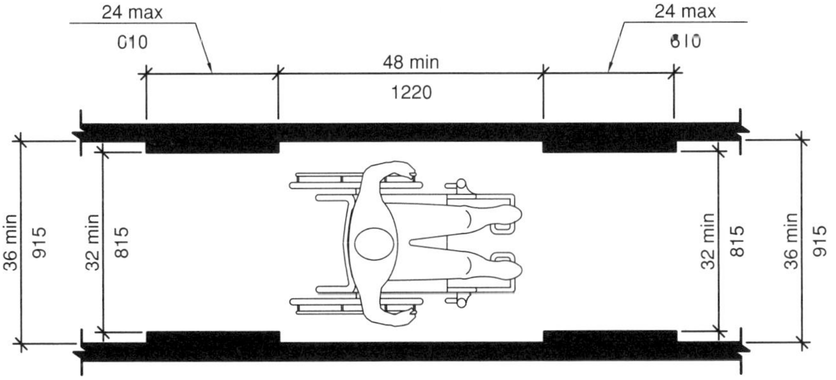

Figure 1.11: ADA Figure 403.5.1. This figure shows the allowable width reduction along the accessible route.

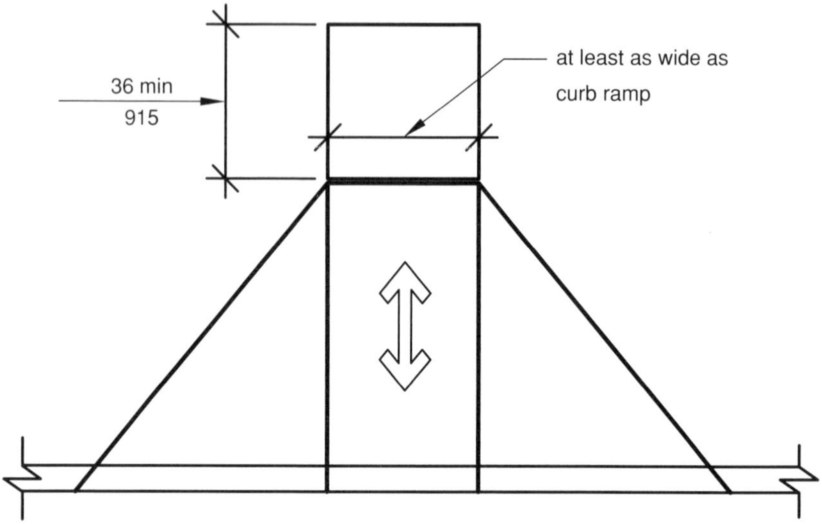

Figure 1.12: ADA Figure 406.4. This figure shows the landing required at the top of the curb ramps.

Doors used for passage or entry must have a minimum clear width of 32 inches, although most commercial doors are specified as 36 inches wide. A 36-inch-wide door will ensure compliance, since a 32-inch clear width is required for a wheelchair to get through. In addition to the appropriate width, the door hardware must be a type that does not require tight grasping and twisting of the wrist to operate. Also there needs to be enough maneuvering clearance at the door that a person in a wheelchair can easily reach the door handle, open the door, and get out of the way of the door to get through. The clearance to reach the door handle must be unobstructed by any permanent objects, including sinks or counters (see Figures 1.13 and 1.14).

The maneuvering clearances at the door must also be at no more than 2%, since a person in a wheelchair would not be able to reach the door handle without the worry of rolling down a steep slope before opening the door. Door opening forces should also be 5 lbs. maximum, and the door must not close in less than 5 seconds. An exterior door does not have the same requirements, since there are many factors that affect the opening force of an exterior door. Automatic doors are sometimes installed as the exterior doors to make it easier for a person with disabilities to open them and maneuver into the building (see Figure 1.15).

GENERAL SITE

At accessible facilities where parking is provided, accessible parking will also have to be provided. The two main considerations of parking are the minimum number of accessible parking spaces required and their location in relation to facility entrances. The minimum number of parking spaces is determined by The ADA table 208.2 (refer to Figure 1.16). This table is used by looking at the total number of parking spaces provided in a parking facility and allocating a minimum number of accessible parking spaces accordingly. Both a surface parking lot and a parking garage are considered facilities.

Figure 1.13: This door handle is obstructed by the paper towel dispenser, since it is closer than 18 inches, which prevents a person in a wheelchair from reaching it to open it.

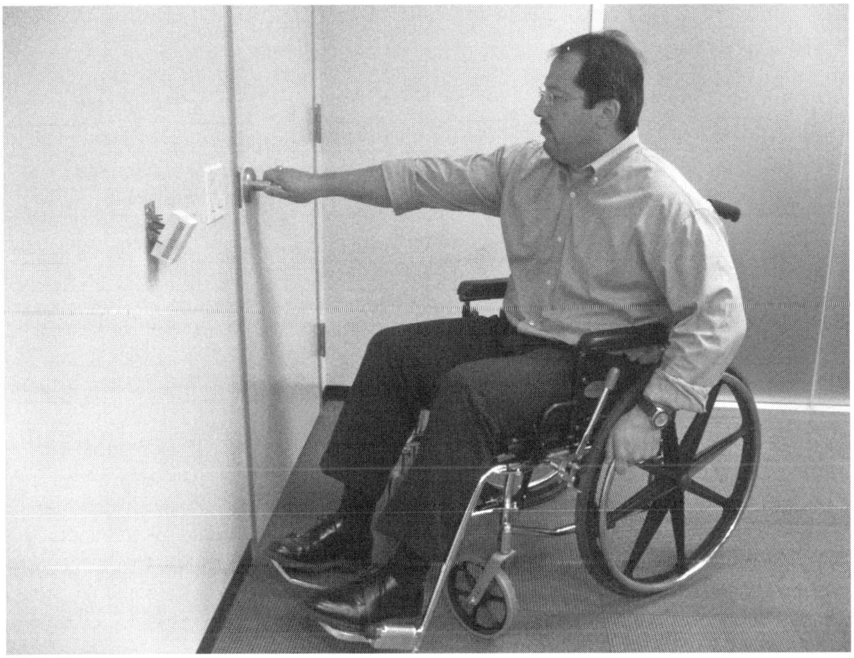

Figure 1.14: This door has plenty of room for a person in a wheelchair to reach the door handle and open the door.

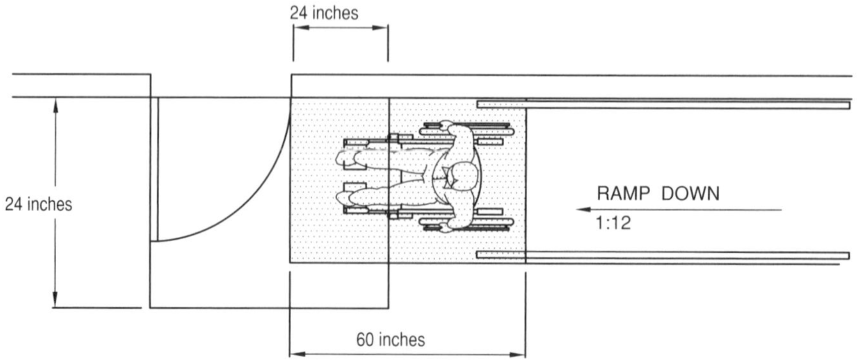

Figure 1.15: A ramp exiting close to a doorway, must be far enough away to allow for enough clearance at the door that a person in a wheelchair can open it to enter the building.

When designing a building or a campus of buildings, the planner will locate the building and then arrange the parking closest to it. In order to determine the minimum number of accessible parking spaces required, the planner will have to ask how many parking facilities will be provided and which building entrance each will serve. When there is only one building, there is technically only one large parking facility, if only surface parking is provided. If there is a combination of surface parking and parking garages, then the entire surface parking will be considered one facility, and each individual parking garage will be counted as a separate facility. If there are multiple buildings on the site, the parking locations should be determined by making sure at least one accessible parking space will be provided at each building and as close to its entrance as possible. There will be unique situations, such as campus-type settings like universities, hospital campuses, and shopping centers with multiple buildings. Some universities have assigned parking for faculty and students and even for visitors. In that case, each type of lot will have to have accessible parking. Some of the strategies listed in the following chapters may increase the accessible parking count more than the table requires (see Figures 1.17 and 1.18).

Table 208.2 Parking Spaces

Total Number of Parking Spaces Provided in Parking Facility	Minimum Number of Required Accessible Parking Spaces
1 to 25	1
26 to 50	2
51 to 75	3
76 to 100	4
101 to 150	5
151 to 200	6
201 to 300	7
301 to 400	8
401 to 500	9
501 to 1000	2 percent of total
1001 and over	20, plus 1 for each 100, or fraction thereof over 1000

Figure 1.16: ADA Table 208.2. This table is used to determine how many accessible parking spaces are required in a parking lot or parking garage.

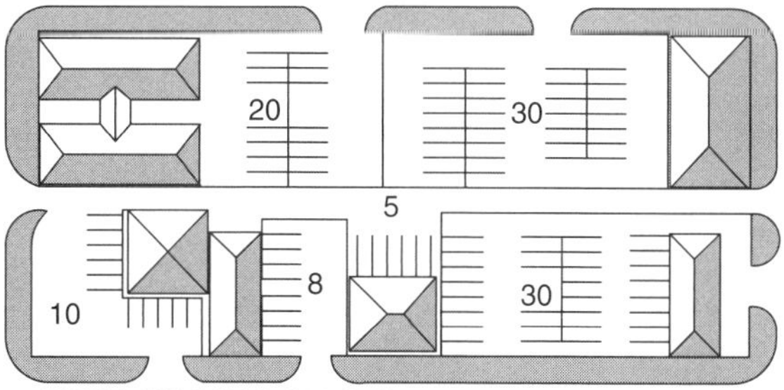

Figure 1.17: The campus of buildings has a total of 103 parking spaces, if you take the entire site as a whole. This would require five accessible parking spaces, which would be dispersed among the six buildings on the site.

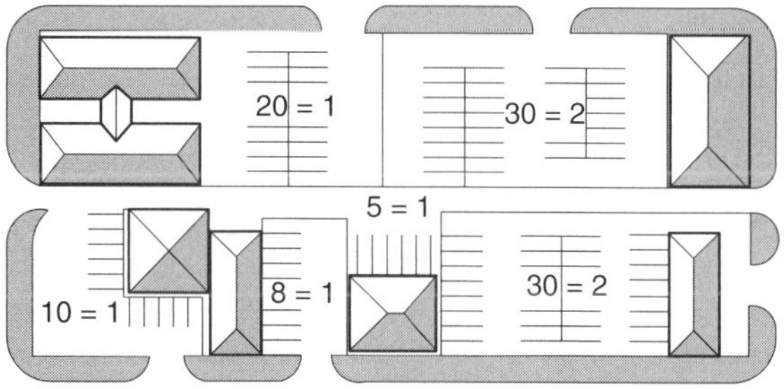

Figure 1.18: If the parking count is determined by building and parking lot, then the number of accessible spaces would increase to eight for the entire facility.

Once the number of parking spaces and their location have been determined, the layout of the parking is figured out. There are two types of parking spaces we design for and provide for the disabled. One is the standard parking space, and the other is the one designated for a van. A standard parking space is 8 ft. 0 in. wide and has an access aisle that is 5 ft. 0 in. wide to enter and exit the vehicle. Some disabled patrons use vans as their mode of transportation. Vans have a wheelchair lift mechanism that is around 48 inches wide. This mechanism will require a wider parking space (see Figure 1.19).

For every six accessible spaces that are provided, at least one has to be designated for vans. Van spaces are 11 ft. 0 in. wide. This will ensure the proper amount of space for wheelchair lifts. Both the parking spaces and the access aisle must be an area that has a slope no steeper than 2% or ¼ inch per foot. This amount of slope will enable a person in a wheelchair to place the wheelchair on the access aisle without the risk of it rolling down hill. After a wheelchair is safely placed on the access aisle and the wheelchair user has transferred into it, that person is ready to travel to the accessible entrance closest to the parking space.

The ADA recommends that accessible routes from the accessible parking spaces to the facility's entrance be located so that a person in a wheelchair does not have to wheel behind someone else's parked car or be placed in a more hazardous situation than anyone else. The same route that the general public would take to get into the facility should be the same route that a person in a wheelchair would take. However, because they are lower than standing person, if people in wheelchairs have to wheel behind a parked car other than their own, a driver may not see them when backing out of the parking space.

Figure 1.19: A van requires more space than a standard car because of the lift mechanism required for the wheelchair to enter or exit the van.

This advice is found in the advisory section of the ADA Standards, but some states require it as part of their standard guidelines.

If the parking space is not in the same level as the sidewalk, a curb ramp will be required to access it. One of the most common mistakes that occur with curb ramps is locating them within the access aisle of parking spaces. The flares of a curb ramp or the curb ramp itself are not allowed to encroach on either vehicular ways or access aisles. Also, access aisles are required to have a 2% slope in all directions. If a curb ramp is located in the access aisle, both of those rules are violated (see Figure 1.20). These types of curb ramps, called built-up curb ramps, are typically found on the existing facilities. Newer facilities plan for a curb ramp that is part of the sidewalk.

Once the disabled person is on the sidewalk, the route to the entry is the next consideration as we design for accessibility. The sidewalk should have a surface that is stable, firm, and slip resistant. "Stable and firm" means that once pressure is applied to a surface and it is released, the surface goes back to the way it was or remains unchanged once the pressure is taken off.

Figure 1.20: A curb ramp should not be located in the access aisle, since doing this gives the aisle a slope steeper than 2%.

Some examples of materials that are stable are concrete, grass, and even crushed granite, if it is compacted properly. Some examples of surfaces that would not be a good accessible route because they are not stable are gravel (including decomposed granite or any derivative of gravel), sand, and muddy dirt. "Slip resistant" is a bit harder to define and determine. In the 1991 version of the ADAAG, there was a coefficient of friction found in the appendix that they recommended be used for flooring materials. The relationship of the foot to the surface is called "traction" or "friction." Friction is the resistance to lateral movement caused by the contact between two surfaces. Dividing the horizontal force by vertical force, we get a number called the coefficient of friction (COF). Concrete, with .8 COF, would have more traction, and be less slippery, than ice, with a COF of .3. However, it was later determined that slip resistance is hard to test, and the coefficient of friction recommendations is no longer part of the Standards. Despite many reservations, most codes recognize a static coefficient of friction of .5 as legal and enforceable for slip-resistant pedestrian walkways. This does change for sloped surfaces. OSHA and other safety standards have recommendation for the COF of surfaces, but the ADA no longer does.

The path should not only be free from obstructions but also should have plenty of room for multiple pedestrians using it. The minimum width is 36 inches, but that amount of space is only adequate for one wheelchair. For multiple-pedestrian access, a 60-inch-wide sidewalk is recommended. Another consideration along the path of travel is any openings that might be found on the ground. Some sidewalks incorporate drainage through grates. These grates should be placed so that the openings are perpendicular to the path of travel so that the wheels of wheelchairs do not get caught in the grooves (see Figure 1.21).

Not only should there be no openings that would be a hazard for wheelchairs, but also no part of the sidewalk should be higher than ½ inch. Depending on the type of ground that the sidewalk is built upon, there might be some settling and heaving. These are not usually addressed as part of the design criteria, but they may become a maintenance issue as the sidewalk ages. The accessible route and the circulation path of travel should lead directly and unobstructed to the front door of desired destination within the facility, even if it's located in different level, and they should coincide with the general public's path of travel (see Figure 1.22).

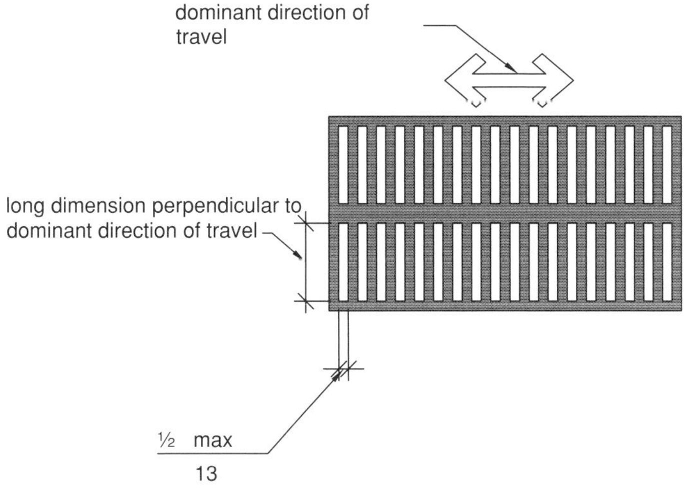

Figure 1.21: ADA Figure 302.3. Any openings, including grates, along the path of travel should not be wider than ½ inch. The figure shows a grate, but this also applies to control joints, grout lines of pavers, and other openings along the route.

Figure 1.22: This existing sidewalk is not accessible because of the heaving that occurs, which makes it higher than ½ inch.

Changes in Level

If there are ever any changes in level along the accessible route, there are some accessible options. A change of level less than ¼ inch is acceptable without any problems. A level change that is between ¼ inch and ½ inch will require a bevel as shown in the ADA figure 303.3. Any level change more than ½ inch will require a ramp, elevator, or other means of accessibility (see Figure 1.23). Ramps must also follow the same guidelines as the accessible route itself. It should not be narrower than 36 inches wide; it must have handrails on both sides and landings on the top and bottom. It should also have edge protection if the ramp is open on both sides.

ACCESSIBLE ENTRANCES

According to the ADA section 206.4 60% of new entrances must be accessible. If not all entrances are accessible, they should have signage to lead people to the accessible door. Some facilities have multiple entrances, and will be challenging to determine which entrance should be designated as accessible in order to not discriminate against those who are disabled. Certain building types are more straightforward than others. The chapters that follow will describe some of the unique circumstances related to entrances and the best way to proceed in the design and construction of the entrances.

Automatic door or power-assisted doors are typically used in facilities, but they are not required. These doors are helpful because they open the door for people with disabilities and eliminate the need for them to maneuver to open the door. This could be helpful in existing

Figure 1.23: A ramp is required when the changes in level exceed ½ inch.

facilities where the existing entryway may exceed the 2% maximum slope required at the entrance. Also, it is very helpful for exterior doors, since the opening force may be greater than that which a person with weak upper-body strength could open. The 5 lb. required opening force for interior doors does not apply to exterior doors, since there are many factors that affect the ability to open an exterior door, which are beyond the designer's control. A door might be harder to open if the wind loads are high. Exterior pressures will also affect the door-opening force. Therefore, there are no requirements for a minimum opening force for exterior doors. All exterior doors will then lead persons with a disability into the interior spaces of the facility.

According to the 2010 ADA Standards in order to use the power-assisted door so that maneuvering clearances are not required, the door would have to remain open when the power was off. This would ensure that, if the power went out, the door would remain open, which then would still allow persons with disabilities to enter the facility without having to maneuver around the door (see Figure 1.24).

Interior Accessible Route

Interior accessible route to all levels of the facility should be provided, and they should be located in the same path of travel used by the general public. This means that a person with a disability should not be made to exit the building, or even an interior space, in order to reach an accessible route to upper levels. If a means of access is provided for other people, the same or equivalent means should be provided for persons with a disability. To access the upper levels, the acceptable accessible route for wheelchair users is an elevator. Elevators have complicated guidelines and many requirements. There are size requirements for person in a wheelchair, height requirements for seated persons but also for persons that are short in

Figure 1.24: This exterior door does not have the proper slope at the landing and could benefit from a power-assisted door opener that will keep the door open if the power is off.

stature, visual elements for persons who are hearing impaired, and audible and tactile mechanisms for the visually impaired. In general, the ADA requires that the elevator be automatic and follow the standards required by ASME A17.1. If there is more than one elevator, all must be accessible, since there is no way to control which elevator will open. The elevator cab size must be large enough to fit a wheelchair with ample room for a person to turn around and operate the car's control buttons (see Figure 1.25). The same ADA requirements for ground surface, reach ranges, and controls as stated previously should be followed.

The 2010 ADA Standards allows for two other type of access to be used for persons with a disability, but only in limited ways. These two are platform/wheelchair lifts and a Limited Use Limited Access elevator (LULA). A LULA is a new option for access, but it is only allowed when the accessible route is exempted. A person may use them only when the facility is not a shopping center, an office of a medical health provider, or a transportation station and meets other requirements as stated in ADA Section 206.2.3. Also, the facility must not have more than three stories, and each story should not be larger than 3,000 square feet. There are other requirements for publically owned vs. privately owned buildings and exclusions that the reader should be aware as well as different State requirements that differ from those of the ADA.

PLUMBING FIXTURES

At accessible facilities, restrooms have to be provided for the disabled. All restrooms that are provided at the facility should be accessible. There is an exception for single user restrooms that are located in a "cluster" which will be explained later in this chapter. The restrooms

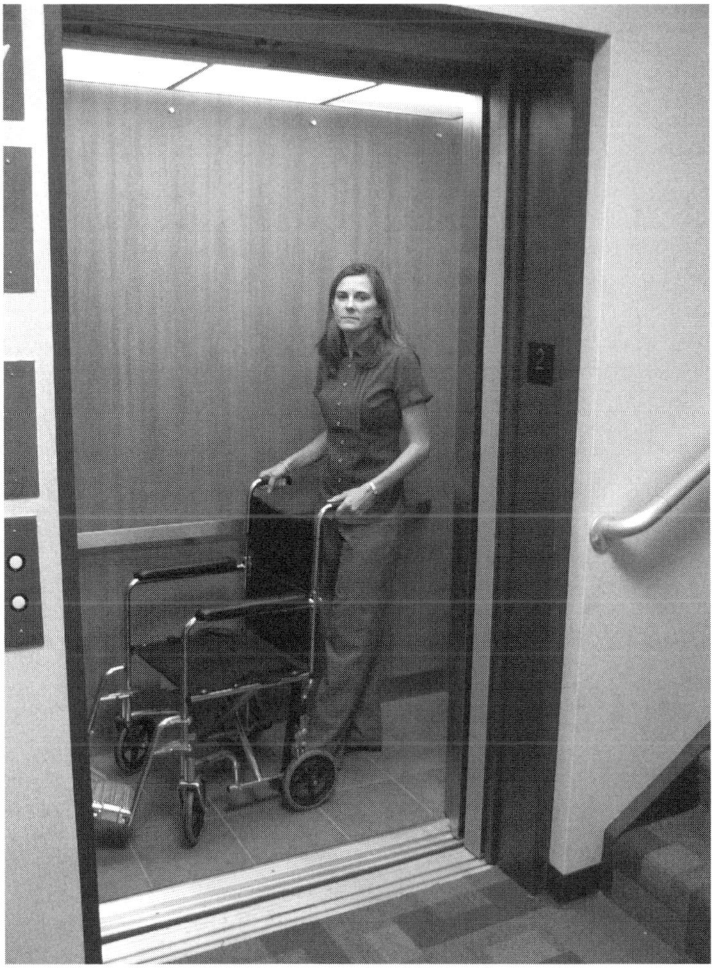

Figure 1.25: This elevator is not acceptable since it is not deep enough for a person to use it unassisted.

should be designed for the primary users. Some restrooms may be used primarily for children, as in elementary schools and maybe shopping centers. If multiple fixtures are provided in a restroom, one of each type of plumbing fixture will have to be accessible. Therefore, if there is an adult toilet and a child toilet, both must have the clear floor space and grab bars per the ADA Chapter 6. In a public restroom, where toilet stalls are provided, one standard accessible compartment must be provided as well (see Figure 1.26).

If urinals are provided and there is more than one, then it must also be accessible. An accessible urinal must be mounted no higher than 17 inches a.f.f., must have an elongated rim that projects 13½ inch, flush controls no higher than 44 inches a.f.f., and a forward approach of clear floor space. If there is only one, then it is not required to be accessible. If there are more than six water closets and urinals located within one restroom, then in addition to the standard accessible stall, a stall that is referred to as "ambulatory" must be provided. This is not for wheelchairs but for people who have other mobility issues, such as using walkers, crutches, or braces (see Figure 1.27).

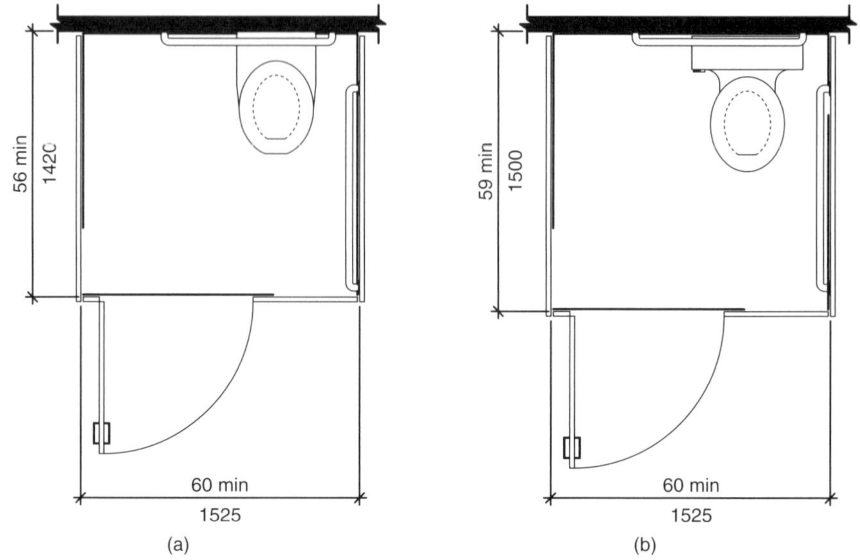

Figure 1.26: ADA Figure 604.8.1.1 shows the required dimensions of a standard accessible toilet compartment.

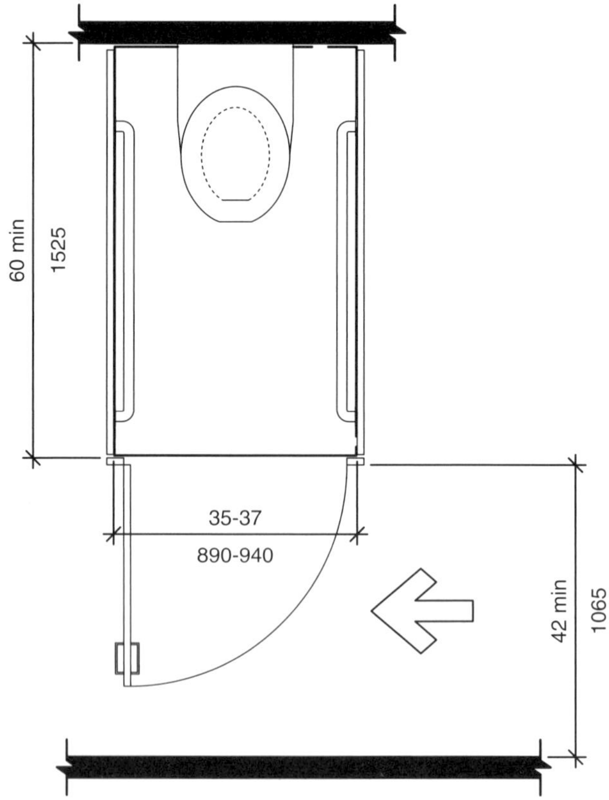

Figure 1.27: ADA Figure 604.8.2 shows the ambulatory compartment requirements.

Single-user restrooms are also allowed and must also be accessible. The definition of a single-user restroom according to the ADA is a restroom with one lavatory, and two water closets or a combination of one water closet and one urinal. In the 2010 ADA Standards, all new restrooms are required to be accessible, including single-user restrooms. However, if you have multiple single user restrooms in close proximity to each other, then only 50% of the single-user restrooms are required to be accessible. The restrooms that are not accessible must have directional sign to those that are. Those that are accessible should have signage with the Universal symbol of accessibility.

Within the single-user restroom, the door may swing into the clear floor space of any fixture as long as there is a 30 inch x 48 inch space beyond the swing of the door. This is so that if a door opens, a person can get out of the way of the door and not get hit. (See Figure 1.28.) In a multiuser restroom, this is not allowed, since there is no way to control who is coming in and when. A single-user restroom can be locked once a person is using it, which prevents a different person from coming in at the same time. In a multiuser restroom, since there is no lock, if the door swings into the clear floor space of the lavatory, for example, and a person in a wheelchair is washing her hands, the person washing her hands could get hit by the door.

The Accessibility Standards also have provisions for showers. There are two types of showers. One is a transfer shower, which is what the name implies: a person will park their wheelchair next to the shower stall and will "transfer" to a foldable seat in the shower itself. Those showers should only be 36 inches x 36 inches, no more or no less. (See Figure 1.29.) This is because, when a disabled person is seated in the transfer shower, he or she will not be able to reach the controls if the shower is larger.

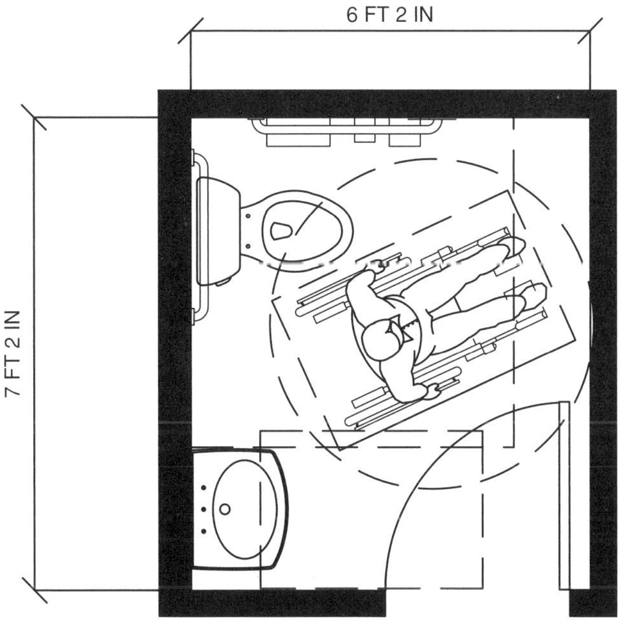

Figure 1.28: A single-user restroom is allowed to have the door swing in, as long as the restroom has a 30 inch × 48 inch space where a wheelchair can be away from the swing of the door.

Figure 1.29: ADA Figure 608.3.1. A transfer shower should not be larger than the required dimensions; otherwise, the wheelchair user may not be able to reach the controls.

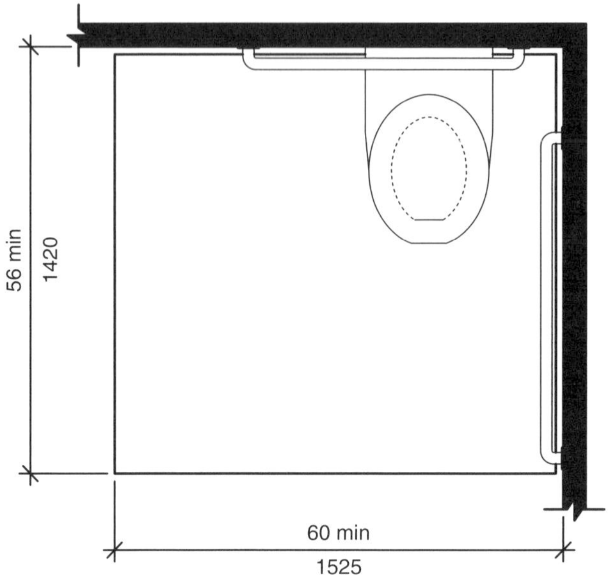

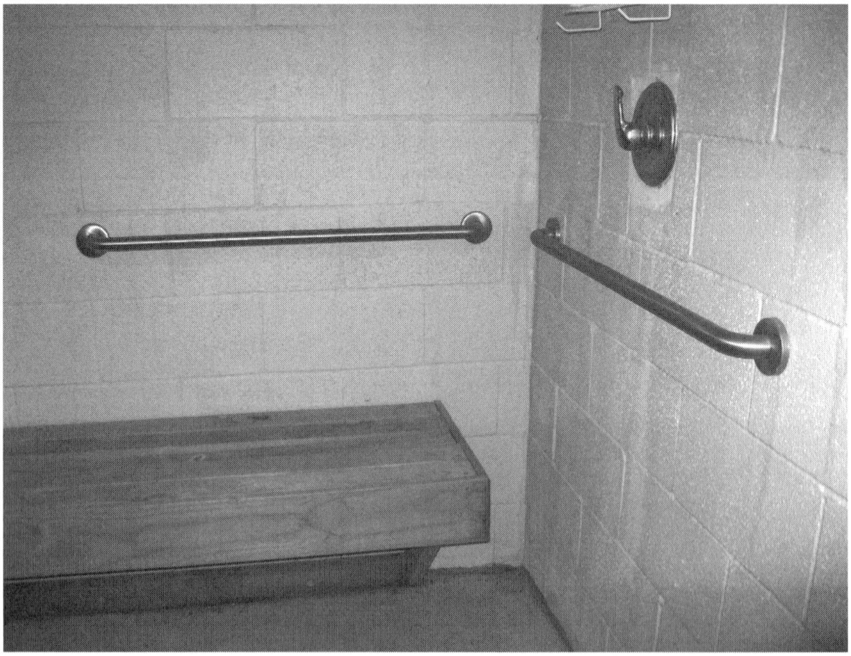

Figure 1.30: This roll-in shower has a seat that is not foldable and is, therefore, an obstruction in the floor space.

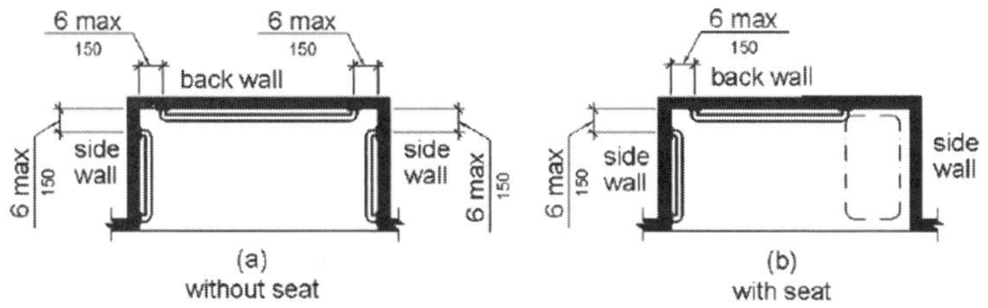

Figure 1.31: ADA Figure 608.3.2. A roll-in shower is designed for wheelchairs to wheel into them. Grab bars will not be required behind the foldable seat if one is provided.

The other type of shower is a roll-in shower. Those are also what the name implies: a person will roll the wheelchair into the shower stall and bathe in it. There should not be any obstructions, so that the wheelchair can fully enter the shower and be usable (see Figure 1.30). So, no curbs are allowed, except a 1/2" maximum curb, neither is a fixed unfoldable seat allowed. If a foldable seat is provided, the controls must be located within the reach range from the seat itself. The maximum size allowed is 27 inches from the back of the seat wall. (See Figure 1.31.)

COMMUNICATION FEATURES

In order for persons who are visually and hearing impaired to maneuver inside a facility that requires access, they must have communication features, such as signage with Braille, strobe lights, and telephones that allow them to communicate. 2010 ADA Standards Chapter 7 gives guidelines on what these communication features must provide.

Permanent rooms must have signage with raised text and Braille as well as contrasting colors for the background and the text, for wayfinding purposes. The sign should be located adjacent to the strike side of the door in order for people to avoid getting hit while reading the sign. An exception in the standards allows for signage to be mounted to the door if the sign is on the push side approach, and the door has a closer. (See Figure 1.32.)

Another requirement for signage is an 18 inch x 18 inch clear floor space in front of the sign. This allows a person to read the sign without any obstructions (see Figure 1.33).

Figure 1.32: This photo shows a sign that is mounted to the pull side of the door where a person could open the door as the visually impaired person is trying to read the sign.

Figure 1.33: This drinking fountain encroaches on the 18 inches x 18 inches required clear floor space in front of the sign, which impedes the reading of the sign.

Lettering on the signage must be in a san serif font, which does not have additional style elements that could prevent someone who is visually impaired from reading the sign clearly. The type of Braille required is Grade 2 Braille, which essentially is English. If a sign has a pictogram, it must be located above the text, and it must not be smaller than 6 inches. The sign should be mounted so that the tactile portion of the sign is no lower than 48 inches and no higher than 60 inches a.f.f. This will ensure that persons with shorter stature can read the sign as well.

SUMMARY

These general guidelines will apply to many different conditions and situations, which will be described in the chapters that follow. The rest of this book will guide you on how to use these very general guidelines and make them more specific to unique building conditions. The format of the book is meant to walk you through a building and site as if you were the person with a disability and show how you would utilize the facility.

Retail and Mixed-Use Facilities

2

by Marcela Abadi Rhoads, AIA RAS

INTRODUCTION

In the United States, there are millions of consumers who spend time shopping and working at shopping centers every day. They are the lifeline of retailers and commercial facilities. The demographics of those consumers are very diverse, but one thing is clear: the population is aging and more citizens are becoming disabled. Prior to the Americans with Disabilities Act, those citizens with disabilities struggled with barriers that impeded their ability to engage in the same activities as able-bodied consumers. The ADA essentially brought equality to the consumer world. With design guidelines in place, design professionals and building owners were given the directive to eliminate architectural barriers in commercial facilities and places of public accommodation. Barriers such as steps in front of retail shops, clothing racks too close to each other, lack of tactile signs for the visually impaired, or high checkout counters. These and other barriers prevented the disabled community from having the same quality of life as everyone else.

Shopping centers are defined as commercial facilities as well as public accommodations in the ADA, and this chapter will focus on how to apply the ADA guidelines to these facilities.

ADA's Definition of Shopping Mall or Shopping Center is:

A. A building housing five or more sales or rental establishments.

B. A series of buildings on a common site, either under common ownership or common control or developed either as one project or as a series of related projects, housing five or more sales or rental establishments. For purposes of this section, places of public accommodation of the types listed in paragraph (5) of the definition of "place of public accommodation" in section §36.104 are considered sales or rental establishments. The facility housing a "shopping center or shopping mall" only includes floor levels housing at least one sales or rental establishment, or any floor level designed or intended for use by at least one sales or rental establishment.

In our analysis, we will focus on three types of retail facilities: shopping malls, strip shopping centers, and lifestyle centers. Along with the lifestyle centers, we will also spend some time discussing work areas and office spaces.

A shopping mall is one building located on one site. The parking surrounds the building, which typically has multiple entrances. The site arrival is typically vehicular and shopping occurs in the interior. A strip shopping center is also one building, but it is arranged in a linear fashion with exterior pedestrian access. Parking is found in front of the stores, and the building is typically one story. A lifestyle center, or mixed-use development is similar to a strip shopping center, but instead of one linear building on one site, we find several linear buildings arranged all around the site. Parking is found in front of each building, which becomes the first destination and then people walk from building to building. The buildings are generally multistory with retail on the ground level and either office or residential on the upper floors.

These three facilities are very similar, but they have different challenges regarding accessibility design. They all have parking that will be laid out, but the strategy for locating it differs from one facility to the other. The interior spaces for all three will have similar accessible elements. They will each have checkout counters, maybe dressing rooms and display racks. The facilities will have employee work areas and possibly a restroom for employees, as well. The multistory facilities will have accessible routes leading to upper floors, as well as common use areas such as public restrooms and food establishments. Along with these similarities, there are challenges brought on by the differences. Each one has a different site arrival strategy. Even though parking will be laid out the same, the way it is planned is different for each facility. Routes to the stores and accessible spaces will also differ for each type of facility.

Thus, the most important challenge for the designer is to understand how the facility will be used and how the patrons will experience each one. For the purpose of this chapter, we will describe how to design a brand-new facility. For remodels of existing facilities, refer to Chapter 8 on remodels, which will explain how a new tenant finish out will affect the facility plus other challenges that come along with remodels.

SHOPPING MALLS

Shopping malls were developed after World War II, when the suburban phenomena began to take hold. Automobiles became the favorite mode of transportation, thus shifting commerce from outdoor pedestrian-type shopping on Main Street to the interior market place, or mall. Shopping malls have anchor stores that are flanked by smaller retailers, and also incorporate food areas and play areas for children. With those things in mind, the designer will begin the design process by analyzing how patrons will approach the site and enter the building (see Figure 2.1).

Site Arrival Points

The ADA requires that at least one accessible route be provided within the site from public streets or sidewalks. An accessible route to the accessible entrances served must connect

Figure 2.1: Shopping malls are required to be accessible since they are a place of commercial activity.

each site arrival point. The ADA advises that if there are multiple arrival points including multiple bus stops near the site, then each one should be located along an accessible route, and each must connect to the accessible entrances. Determining which site arrival point a person with disabilities will use is difficult. In order to not discriminate, therefore, all arrival points should be made accessible. If pedestrian access is not provided and the only means of access is vehicular, then the site arrival point will begin at the parking space including parking spaces located at parking garages. There is an exception in the Standards that states that if the site arrival into the facility or building is vehicular then no connection to the pedestrian public right of way is required. This exception does not apply to shopping centers since there is a possibility that pedestrians can access the center or mall without a vehicle (see Figure 2.2).

Minimum Number of Parking Spaces Closest to the Entrances

The two primary concerns with parking in a shopping mall are the minimum number of accessible parking spaces required and their location in relation to the mall entrances. The minimum number of parking spaces is determined by using ADA Table 208.2, as discussed in Chapter 1 of this book. This table includes surface parking lot as well as parking garages.

Figure 2.2: Most shopping centers are accessed by vehicle, but a pedestrian route to the public right of way will be required also.

Sometimes malls have a combination of surface parking and parking garages, which are called "facilities."

When designing a shopping mall, planners locate the building and then arrange parking around it (see Figure 2.3). To determine the minimum number of accessible parking spaces required, they must first decide how many parking facilities there will be in a shopping mall. Because a shopping mall consists of only one building, there is technically only one large parking "facility" when only surface parking is provided. If, however, there is a combination of surface parking and parking garages, then the entire surface parking will be considered one facility and each individual parking garage is a separate facility.

Another way that parking count can be determined is by deciding that each mall entrance has a parking facility in front of it. This makes the accessible parking count greater, but also ensures ample parking spaces for persons with disabilities (see Figure 2.4).

After the minimum number of parking spaces has been determined for the entire shopping mall, locating the accessible parking spaces closest to the accessible entrances is the next challenge. Each accessible entrance should have accessible parking spaces close to them.

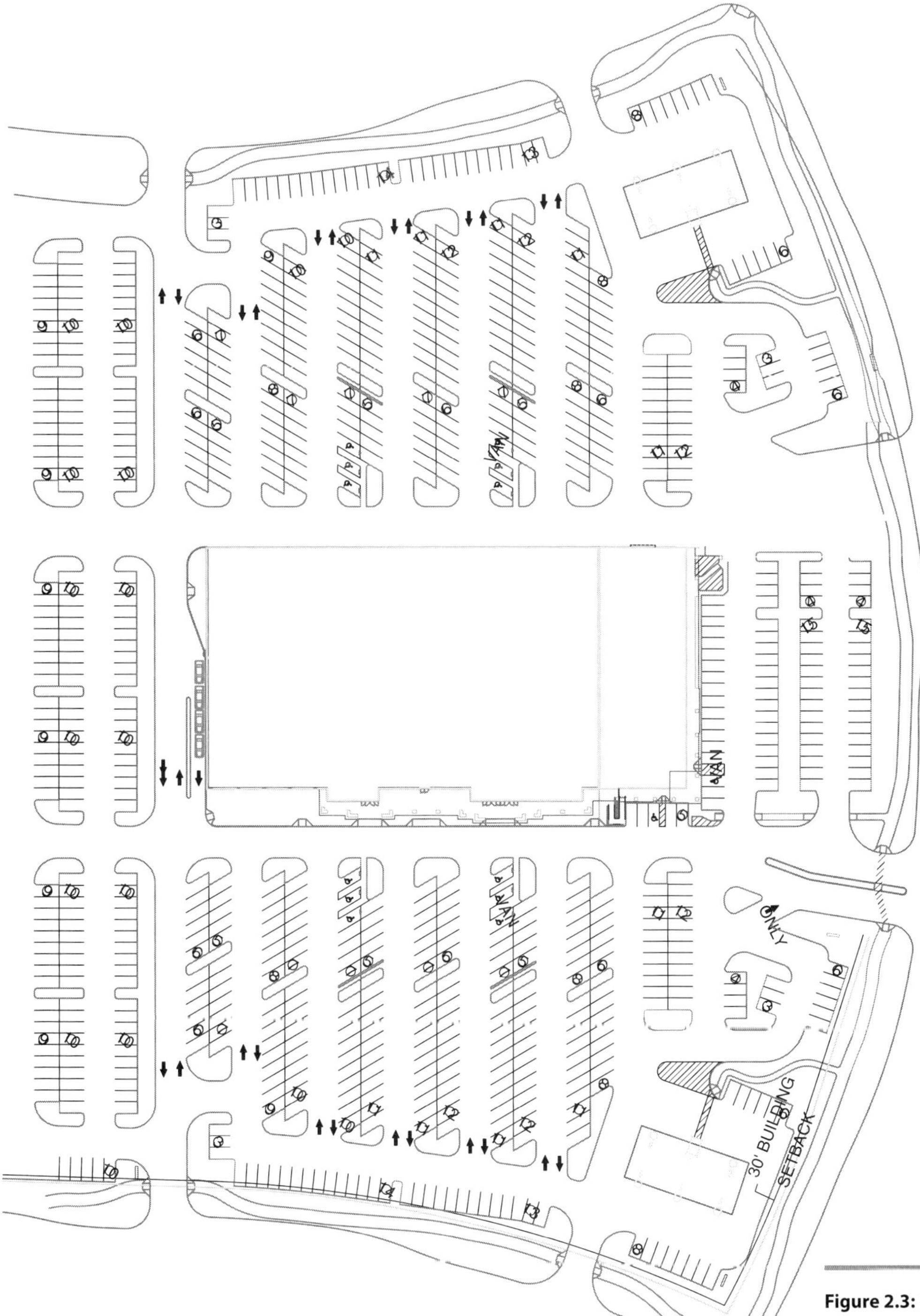

Figure 2.3: Parking is typically located all the way around the shopping mall, with accessible parking closest to the entrances.

Figure 2.4: Accessible parking should be arranged closest to the mall entrance.

If only the minimum number of parking spaces are provided, they must be dispersed among all the accessible entrances provided. In a situation where only the minimum number of accessible parking spaces are provided, there may be some entrances that do not have accessible parking spaces near them. In that case, the number of accessible parking spaces might need to be increased in order to ensure that each accessible entrance has nearby parking spaces. Once the location of the parking spaces is determined, the layout of the parking will be similar for all three types of centers.

Accessible Route to Entrances

It is advisable that accessible routes from accessible parking spaces to a mall entrance be located so that a person in a wheelchair does not wheel behind another parked car or find himself in a more hazardous situation than anyone else. People in wheelchairs are visibly lower than people standing or walking. Therefore, wheeling behind a car that is not their own presents a unique hazard to people in wheelchairs, because a driver backing out of a space cannot see them (see Figure 2.5). This provision is found in the ADA advisory and is a standard guideline in some states.

Figure 2.5a: It is advisable that the accessible route be located in front of the parking in order to avoid the risk of a person getting hit by the car exiting the parking space if a person is wheeling or walking behind a parked car that is not their own.

Figure 2.5b: Parking spaces should have wheel stops to prevent cars from blocking the accessible route that is located in front of the cars.

The route that the general public uses to get into the shopping mall should be the route that a person in a wheelchair will use. Unless the parking space is on the same level as the store entrance, a curb ramp is typically provided for access to the sidewalk and path to the store (see Figures 2.6a and 2.6b).

Figure 2.6a: An accessible route from parking to sidewalk generally goes up a curb ramp.

Figure 2.6b: This accessible route does not have a curb ramp where it crosses a curb.

A curb ramp must have a 36-inch landing at the top of the ramp in order to allow a person in a wheelchair to travel from one end of the sidewalk to the other without having to travel over the ramp (see Figures 2.6c and 2.6d).

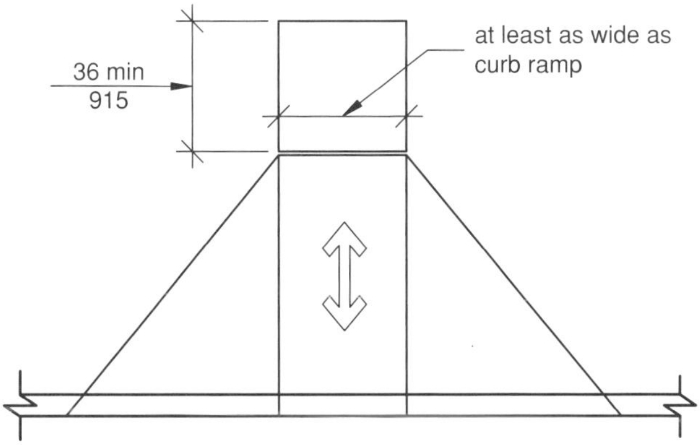

Figure 2.6c: ADA Figure 406.4 This figure depicts the new requirements for a landing at the top of a curb ramp.

Figure 2.6d: A curb ramp should have a 36-inch landing at the top of the ramp. This allows a pedestrian to go from one side of the sidewalk to the other without crossing over the curb ramp.

A person using a wheelchair must have a cross slope no greater than 2%. This enables the person to maneuver across a surface without losing balance and potentially tipping over. Therefore, curb ramps must have a 36-inch landing at the top of the curb ramp. The 36-inch landing should also have a 2% slope in order to have the cross slope of the sidewalk be the proper slope of 2% as well (see Figures 2.6e and 2.6f).

Figure 2.6e: A curb ramp that ends in front of a patio fence will not allow a person in a wheelchair to go from one side of the sidewalk to the other easily.

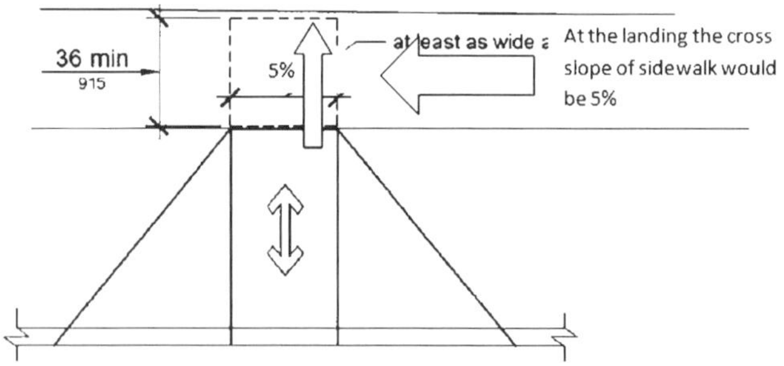

Figure 2.6f: Even though the landing is not required to have a specific slope, it is clear that it should be a slope of 2% or less when it is part of a cross slope of a walking surface. If the landing is only part of the running slope, then the slope can be 5% or less.

Once the disabled person is on the sidewalk, the route to the entry is the next consideration as we design for accessibility. Sidewalks leading to entrances at shopping malls should have the proper slopes as well as being free from hazards from grates or even branches of trees along the way (see Figures 2.7 and 2.8).

Figure 2.7: An accessible route should be a minimum of 36 inches wide. The sidewalk shown in the photograph is only 24 inches wide.

Figure 2.8: Gaps along the path of travel to the mall must be avoided. The wood expansion joint located at this sidewalk decayed away and created a gap wider than ½ inch.

Accessible Entrances

According to the ADA section 206.4, 60% of the entrances must be accessible. If not all entrances are accessible, those that are not should have signage to lead people to the accessible door. This is a difficult situation when designing a shopping mall to accommodate the disabled. A shopping mall has multiple entrances, and they are typically all used as a "main" entrance, depending on where one has parked. Therefore, in order to have equal access in a shopping mall, all entrances that are used by the general public will have to be accessible even if the standards require fewer.

Since exterior entrances are not scoped for opening force in the ADA because of factors that are beyond the control of the mall operator or designers, automatic doors are recommended to allow for patrons to open the exterior doors without much effort or assistance. The controls or push button for the automatic or power-assisted doors needs to have clear floor space that will allow a person in a wheelchair to push the button, be clear of the door, and enter the mall before the door closes (see Figures 2.9a and 2.9b).

Figure 2.9a: A power-assisted door-opening mechanism should be located at a space close to the entrance but also with a slope of 2% or less.

Interior Accessible Route to Spaces

Because all activities in shopping malls occur on the interior, this type of retail facility differs from the other two that will be discussed in this chapter. Many shopping malls are generally multistory facilities. There will be shops at the ground level as well as on the upper levels. They may also have kiosks or portable shops throughout the open spaces and hallways (see Figure 2.9c).

Figure 2.9b: If not all doors are accessible in a shopping center, clear signage directing people to the accessible entrance should be provided.

Figure 2.9c: Kiosks will have to be accessible, and if there are any transaction counters, they should be at the proper height per ADA Section 904.

There are also common use areas, such as restrooms, on multiple levels. Therefore, an accessible route to all levels of the mall must be provided and be located in the same path of travel as that used by the general public. This is primarily why the elevator exception excludes shopping centers. Some shops may be two-story retail stores with an interior stair or escalator within. If the store only has a stair that leads to the second floor, but also has a second entrance from the mall into the second story, the old Standards allowed people to exit the first level into the mall, find an elevator up to the second floor, and reenter the store. One accessible route was required between stories because it was in a shopping center. Now, if the route is on the interior of the shop, then the accessible route will also have to be on the interior of the shop. A person with disabilities should not be made to exit the store, go up an elevator located in the main mall, and then return to the store through the second-level entrance from the mall side. To access the upper levels for the mall, the acceptable accessible route for wheelchair users is an elevator. Escalators will never be considered part of an accessible route inside a shopping center (see Figure 2.10).

Figure 2.10: If there are any level changes within the store, an accessible route should connect each level. These steps cannot be the only access to the upper level of the store.

Figure 2.11: Display shelves don't have to be accessible except for having an accessible route to them and between them.

Retail Spaces

The ADA section 206.4.5 requires that at least one accessible entrance be provided for each tenant space. Inside the retail spaces, you might find display shelves, customer counters, and maybe dressing rooms, as well as employee areas (see Figure 2.11).

In a self-service shop, where customers shop unassisted, then the shelving and racks are not required to be at an accessible reach range, but they will have to be along an accessible route. An accessible route within the store still requires 36 inches minimum distance between racks and display cases (see Figure 2.12a).

If any common-use elements such as drinking fountains are located inside the retail space, those should not impede access to the display cases or racks, and should have the proper clearances for access (see Figure 2.12b).

Figure 2.12a: A 36–inch-wide accessible route between display cases is required for access.

Figure 2.12b: Drinking fountains should have proper clearances.

Checkout and Sales Counters

Checkout and sales counters are required to be on the accessible route but must also have the proper heights that will allow a person in a wheelchair or a person with lower stature to approach the counter. At least one counter needs to be 36 inches high and should extend the same depth as the sales countertop. Because the sales counter should be integral part of the main counter, a folding counter or a counter that pulls out specifically for the disabled is not permitted for new construction (see Figures 2.13 and 2.14).

The width of the counter is determined on the approach. If you have a forward approach, then the width of the counter will have to be 30 inches and must have a knee space that complies with section 306. However, if there is a parallel type approach, then the width of the accessible sales counter should be 36 inches and knee space is not required.

What determines the approach is the clear floor space. If there is enough space for a forward approach, it is advicable to be provided. A forward approach is typically found in retail stores with one cashier counter. If there are multiple checkout counters, then a parallel

Figure 2.13: A shelf on the side of the counter that is not integrated to the main counter is not acceptable as the accessible checkout counter.

Figure 2.14: A service counter at a store should be no higher than 36 inches a.f.f.

approach is typically used since the space between the aisles is what will determine the amount of clear floor space.

Dressing and Fitting Rooms

The retail space might also have dressing rooms. Five percent of each type of dressing room should be accessible. These dressing rooms must be large enough that a person in a wheelchair can enter it and be able to maneuver inside and exit. The dressing room must have a 180-degree turning space, or a "T" turn. The door should not swing into the room, unless the room is large enough for the wheelchair to get out of the way of the door swing. This would be accomplished with an additional 30-inch x 48-inch space beyond the swing of the door. If the door provided for the dressing room is a partition door that does not have traditional hardware, pulls should be provided so that a person can easily close the door once inside. Partitions and doors should be designed to ensure people using accessible dressing and fitting rooms privacy equivalent to that afforded other users of the facility (see Figure 2.15).

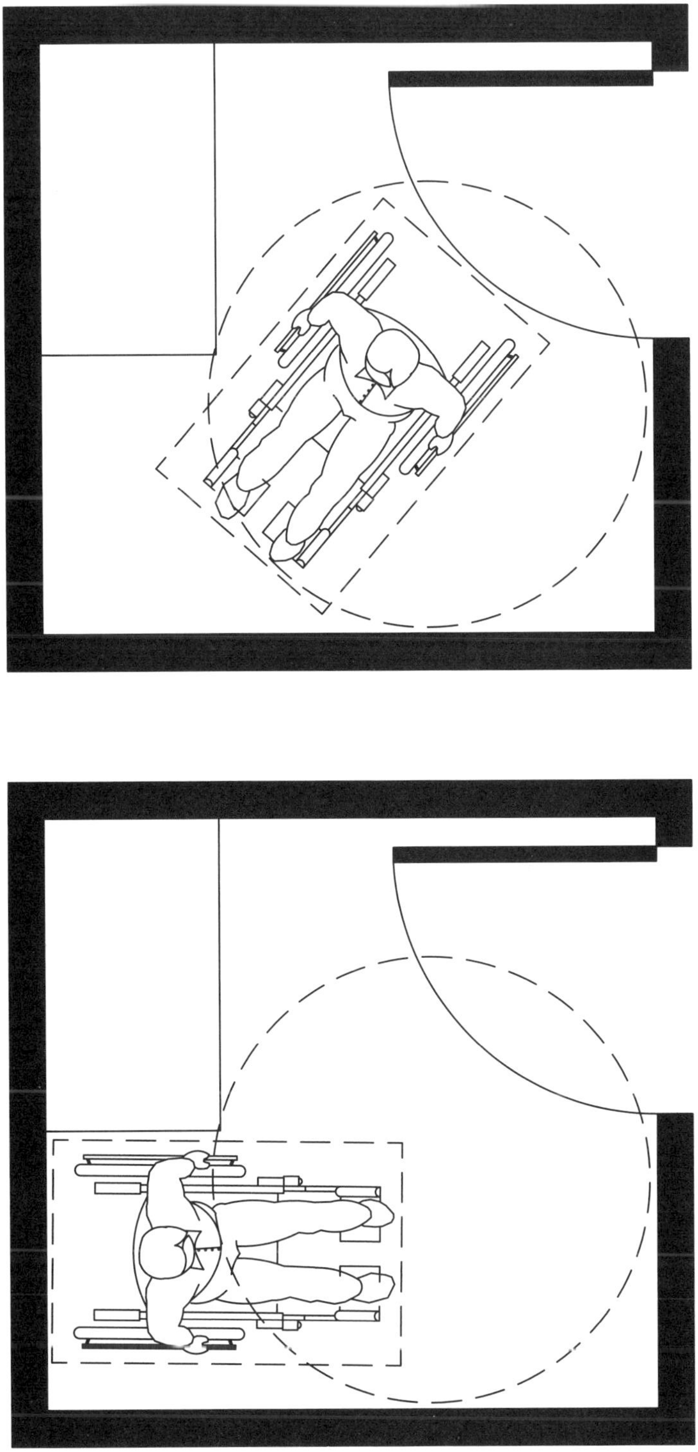

Figure 2.15: Dressing rooms must have enough room for a wheelchair to enter and turn around, but also enough room to transfer onto the bench from the side.

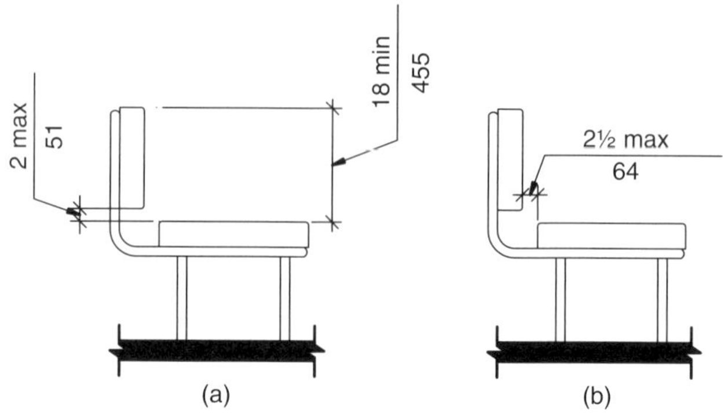

Figure 2.16: ADA figure 903.4 shows the back support required at a freestanding bench.

The dressing room would also have a bench that is between 17 inches and 19 inches high. This height is for wheelchair users, but designers should also keep in mind the children or people with short stature who might also use the space. The ADA does allow for shorter benches in those situations. The bench must be fixed and 42 inches long minimum. If the bench is not attached to the wall, a back support must be provided (see Figure 2.16).

A side approach to the bench will also be required. Where coat hooks or shelves are provided in dressing, fitting, or locker rooms without individual compartments, at least one of each type should be accessible and within reach ranges.

Employee Areas

The employee work area in a retail store is a confusing thing to design for accessibility. Most shop owners think that accessibility is only required for the public spaces, but the common use spaces in the back also must comply. Employee work areas are exempted, and the only requirement is the ability to approach, enter, and exit (see Figure 2.17).

Work areas such as stock rooms, workrooms, or offices do not have to comply with reach ranges or heights of counters. The maneuvering clearances at the door to enter have to comply per ADA section 404, but nothing else within the work area is required to comply (see Figure 2.18a).

Even though work areas are exempt, employee areas that are not work areas require access. An employee restroom and employee break room are both areas that are not considered work areas, since these are not used for activities or duties that employees typically get paid to perform. Therefore, since they are not employee "work" areas, they must be accessible, even if patrons will not use them.

The Title III of the ADA which requires that buildings be made accessible, gives exceptions to the employee work areas with the only requirement being the ability to approach, enter, and exit the work area as previously stated. But work areas are not exempted from the Title I of the ADA, which prohibits discrimination on the basis of disability for employment. Work-related activities such as using a time clock, inputting information in a point-of-sale (POS) station, or working behind a counter will not require special heights or clearances for access. Therefore, even though the design standards do not require accessible elements within the work area, if a person with a disability is hired, the work area will need to be adapted, so they will be able

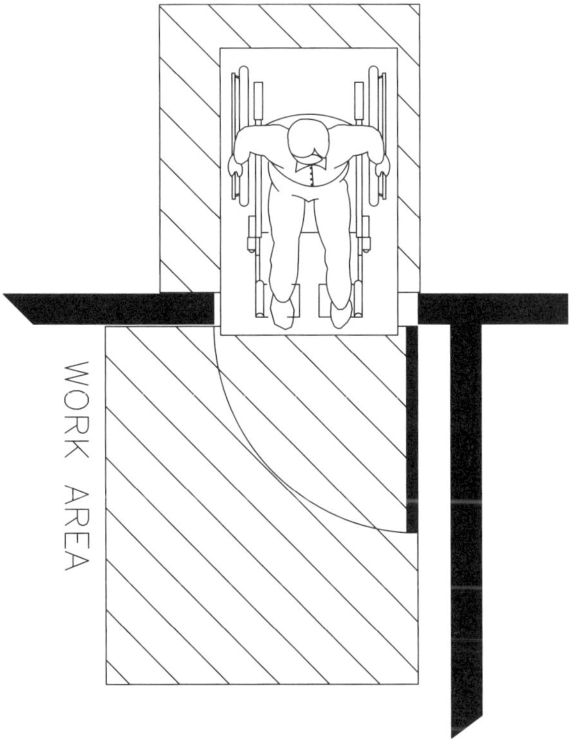

Figure 2.17: The maneuvering clearances at doors to enter the work area is required, but the interior space is not required to be accessible until such time when a disabled employee is hired. It is, however, advisable to provide interior clearances.

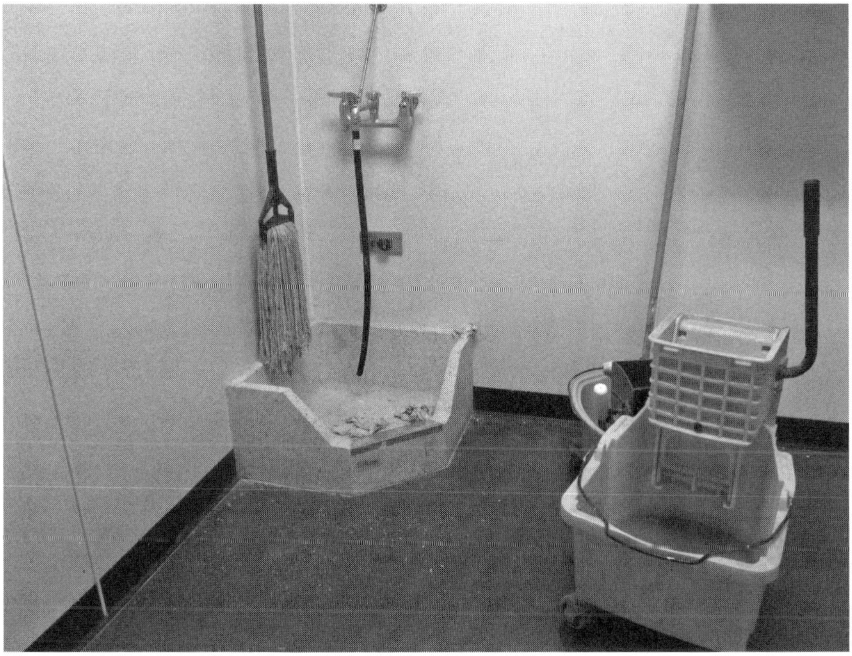

Figure 2.18a: A janitor's closet is considered a work area and requires approach, entrance to the room, and exit accessibility. Items within the room are not required to be accessible.

to work in the store. However, common-use areas used by employees such as break rooms and employee restrooms will have to be accessible, since these are not considered work areas (see Figures 2.18b, 2.18c, and 2.18d).

The break room for employees will be required to be accessible and provide counters at the proper heights as well as the proper amount of storage and reach ranges. The employee restroom is also considered a non-work area. Therefore, if an employee restroom is provided, it must meet all the requirements listed in Chapter 6 of the 2010 ADA Standards. At least

Figure 2.18b: A time clock is not required to be mounted at 48 inches a.f.f., but if a person with a disability is hired, it will need to be located at the proper accessible height.

Figure 2.18c: A POS station does not have to be at an accessible height, since it is a work area.

Figure 2.18d: A commercial kitchen in a food court restaurant is considered a work area and, therefore, only approach, entrance, and exit have to be accessible.

one lavatory, one water closet, and one mirror should be accessible within the employee restroom (see Figure 2.19).

Storage that is located inside the employee restroom cannot be considered part of the employee work area, since it is not located in a work area. Therefore, if a restroom has a cabinet above the water closet, it will not be accessible since it will not meet the required reach ranges without becoming a hazard to the person using the water closet. By the same token, if there is an employee coat closet located within the common spaces, it will also be required to be accessible and have the proper reach ranges. A shallow closet which allows passage will also require a 32-inch minimum doorway in order to provide access to the interior rod (see Figures 2.20 and 2.21).

Figure 2.19: An employee break room is not exempt from having to be accessible. Knee and toe clearances per ADA section 306 and heights at the sink per ADA section 606 should be provided and reach ranges for accessories per ADA 308 should also comply.

Figure 2.20: Storage above the water closets must be within reach range of 44 inches over an obstruction, but this would cause a hazard to the user. This type of storage is not recommended.

Figure 2.21: A coat closet will be considered common use if it is located within a common area and if the function of storing personal items is not part of the workers' job description.

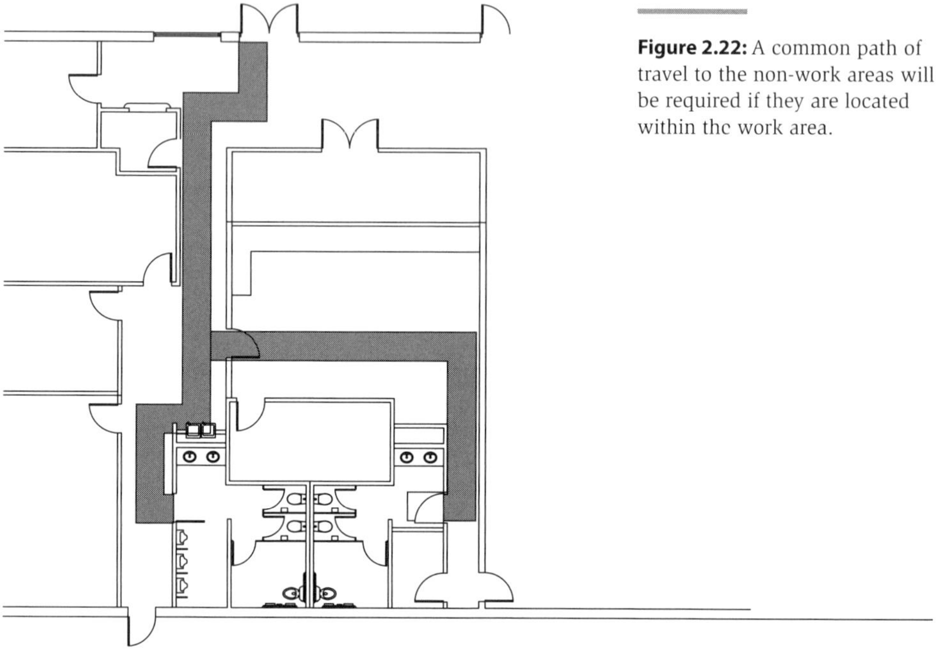

Figure 2.22: A common path of travel to the non-work areas will be required if they are located within the work area.

If any common-use areas such as restrooms, telephones, drinking fountains, or break rooms are located within the work area, a 36-inch path of travel from the entrance to the common use elements is required (see Figure 2.22).

Other considerations along the path of travel within the employee areas that are not work areas are protruding objects. Any element that is mounted higher than 27 inches could be a protruding object for the blind if the object is located along a circulation path inside the restroom. Remember that circulation paths are not just for wheelchairs, but for any pedestrian. A blind person looking for the water closet or a lavatory could use the walls of the restroom, so they must all be free from hazards (see Figure 2.23).

Common-Use Spaces

Along with the common use spaces in each store, the shopping mall has public spaces for the patrons. There are restrooms, food court, and play areas that will need to be designed for accessibility. The common areas need to be designed for the primary users. Restrooms in shopping malls are designed for families. The public restroom is designed for a mixed group of people, mainly adults. However, family restrooms are single-user restrooms that also have fixtures for children. In the family restrooms, you will often find an adult water closet and lavatory as well as a child-height water closet and lavatory. Each type of plumbing fixture must be compliant (see Figure 2.24).

ADA Section 604.9 describes water closets for children's use. It advises heights and reach ranges according to the age group. The ADA standards state that it is advisable to have

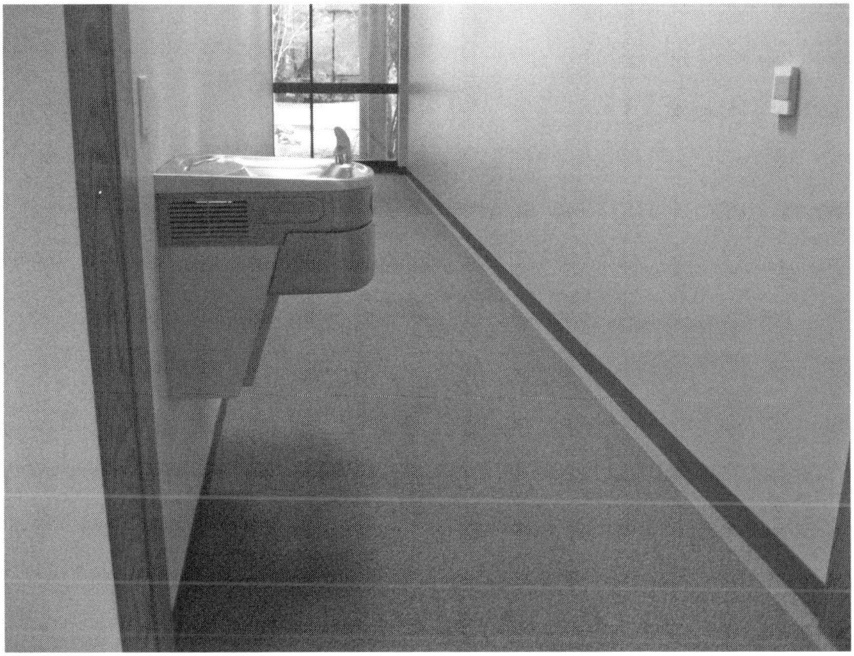

Figure 2.23: The common path of travel should be free from hazards for the visually impaired. This drinking fountain might be a hazard to a blind person if either of the units is mounted higher than 27 inches above the ground measured to the bottom of the fountain.

Figure 2.24: Family restrooms are unisex restrooms that are geared toward parents with their children. If a child fixture is provided, it must also be accessible and meet the children's requirements.

lavatories with children's heights and reach ranges within the restroom. Since this is only advisory, they are not required; however, if they are provided they must be compliant. Chapter 3 of this book covers all the children's requirements and provides a reference table that describes all the provisions in one place.

Some shopping malls have multiple family restrooms and unisex restrooms as well as the multiuser restrooms. A new provision in the 2010 ADA Standards is single user restrooms found in a cluster. If multiple single and family user restrooms are located in the same area of the shopping mall, only 50% of the single user restrooms need to be compliant. These must be located in the same area, and it does not pertain to restrooms throughout the mall. If they are not all accessible, then signage must be provided on the nonaccessible restrooms that directs people to the accessible restrooms and signage with the universal symbol of accessibility should be provided at the accessible restrooms.

Inside the general public restrooms, or even the family restrooms, there might be a baby changing station. These are considered the same as fixed counters. The fixed counter is considered a non-employee "work surface," since the patron will be using it to change their child's diaper. The provisions found in ADA Section 902 explains that these counters must have a forward approach and the proper knee clearances, but also be mounted no higher than 34 inches a.f.f. If they are provided, they should be outside of the toilet compartment. If the baby changing station is located inside the toilet compartment, there should be enough clearance within the toilet compartment for a forward approach to the diaper changing station (see Figure 2.25a).

Public telephones are still provided in many shopping centers, and they are still required to be accessible by the ADA Standards. Section 217 provides the scoping for how many telephones will have to be accessible and the requirements for volume controls and TTY (see Figure 2.25b).

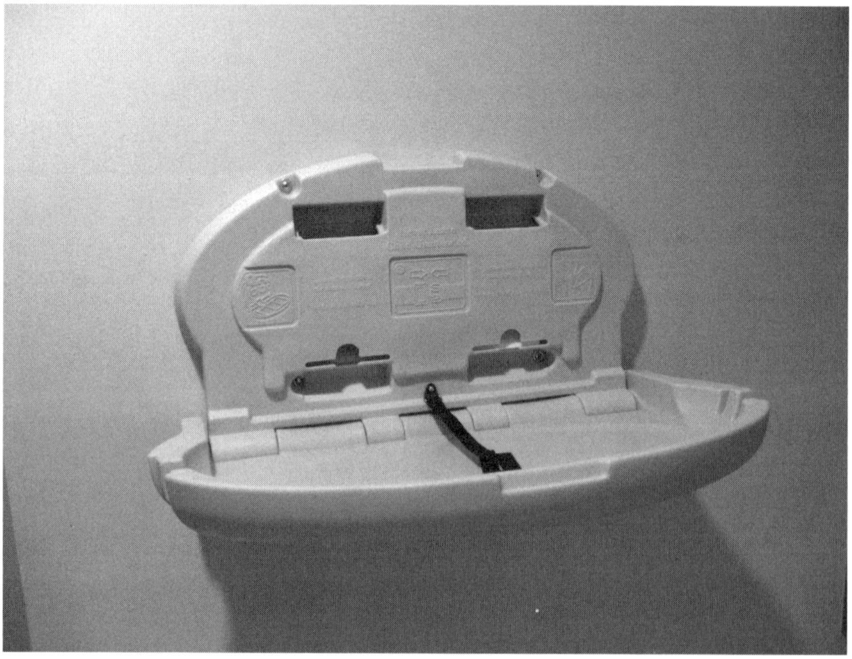

Figure 2.25a: A baby changing station is considered a "non-employee work counter" and must be mounted so that when opened it is not higher than 34 inches per ADA section 902 and a forward approach and knee clearance per ADA section 306 have to be provided as well.

Figure 2.25b: Telephones are required to be accessible if provided.

A common area will also have drinking fountains that will have to be compliant. In a shopping mall, as discussed before, there will be different users at different age groups. The drinking fountain should be provided for each type of group. There should be a drinking fountain for the adult wheelchair user, the child wheelchair user, and the person who is standing. A forward approach with a proper knee clearance should be provided, except for children, who can use the drinking fountain with a parallel approach. Providing a child drinking fountain is not required, but if it is provided, it should not replace one of the other required fixtures. It should be a third drinking fountain (see Figure 2.26).

Figure 2.26: Multiple drinking fountains for different users are not required, but they are advisable.

Food Court

A food court in a shopping mall is like a series of restaurants and a dining area. Elements that need to be accessible are dining surfaces, service counters, food service lines, and self-service shelves and dispensing devices. The accessible dining surfaces are any counter or fixed table that is used to consume food. There should be a clear floor space positioned for forward approach and furnishings should have a knee clearance. You are not required to comply with knee spaces or heights for children under five and can use a parallel approach to use the dining counters for them. However, most of the food court counters are also service counters, which only hand the food to the customer in order for them to go elsewhere to consume it (see Figure 2.27a).

An accessible counter where food is sold should be in the same location as the main counter where everyone else receives their order. Customers with disabilities should not be made to feel separate by being asked to move to a different counter to be served (see Figure 2.27b).

Figure 2.27a: Food courts have service and dining counters and must have the proper clearances and heights.

Figure 2.27b: This counter, which is where most people receive their order, is higher than the required height. Persons with disabilities would have to get their order in a different location.

Once people receive their order, they must find a place to sit in the food court; 5% of all fixed seating and fixed tables must be accessible. This means that they must be at the proper heights as described in ADA Section 902, as well as have forward-approach knee clearances as described in ADA Section 306. Sometimes there are standing counters, or bars, where people may sit and eat, which also must be accessible. The rule states that 5% of the counter must be accessible, but this may not give you the proper width. Since a forward approach knee clearance is required. In that case, 30-inch minimum width dining counters should be provided at the proper heights. This should also be done for fixed booths and tables (see Figures 2.27c–2.27e).

Food service lines should also be accessible and be at the proper heights per ADA Sections 902 and 904. If there is a queue, the width should be no less than 36 inches, and when it changes direction, it should have a 60 inch x 60 inch space (see Figure 2.28).

Self-service shelves, such as for tableware, dishware, condiments, and food and beverages, must be located within the reach range specified in ADA section 308 (see Figure 2.29). Self-service buffets or salad bars should also be at the proper height and all items should be within reach range.

Figure 2.27c: A high counter should have a portion at a lower height for wheelchair users.

Figure 2.27d: A bar where customers sit and consume their food should also have a portion that is lowered for the disabled customer to sit.

Figure 2.27e: Fixed booths should provide the proper widths in order for a person in a wheelchair to join his or her party.

Figure 2.28: Food service lines may be provided at food courts and should have the proper widths for use by people who are disabled.

Sometimes the sneeze guard poses issues with access, since it becomes a slight obstruction. With planning, the sneeze guard shouldn't pose a problem to the customers.

Within the food establishment, the rest of the spaces, such as the kitchen or the area behind the counter, are considered work areas and do not have to be accessible. As described earlier, only common areas inside the work area have to be accessible.

Play Areas

Play areas at shopping malls are considered common areas and are required to be accessible. There should be an accessible route to the play area itself and to the ground-level play components. Ground-level components are those that are accessed from the ground. The play components provided should have the system of transferring on and off the play components. Creating a transfer system for soft contained play areas can be accomplished simply by having them set at a certain height (see Figure 2.30).

In soft contained play structures such as in shopping centers, the transfer system can be used as part of the accessible route. In play areas, clear floor areas, turning spaces, and accessible

Figure 2.29: A condiment table should have all items within reach range.

routes can all overlap each other. This will allow the play area not to be one large accessible route. Some play areas are contained and have elevated components as well. A transfer system, as described in Chapter 7 of this book, will be sufficient for entering the play equipment (see Figure 2.31).

STRIP SHOPPING CENTER

A strip shopping center is a group of retail buildings that are interconnected by an exterior pedestrian walkway. The ADA defines them as:

> . . . a series of buildings on a common site, connected by a common pedestrian access route above or below the ground floor, that is either under common ownership or common control or developed either as one project or as a series of related projects, housing five or more sales or rental establishments.

Figure 2.30: Play areas at shopping mall should have an accessible route and clear floor space adjacent to the play components.

Figure 2.31: Elevated and enclosed play areas and play components must be accessible.

They are similar to shopping malls, except that all the circulation occurs on the exterior of the stores. The main difference is how to approach the site and how to locate the parking (see Figure 2.32).

Most of the time a strip shopping center is a single-story building separated into units for different tenants. Sometimes, however, the shopping center has two stories. Both stories have to be accessible and be connected via an accessible route (see Figure 2.33).

Site Arrival Point

The site arrival for a strip shopping center can be either pedestrian or vehicular. If there is a pedestrian route or a bus stop near the shopping center, at least one accessible route from the bus stop to the entrances of the stores has to be provided (see Figure 2.34).

If sidewalks and curbs are provided, any time the accessible route crosses the curb, a curb ramp has to be provided. The distinction of who is responsible for these elements can be

Figure 2.32: A strip shopping center is one that has stores attached to each other with exterior entrances and exterior accessible route.

Figure 2.33: Second stories at strip shopping centers are also required to be accessible.

confusing in a strip shopping center because bus stops and sidewalks that are part of the accessible route can often be part of the public right of way and not the responsibility of the landlord or owner of the center. If the elements are owned by the city or municipality where the shopping center is located, then that municipality will be responsible for making them accessible.

There are also times when there is a pedestrian sidewalk but also a steep climb up to the shopping center. The ADA Standards allows for this type of shopping center to be regarded as vehicular only. If there is a bus stop at the public right of way, a second bus stop could be placed within the center drive in order to provide accessible pedestrian access to and drop-off at the shopping center (see Figure 2.35).

Figure 2.34: A bus stop near a shopping center will necessitate that a pedestrian access be provided to the tenant entrances of the shopping center.

Figure 2.35: A steep entrance to the shopping center from the public right of way makes it difficult for pedestrians to access the shopping center directly from the street.

Parking

For a strip shopping center, the parking analysis is similar to that of a shopping mall because it is also one building, even though it is configured in a linear fashion rather than in a cluster. The strip shopping center is considered one facility and should also follow ADA Table 208.2. The challenge is where to locate the parking spaces. If the guideline states that the spaces should be located at the shortest route to the entrances, the question is: When there are multiple tenants along the face of the center and each tenant has an entrance, which one is the closest one? The best approach is to disperse the parking spaces in a logical fashion. If the shopping center has 10 stores, and the parking lot requires four accessible spaces, maybe two could be placed at the center of the first five and the rest at the center of the last five (see Figure 2.36a).

Some strip shopping centers do not provide any accessible parking spaces in front of their stores. This prevents access for persons with disabilities (see Figure 2.36b).

If the parking is located below the sidewalk level, a curb ramp will have to be provided to access the tenant entrance. The curb ramp should be located in such a way where a 36-inch landing at the top will be provided. As explained previously, this allows a pedestrian or a person in a wheelchair to go from one side of the walkway to the other without having to pass through the curb ramp (see Figures 2.36c and 2.37).

Accessible Route

A strip shopping center will sometimes present a challenge when the site is arranged in different levels. Some tenant spaces will be above the sidewalk level. Sometimes different tenants will have different finished floor elevations. In each of these situations, an accessible route to the tenant space is required (see Figures 2.38 and 2.39).

Tenant Entrances

Each tenant entrance must be accessible and be located close to an accessible parking space. Accessible routes from the parking to the entrance must have a minimum of 36 inches clear space. If bollards are located in front of stores, these should not impede or decrease the width of the accessible route. Other common elements that decrease access could be a patio fence. The outdoor eating area should be located so that a 36-inch walkway is provided in front of it (see Figure 2.40).

Entry doors must follow the standards stated in ADA Section 404, except for the door opening force. Since there are factors that the owner and designer have no control over, such as differential air pressure and wind, it will be impossible to provide a certain opening force. Therefore, the ADA does not provide rules for exterior hinge doors in relation to opening force. The standards, however, still require maneuvering room when entering the establishment. A clear floor maneuvering space in front of the door should be provided, and it should not exceed 2% of the slope (see Figure 2.41).

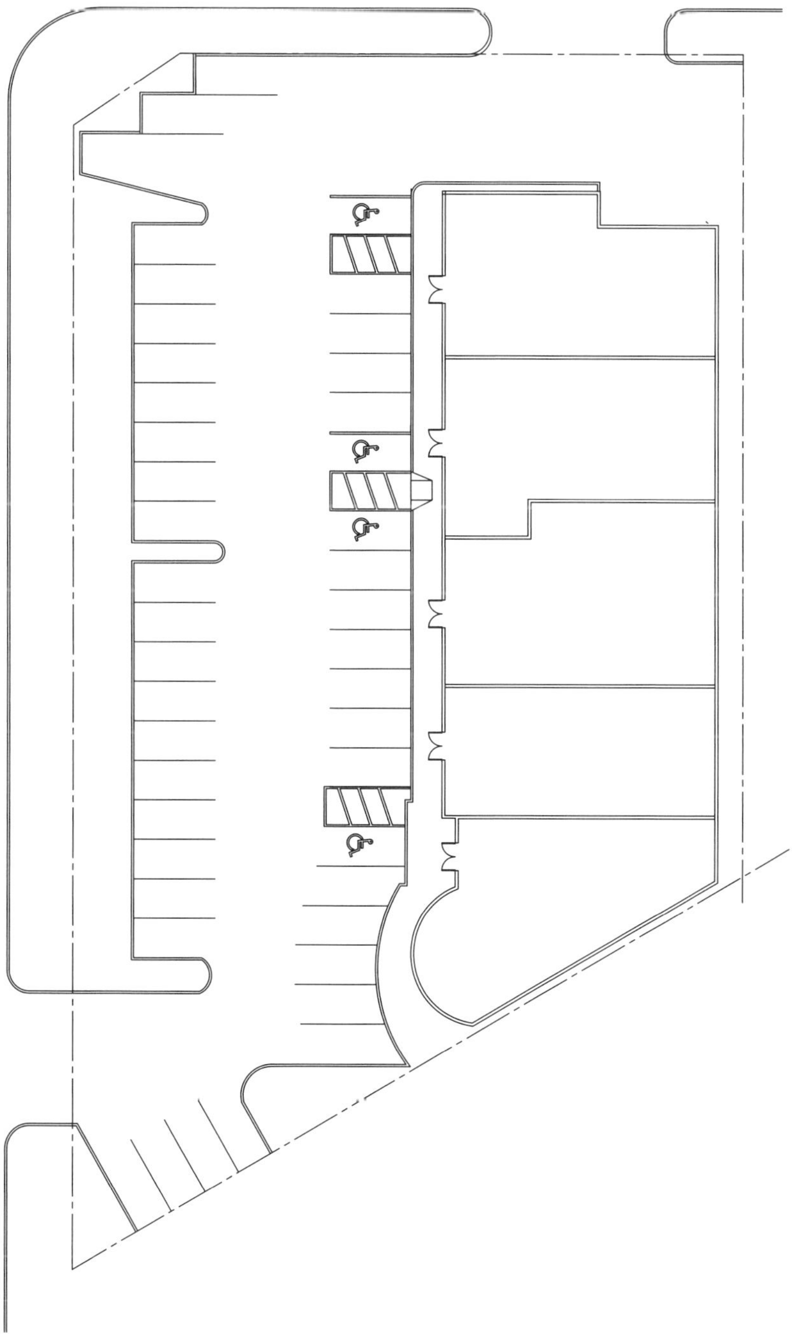

Figure 2.36a: Laying out parking spaces at a strip shopping center can be a challenge. It is best to disperse them where they will be as close as possible to most entrances.

Figure 2.36b: This strip shopping center does not provide any accessible parking spaces.

Figure 2.36c: Accessible parking spaces must have an access aisle that is clear from obstruction, and it is recommended that they have a direct connection to the sidewalk.

Figure 2.37: The planter in front of the curb ramp is decreasing the landing depth. There should be 36 inches of clear width in order to allow access.

Figure 2.38: Steps along the accessible route to the tenant stores should be avoided. If they exist, a second means of access via a ramp should also be provided.

Figure 2.39: A long walkway could be used as a means of access as long as the running slope is not greater than 5%.

Figure 2.40: An outdoor patio should not decrease the accessible route to other tenant spaces.

Figure 2.41: A ramp leading up to the tenant door should have a landing, and the door should have maneuvering clearances that do not exceed 2%. In this case, the person who is trying to open the door will roll downhill before being able to enter the store.

LIFESTYLE CENTER

A lifestyle center is a multi-building facility that incorporates a pedestrian shopping and living experience. They are very similar to strip shopping center, except that they are a group of many strip shopping centers on one site. For the most part, they are retail shops along the street level with residential and office space on the upper levels. Each building has shops that face the parking lot with parking spaces right in front (see Figure 2.42).

Parking

Lifestyle center parking layout is the most complicated one. In a lifestyle center and strip shopping centers, the parking is determined by proximity to each building's entrance. Since the parking is primarily found right in front of the stores they serve, the parking is organized in a way that enables patrons to park and quickly access their destinations. Parking in a lifestyle center is decided for the entire facility keeping in mind that the users will be parking near their destination. Whatever store they plan on visiting first is where they will be parking.

Utilizing ADA Table 208.2, the minimum number of accessible spaces will be determined. As the designers plan the parking and determine how many accessible parking spaces will be required, they will be tempted to consider the entire site as one facility. If they do that, they might not have the proper number of parking spaces required per building for persons with disabilities. The best way to determine the minimum number of accessible spaces required in a lifestyle center is to count the number of parking spaces located or designated for each building on the site. This will ensure that each building will have at least one accessible parking space associated with the building (Figure 2.43 and 2.44).

Another challenge of parking layout in a lifestyle center is the location in relation to the store entrances. Accessible parking spaces are required to be located at the closest routes from the entrance. In lifestyle centers, the entrances are found in front of the parking spaces. However, at the planning stage of the center, the tenants and entrances may not have been figured out. Therefore, it will be difficult to determine where the parking should be in relation to entrances since the center is composed of shell spaces at first. In this scenario, the best solution is to place the parking spaces in the middle of each building, which will ensure equidistant travel distance to the entrances when they are established.

Parking garages may be another option for parking in lifestyle centers as in shopping malls. The location of a parking garage should be planned so that it is close to the route from the

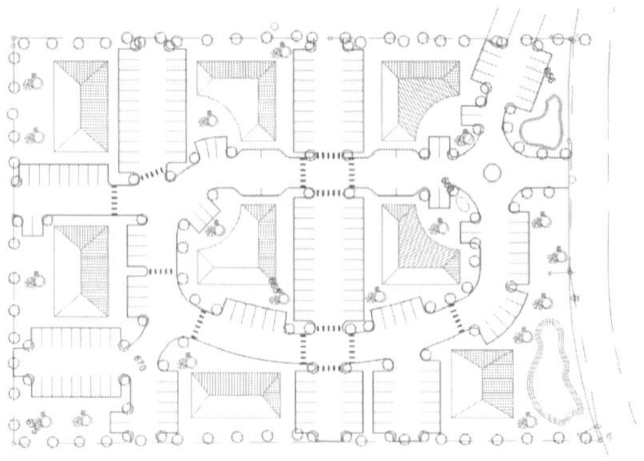

Figure 2.42: Lifestyle centers have multiple buildings on one site with retail on the ground level and offices or residences on the upper levels.

Figure 2.43: This portion of the lifestyle center does not have any accessible parking spaces in front or near the building.

Figure 2.44: Routes from parking to the different buildings is recommended to be marked and curb ramps are required whenever the accessible route crosses a curb.

parking garage to the entrance of the shopping mall or the tenants. If the parking garage has a pedestrian access, then each of the entrances for pedestrians will have to be accessible. An accessible entrance to a parking garage should have a curb ramp if the route crosses a curb. Parking spaces within have to follow the requirement on the table, except that all van-accessible spaces can be located in one area and one level. One thing to remember is the headroom for vans to get into the garage must be 98 inches high, but also headroom for tall persons who are visually impaired may not be lower than 80 inches. Parking garages also have multiple stories. If the garage does not have an elevator, then all the accessible spaces must be located on the accessible floor. If there are elevators, then the accessible spaces can be dispersed among floors. The accessible spaces must be located on the shortest distance from the elevators and the exit from the garage. They must be placed in a level area and must also have a level access aisle.

Accessible Route

Because a lifestyle center is a facility where pedestrians walk between buildings when they are shopping or going to their residences, an accessible route should be provided from parking spaces to all entrances as well as between buildings. Elements along the accessible route should not reduce the width of the route to less than 36 inches. If there is a route that is longer than 200 feet, it is required to have a 60–inch-wide space so that two wheelchairs can pass each other (see Figure 2.45).

Figure 2.45: A lamp post is impeding access along the accessible route.

Residential Facilities/Offices on Upper Floors

The upper levels of the lifestyle are sometimes residential facilities. These do not have to meet the requirements of the 2010 ADA Standards because they are generally privately owned and are scoped in the Fair Housing Act. The Fair Housing Act is beyond the scope of this book, but Chapter 5 of this book explains the residential requirements of the ADA.

The areas of the residential facility that will have to comply are the common areas such as the leasing office and public restrooms. If the leasing office is located on the upper level, an accessible route will have to be provided. Usually this will be a passenger elevator. Because the leasing office is a public accommodation for persons who will eventually purchase or lease a residence in the building, access is required. The elevator exemption cannot be used if there is no other space that allows a person to discuss leasing opportunities. The route should lead directly to the front door of the leasing office, which should have the proper maneuvering clearances at the pull side of the door as well as the push side of the door. The route should also have properly laid carpet, so it is not a hazard to pedestrians or wheelchair users (see Figures 2.46a and 2.46b).

Figure 2.46a: Carpet should be laid down and attached securely to the floor.

Figure 2.46b: Carpet that is not laid down properly could prevent a door from opening the entire 90 degrees.

Inside the office, the common and public areas must be accessible, but the work areas just require the ability to approach, enter, and exit the space, just as described earlier. A reception desk must have both a public side and an employee side. Only the public side of the reception desk has to comply with the service counter requirements listed in ADA Section 904 (see Figures 2.46c and 2.47a).

Any amenity that is provided for the customer or visitor will be considered a common-use space and access will be required. Some offices have waiting rooms with coffee bars, telephone counters, or even televisions as a service to the customers. These all should be accessible and follow the guidelines in the ADA (see Figure 2.47b).

Figure 2.46c: A reception desk or transaction window should be mounted no higher than 36" a.f.f.

Figure 2.47a: The reception desk is not required to be accessible on the side where the receptionist is sitting.

Figure 2.47b: A service telephone counter should be mounted at 34 inches high, and a knee space should also be provided.

Private offices are not required to be accessible, except for the door and the maneuvering area around it. Doors to other spaces within the work area that are not a private office, such as a conference room are considered common-use spaces and require access. Most conference rooms do not have any built in millwork. Only the built in elements will have to comply (see Figure 2.48).

Restrooms inside an office space will typically be used by both employees and visitors. They are required to be accessible even if they are not used by visitors. Appropriate clearances at the lavatories and water closets have to be provided. Sometimes the tenant or operator of the office will use his or her restroom as a storage room as well. That would be acceptable as long as the clearances at the fixtures remain clear from obstructions (see Figure 2.49).

Public and unisex restrooms should also be free from protruding objects and whenever possible recessed fixtures should be provided (see Figure 2.50).

Figure 2.48a: Pocket doors should have hardware that, once the door is open, will allow the 32-inch minimum clearance to enter.

Figure 2.48b: Pocket door hardware should be able to be used without tight grasping and twisting of the wrist.

Figure 2.48c: Private offices are work areas and require only an accessible approach, entry, and exit. Furniture inside will not be required to have a certain height or knee clearances.

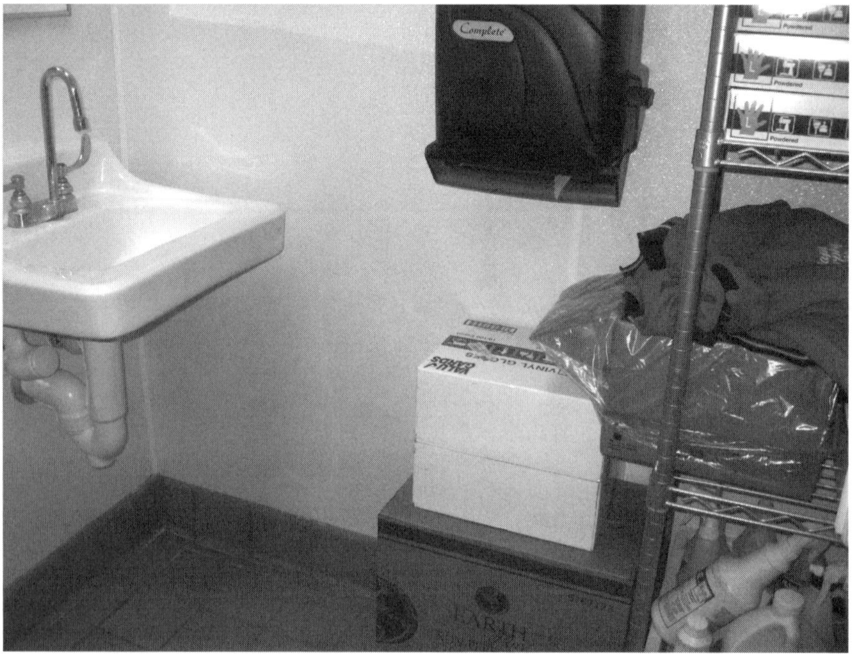

Figure 2.49: A lavatory in a restroom should not be obstructed by any stored materials.

Figure 2.50: Using recessed fixtures ensures that no protruding objects will be found along the circulation path of the restroom.

Requirements for all the other items on the interior are similar to those of retail space work areas and common areas discussed in prior sections.

SUMMARY

To design retail centers for persons with disabilities, one must take into consideration the way the patrons use the facilities. Each facility that we discussed has with it its unique challenges, but for the most part they are similar in the way people will use them. The main idea is to allow equal access and equal opportunity for the disabled users. The amenities in retail and commercial facilities should be available to everyone in the same number and in the same location as everyone else. This allows a sense of independence and dignity, and makes a more usable and inclusive environment that everyone can enjoy regardless of their challenges.

Reference Sections Chapter 2

The 2010 ADA Standards reference several sections for one topic. This reference table assists the designer in finding the pertinent sections pertaining to one specific area. To use the table, find the topic and below are all the different sections that the standards refer to.

SHOPPING CENTER	
DOJ § 36.401 New construction	
Section Number	**Section title and description**
(d)(1)(ii)	Definition-Shopping Center
(d)(1)(ii)(B)	Definition
(d)(2)(i)	Regarding elevators
(d)(3)	Elevator exemption
DOJ 36.404 Alterations: Elevator exemption.	
(a)	Elevator exemption
(a)(2)	Definition
(a)(2)(iii)	Definition
ADA Chapter 2: Scoping	
206.2.3	EXCEPTIONS (1) In *private buildings or facilities* that are less than three *stories* or that have less than 3000 square feet (279 m2) per *story*
206.2.1	ADVISORY: Site Arrival Points Exception 2.
PLAY AREAS	
ADA Chapter 1: Definitions	
Definitions	**Play area**
ADA Chapter 2: Scoping	
105.2.3	ADVISORY
204.1	EXCEPTIONS (2)
206.2.17	Play Areas
206.2.17.1	Ground Level and Elevated Play Components
206.7.8	Platform Lifts
233.1	ADVISORY: General
240	Play Areas
240.1	General
240.1	EXCEPTIONS (1)
240.1	EXCEPTIONS (2)
240.1.1	Additions
240.1	ADVISORY: General
240.1.1	ADVISORY: Additions
240.2.1	Ground Level Play Components
240.2.1	ADVISORY: Ground Level Play Components (continued)

ADA Chapter 2: Scoping	
240.2.1.2	Additional Numbers and Types EXCEPTION
240.2.1.2	ADVISORY: Additional Numbers and Types
ADA Chapter 3-10: Technical	
1008	Play Area
1008.1	General
1008.2	Accessible routes
1008.2.4.1	Ground Level EXCEPTIONS (1)
1008.2.5	Ramps
1008.2.6	ADVISORY: Ground Surfaces
1008.4.2	ADVISORY: Clear floor or ground space

Primary Education

3

by Wally Tirado, ICC RAS

INTRODUCTION

In the United States, "primary education" typically describes the first six years of formal education. The National Center for Education Statistics estimates there are over 67,000 primary schools (also referred to as elementary or grade schools) serving almost 3.5 million students. Arguably, schools have more impact on their occupants and the functions of the building than any other building type.

As a building type, primary schools typically educate students ages 5 through 14 or kindergarten through eighth grade. However, larger urban areas often separate grades six through eight in a middle school or junior high school. Preschool education has recently begun to be offered in primary schools. Preschools, which are usually not mandated by law, typically are much less formal and are not considered part of primary education in general.

Historically, the education of children with disabilities was characterized by mistreatment and neglect. Where programs and facilities did exist to serve disabled children, they tended to be separate facilities. "Handicapped" schools were thought to be better suited to children with disabilities.

When public schools began to open to disabled children, these schools were not prepared to educate students with disabilities. Additionally, no one could have anticipated the advancement of medicine that has significantly increased the number of children who survive with serious medical conditions and who are sometimes left with profound disabilities. These same children are now entering into the general education classrooms in primary schools in greater numbers and must be served.

As we detail the functional accessible spaces of primary schools, we'll identify the children's key requirements as well. A table at the end of this chapter details all the advisory children's specifications. The functional spaces to be discussed include, but are not limited to:

- Administrative areas
- Children's areas
- Toilet rooms
- Outdoor play areas
- Transportation facilities

ADMINISTRATIVE AREAS

Administrative areas are the service areas of the primary school in addition to employee work areas. In general, all areas that may be used by students or are used by staff to provide services to students must be accessible, including office reception areas, supply and storage rooms, and staff offices (see Figure 3.1). Employee work areas are those used specifically for

Figure 3.1: The administrative area is a common-use location, since visitors to the school also use it.

work. Corridors, toilet rooms, kitchenettes, and break rooms are not employee work areas and are required to be accessible.

Employee Work Areas

Spaces and elements within employee work areas are only required for persons to approach, enter, and exit the employee work area. In other words, only the doorway and maneuvering clearances for that doorway are required to comply. The elements of the work area will not require access until such time that an employee requires it. There are specific exceptions for portions of employee work areas that are less than 300 square feet and elevated 7 inches above the finish floor. However, this exception must be essential to the function of the space. An example of this would be areas providing security. Additionally, common-use circulation paths are not required within the area if the area is less than 1,000 square feet (see Figure 3.2).

Although not required to be fully accessible, consider designing work areas used exclusively by employees to provide accessible elements and turning spaces when possible. Under the ADA, staff with disabilities are entitled to reasonable accommodations in the workplace. Designing

Figure 3.2: The Art work room sink does not require accessibility, such as knee space and maximum counter heights, since it is considered a work area where only teachers work and not the students.

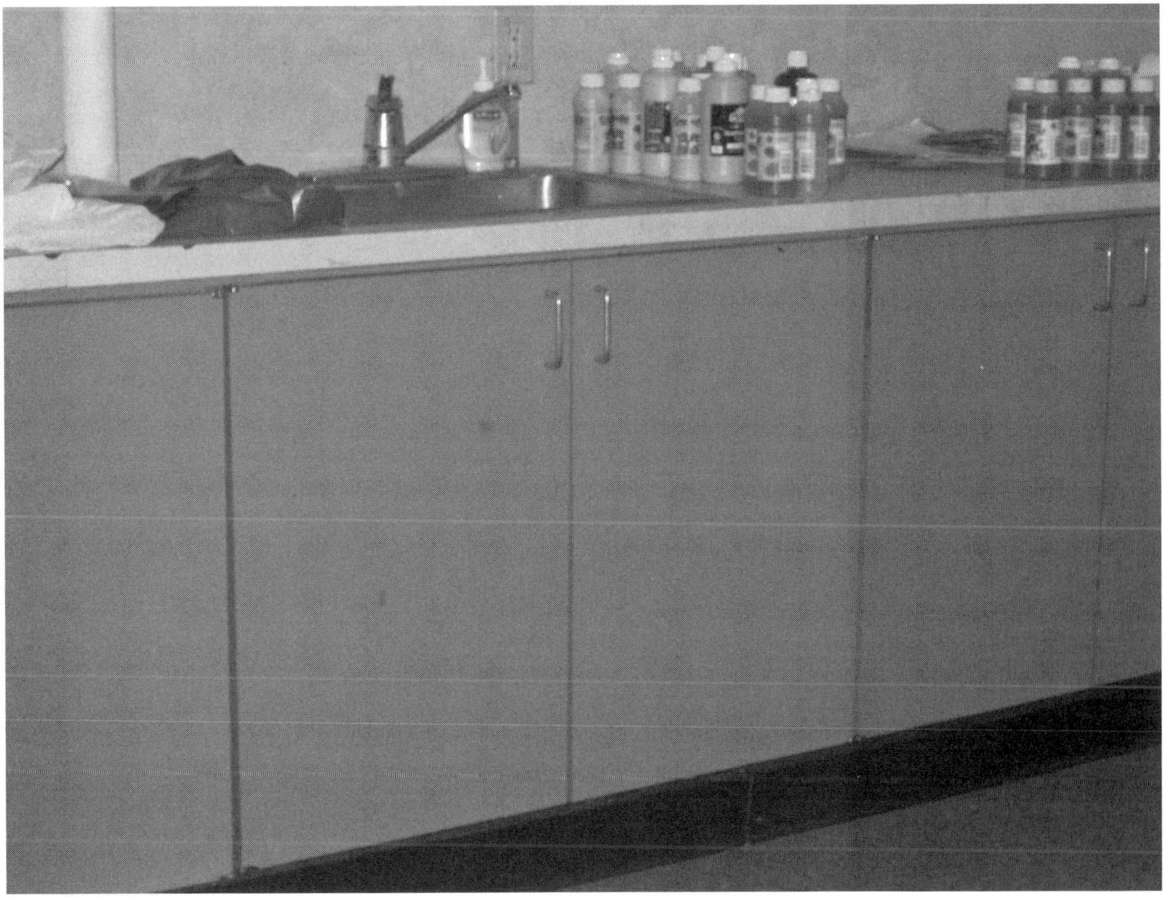

employee work areas to be accessible will avoid more costly retrofits when new employees with disabilities are hired or in the event a current employee becomes temporarily or permanently disabled. Also, keep in mind that parent volunteers are not employees, and by creating nonaccessible spaces, you create a barrier and thereby are not in compliance with the ADA (see Figure 3.3).

Service Areas

Provided spaces such as supply rooms, libraries, book rooms, box offices, and concession stands or other sales or checkout facilities must comply with accessibility requirements. These standards can affect counter surface heights and arrangements, security glazing and windows, and two-way communication systems (see Figure 3.4).

Service counters are to be accessible when designated for use by the public. Often service counters have multiple uses, have multiple approaches, and are used from both sides. It's advisable to provide for the widest range of use and approaches.

Service counters must include a portion that is a maximum of 36 inches (915 mm) above the finish floors. The width of the accessible counter varies depending on whether a parallel or

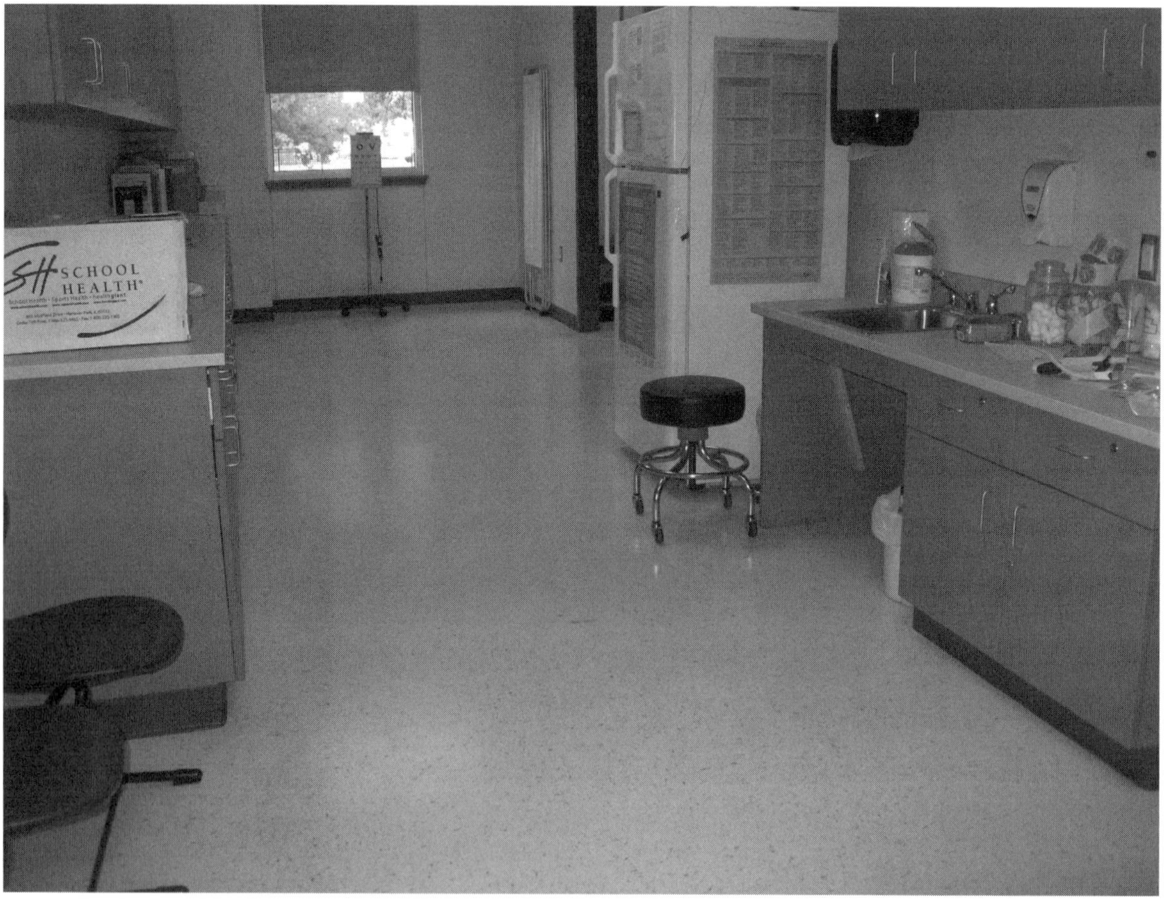

Figure 3.3: A nurse's station is a work area for the nurse, but since students also use it, it is a good idea to provide accessible elements.

Figure 3.4: Service counters at dining areas are required to be at an accessible height.

forward approach is applied. When providing for forward approaches, ensure that knee and toe clearances are provided as specified in Chapter 3 the Building Blocks of the standards (see Figure 3.5).

Service Yards and Loading Docks

Service yards, loading docks, and similar service areas are generally exempt and are not required to be accessible. If those areas are the only entrance to a facility for both public and employee use, such as the service door into a maintenance building, they are required to be accessible.

GENERAL APPLICATION FOR CHILDREN AREAS

There are no specific requirements in the accessibility standards for teaching areas such as classrooms and laboratories. These areas are considered to be common-use areas and must be accessible and also distributed throughout the facility (see Figure 3.6).

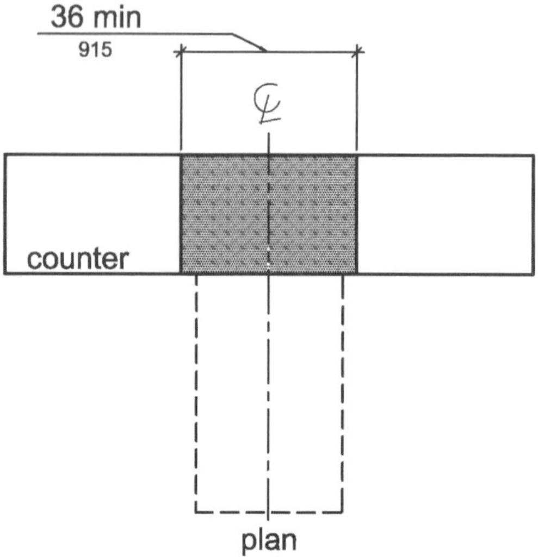

Figure 3.5a: Plan view of accessible counter.

Figure 3.5b: Service counters at the front office must have an accessible portion.

Figure 3.6: Lab counters must have a knee space and be at an accessible height.

When the primary users of a facility are children, such as those in primary schools, an exception to the accessibility standards are provided for these children. The standard exceptions apply only to facilities to be used specifically by children. A staff toilet room, for example, intended for use by adults such as faculty and staff, should be designed to adult accessibility standards, not children's standards. When a facility might be used equally by children and adults, elements such as the accessible means of egress must comply with both adult and children's standards. Application of children's requirements does not eliminate the requirement to accommodate adults occupying the same area (see Figure 3.7).

While we tend to think of schools when applying children's standards, in reality these standards would apply to any place where children congregate occupants. Some examples are daycare centers, children's museums, and even children's reading areas in public libraries. The accessibility standards provide advisory guidance generally for three age groups: ages 3 and 4; ages 5 through 8, and ages 9 through 12. See Table 3.1 at the end of the chapter for a complete reference of the Advisory Specifications for Serving Children Ages 3 through 12.

Figure 3.7: If a child-height drinking fountain is provided, it does not eliminate the requirement for a standard adult wheelchair drinking fountain or the requirement to provide an additional adult-size standing-person drinking fountain. The facility would have to provide three minimum: a standard wheelchair height one, a standing-height one, and a child-height.

Reach Ranges and Operating Mechanisms

Although its use is not required and advisory in nature, the standards provide a table for guidance for building elements to be used primarily by children. This table provides reach ranges, and they are the same for both the forward and side reaches. If elements are provided outside these reach ranges, they must be within the ranges required for adults. Cabinets and shelving used for storage should comply with the approach and reach requirements for adults and/or children (see Figures 3.8 through 3.12).

Dining and Work Surfaces

Children are provided with different clearances when designing dining and non-employee work surfaces. This section also applies to classroom and laboratory workstations. It covers all potential uses by children. Surface heights for children aged 6–12 are to be 26–30 inches in height and provide a knee clearance of at least 24 inches (see Figures 3.13 and 3.14).

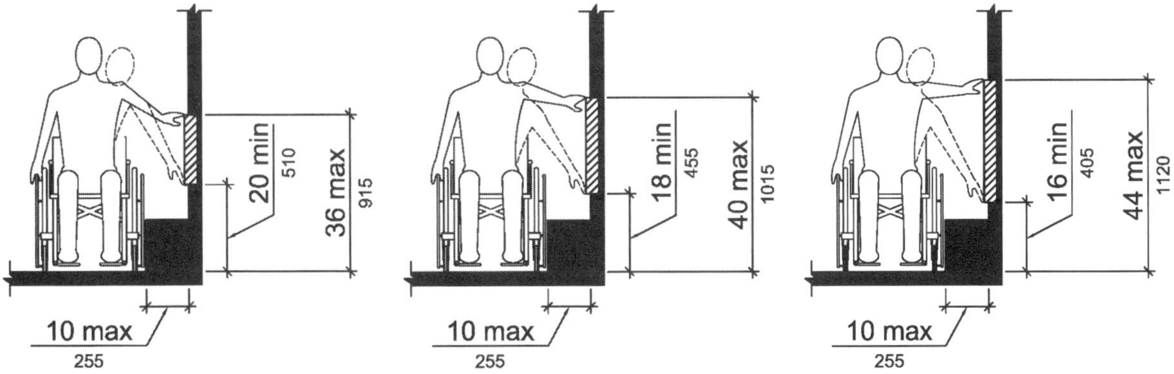

Ages 3 and 4

Ages 5 and 8

Ages 9 and 12

Figure 3.8a, 3.8b, and 3-8c: Children's reach ranges.

Figure 3.9: These cubbies are higher than the recommended reach ranges for children.

Figure 3.10: Shelving at restrooms must also be at an accessible reach range.

Figure 3.11: The standards recommend that hand dryers in restrooms be at a child's height.

Figure 3.12: Five percent of locker opening mechanisms should be within a reach range, but their mechanism should also be the type that does not require tight grasping and twisting of the wrist to operate.

Figure 3.13: Even though tables in classrooms are not fixed, it is recommended that they be accessible for children with disabilities. Bookshelves are not required to be at an accessible height.

Figure 3.14: Tables at libraries should also be made accessible, even if they are not fixed so that children with disabilities can study together.

For those ages 5 and younger, the knee clearance requirement has been removed, provided that the clear floor space for a wheelchair is provided for a parallel approach to the surface. The typical surface height for this age would be lower than 26 inches, which would prohibit both knee and toe clearances. The surface height is not specified and any height may be used (see Figure 3.15).

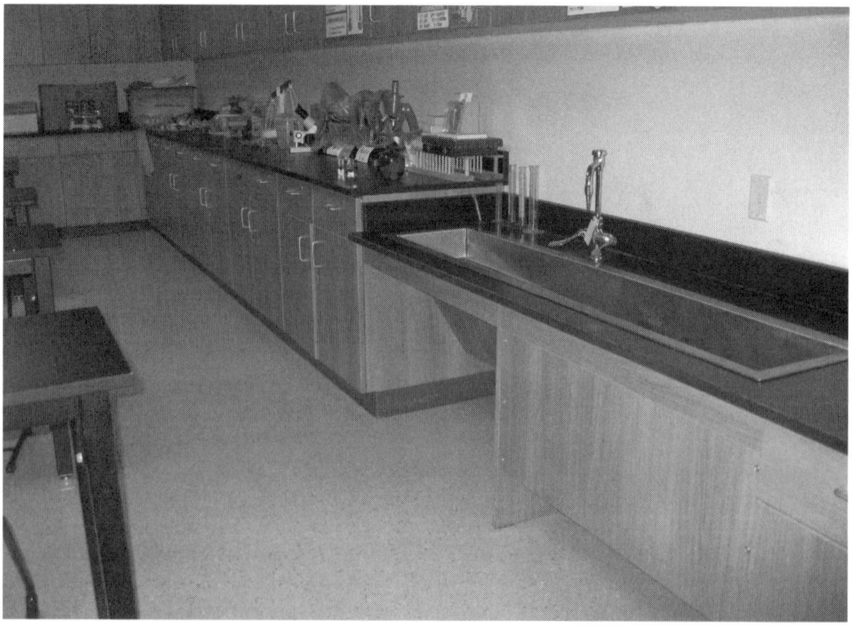

Figure 3.15: Five percent of lab tables should have a knee space as well as be at an accessible height for children.

The accessibility standards detail the technical requirements of both adults and children, giving the dimensions for drinking fountains, water closets, toilet compartments, and lavatories and sinks, as well as dining surfaces and non-employee work surfaces.

TOILET ROOMS AND ELEMENTS

A common design omission is having separate toilet facilities for staff and students but not making both accessible. Toilet rooms serving children 12 years of age and younger have accessibility requirements for different compartment size, grab bar height, water closet location, lavatory height, and other accessory heights and arrangements.

The following section provides guidance for applying the accessibility standards according to age group and identifies the requirements for ages 3 through 12. When providing toilet rooms according to children's specifications, identify the age group most served and consistently apply the specifications to the facility and its components and related elements. While there are specific technical requirements for children's specifications the specific age groups are advisory (see Figure 3.16).

Figure 3.16: It is recommended that toilets for children meet the heights for children, including grab bars.

Drinking Fountains

An exception has been provided for accessible drinking fountains for children's use. A parallel approach is permitted when the spout is 30 inches maximum above the finished floor and 3½ inches from the front of unit. These devices must be located or guarded so that they do not violate the requirements related to protruding objects and also include the minimum clear width of an accessible route (see Figures 3.17 through 3.19). If child height drinking fountains are provided it cannot replace one of the two other required drinking fountain heights.

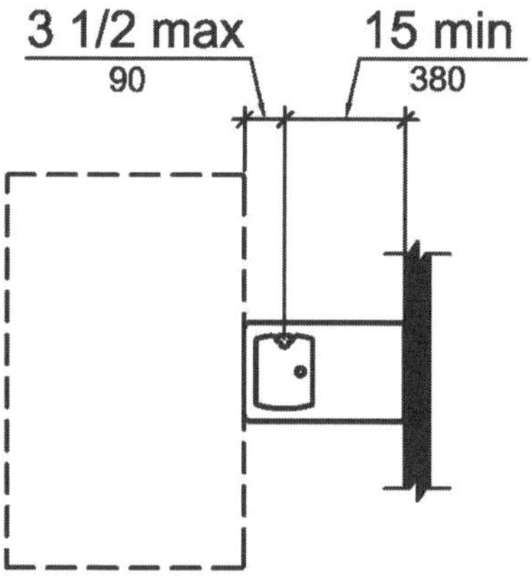

Figure 3.17: Children's drinking fountain spout location.

Figure 3.18: Children's drinking fountain can have a parallel approach.

Figure 3.19: A high and a low drinking fountain are required at schools, and they must be mounted at the adult dimensions. There should also not be protruding objects according to the standards.

Toilet Compartments

Wheelchair-accessible compartments designed for children have requirements that are different from those that are required for adults. First, the compartment is to be deeper than those for adults. They must be at least 59 inches deep or the same as if you were to provide a floor-mounted water closet for adults.

Additionally, these compartments must provide a minimum of 12 inches of toe clearance above the finished floor. These requirements are in place because the foot rests of the children's wheelchair are higher above the ground than an adult's, and they also cannot maneuver under the space of a wall-hung water closet. However, these toe clearances are not required at all if the compartment is larger than 66 inches wide and 65 inches deep. Ambulatory-accessible compartment requirements provided for children have the same technical requirements as for adults (see Figures 3.20 and 3.21).

Water Closets and Accessories

The water closet, grab bars, and dispensers are located differently according to the age group. The provision for dispensers effectively disallows its installation above the grab bar. As the dispenser heights ranges are below the grab bar height. For all age groups, the water closet flush controls are not to be mounted more than 36 inches above the finished floor (see Figures 3.22 and 3.23).

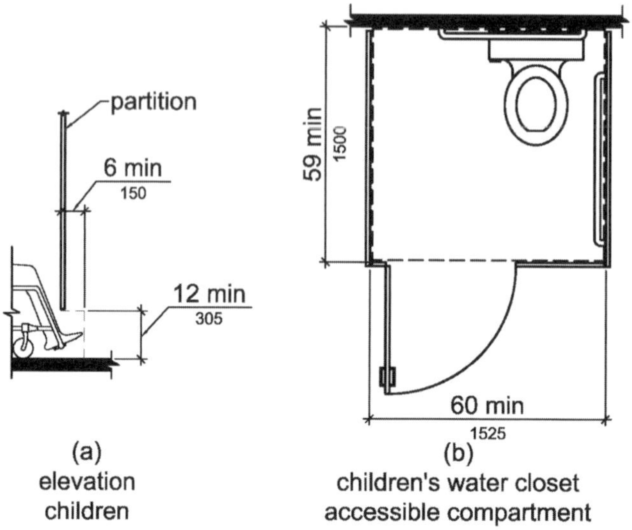

Figure 3.20: Size of children's accessible toilet compartment.

Figure 3.21: Children's toilet compartments are recommended for children with disabilities.

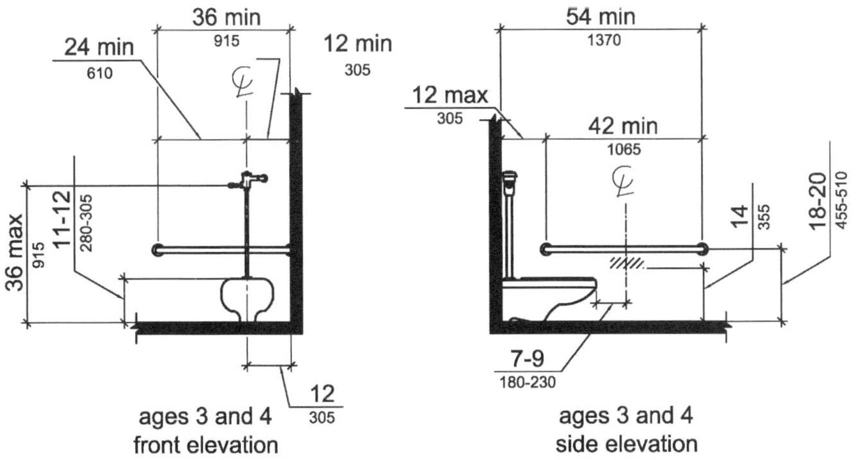

Figure 3.22a: Location of water closet and accessories (Ages 3 and 4).

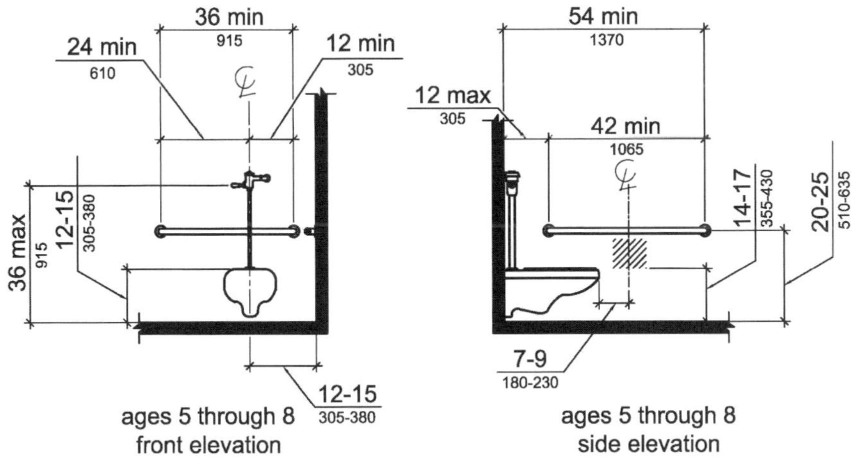

Figure 3.22b: Location of water closet and accessories location (Ages 5 and 8).

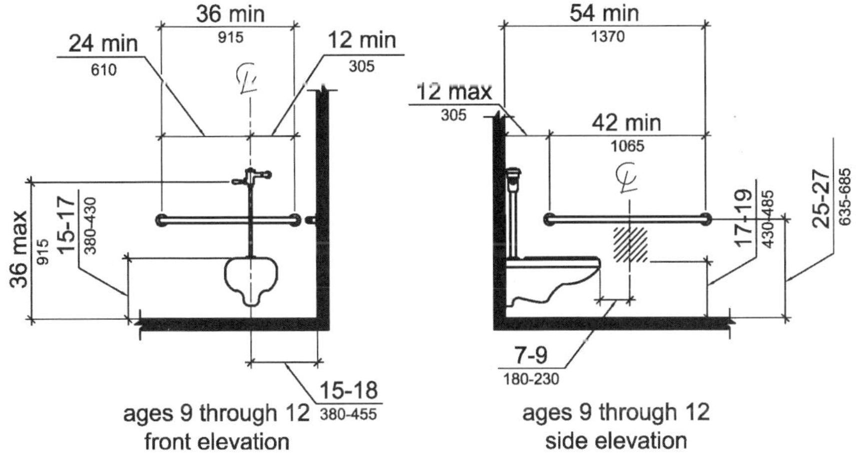

Figure 3.22c: Location of water closet and accessories location (Ages 9 and 12).

Figure 3.23: Water closets for children should not be a tank type if the grab bar heights for children will be used. The distance between the tank and the grab bar should be 12 inches minimum in order to allow for gripping.

Mirrors

Although not required within the standards, a full-size mirror can accommodate a larger group of people, including children. Consider a mirror where the top of the reflecting surface is 74 inches above the finished floor.

Mirrors located above lavatories or countertops must still be installed with the bottom edge of the reflecting surface 40 inches maximum above the finish floor or ground. Additionally, mirrors not located above lavatories or countertops must be installed with the bottom edge of the reflecting surface 35 inches maximum above the finish floor or ground.

Lavatories and Sinks

The standards, by exception, allow a special height and knee clearance for lavatories and sinks primarily used by children. For all children, a lower height and knee clearance is permitted. The same is true for ages 6 through 12. Additionally, for ages 5 years and younger any height lower than 34 inches is allowed with no knee and toe clearances and a parallel approach (see Figures 3.24 through 3.28).

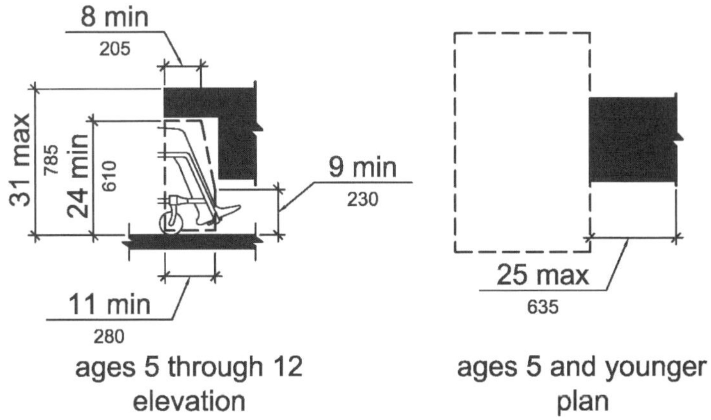

Figure 3.24: Children's lavatories and sink's height and clearances.

Figure 3.25: Child-height lavatories are suggested so that children with disabilities can wash their hands independently.

Figure 3.26: A side approach to a sink is allowed for children five and under.

Dressing and Fitting Rooms

All benches provided within dressing rooms should be the typical height of a wheelchair seat: 17 inches to 19 inches. However, in dressing and fitting rooms serving children, it is permissible for them to be lower. The actual height is not specified (see Figure 3.29).

Signage

Toilet room signs generally indicate "MEN," "MEN'S TOILET," "WOMEN," or "WOMEN'S TOILET," and include male or female pictograms. For signage designating children's toilet rooms in

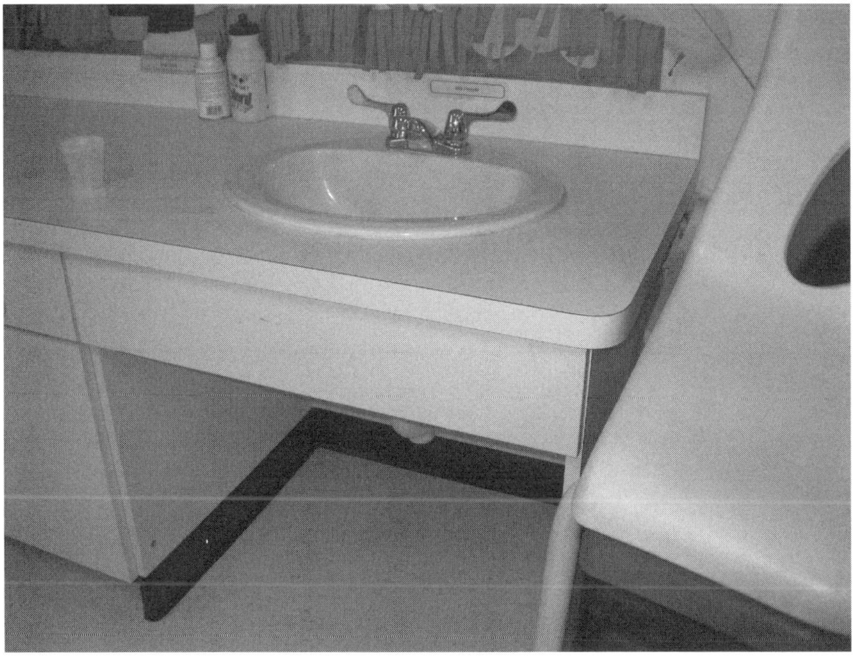

Figure 3.27: A knee space at a child sink is required if the children are over the age of 5.

Figure 3.28: Lavatories that are communal can be used as long as the proper knee clearances, reach ranges, and heights are maintained.

Figure 3.29: Benches in dressing rooms near children's lockers are required to have back supports so that children with disabilities can sit at them without difficulty.

occupancies serving children 12 years old or younger, it is generally acceptable to use the equivalent "BOY" or "GIRL." Pictograms alone are considered insufficient, however. If those pictograms are provided, the appropriate verbal message must be written immediately below the pictogram and its corresponding braille as specified the accessibility standards (see Figure 3.30).

RAMPS AND STAIRS

Where children are the primary users of a facility, a second set of handrails may be provided at stairs, ramps, and other walking surfaces. At the appropriate height, they can provide invaluable assistance and prevent accidents. A maximum height of 28 inches is recommended with a minimum of 9 inches required between upper and lower rails. Special consideration of the double-handrail design should be undertaken, because children may attempt to climb over the rails, especially at stairs (see Figures 3.31 and 3.32).

Figure 3.30: This "Boys" signage has the pictogram below the corresponding text, which is not acceptable.

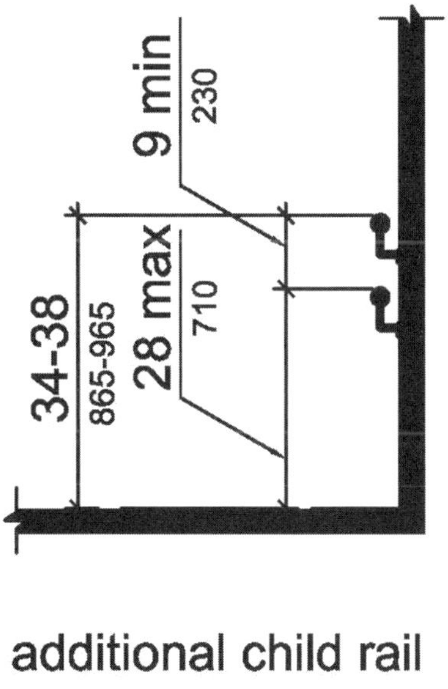

Figure 3.31: Additional children's handrail.

Figure 3.32: It is suggested that handrails for children be lower than for adults.

ASSEMBLY AREAS

Primary schools have cafeterias and performance areas that will sometimes be in the same place. Both those spaces will have to be in compliance with the ADA Standards. The size of the performance areas and whether there is fixed seating or not will dictate if the designer should use the wheelchair and companion seat numbers listed in the ADA Table 221.2.1.1. A certain number of wheelchair seats will be required, as well as a companion seat for each wheelchair seat. The companion seat is for the able-bodied person who accompanies the child or parent attending a performance. Companion seats are typically the same type of seat as all the others, although they can be removable. The wheelchair and companion seat must be integrated into the regular seats (see Figure 3.33).

The stage for performing must also be accessible. If the access is by steps that the audience can ascend from the seating area, an accessible route must also be provided from the same place for people with disabilities (see Figures 3.34 through 3.36). The accessible route may be provided by ramp or wheelchair lift as permitted by section 206.7 of standards.

Figure 3.33: Wheelchair spaces are required to be provided in assembly areas.

Figure 3.34: A stage must be accessible, and access should be in the same place as the main access to the stage.

Figure 3.35: It is suggested that tables in cafeterias be made accessible even if they are not fixed.

Figure 3.36: Cafeteria lines must have the proper width for use by a child in a wheelchair.

Cafeterias can sometimes act as "auditoriums" as well as places for dining. The cafeterias do not have fixed seating typically, but it is recommended that they be made accessible and include provisions for those with disabilities. These provisions are found in standards section 306 for knee and toe clearance and section 902 for dining surfaces.

OUTDOOR PLAY AREAS

Often playgrounds in primary schools are not usable by students with disabilities. Playground equipment may not be easily accessible by students in wheelchairs or by those with mobility problems, who may not easily traverse ground surfaces.

Accessibility standards now address the play area components that must be accessible (see Figure 3.37). Chapter 10 of the standards discusses requirements for playgrounds. The kinds of acceptable play surfaces, requirements for wheelchair maneuvering, and the height and clearances of play tables are identified in depth in Chapter 7.

Figure 3.37: Playgrounds are required to be accessible, including the equipment.

TRANSPORTATION FACILITIES

Primary schools are not often thought of as having transportation facilities. It's easier to make the case with inner city schools; however suburban schools do as well. Many primary schools have both passenger and bus loading zones.

Passenger Loading Zones

Passenger loading zones are designed for loading and unloading. Students being dropped off by their parents and carpools are consistent with this definition. These zones, provided at many primary schools, must provide at least one passenger loading zone every continuous 100 linear feet (30 m) of loading zone. The technical standards for loading zones can be found in section 503 of the standards. Loading zones serving an accessible entrance should be located in the shortest distance from the zone to facility entrance. These are zone areas at which a vehicle will briefly stop, load or unload, then depart. If there is a curb at the loading zone, a compliant curb ramp that is part of the accessible route shall be provided as well. Accessible parking spaces are not passenger loading zones. A canopy is not required, but if one is provided for general public use, it must also comply with accessibility the requirements. (See Figure 3.38.)

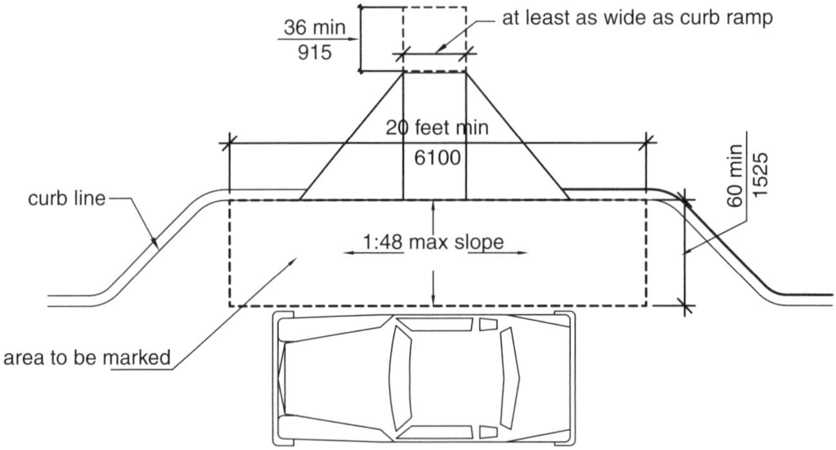

Figure 3.38: Accessible passenger loading zone and aisle.

Bus Loading Zones

Bus loading zones are restricted to use by designated or specified public transportation vehicles, with each bus bay, bus stop, or other area designated for a lift or ramp. Designated public transportation is defined by the Department of Transportation and is intended to mean other than public school transportation. While schools are not required to provide a zone by the standards, consider providing at least one for use of buses that are fitted with a lift or deploy a ramp (see Figure 3.39). Review Chapter 4 for specific requirements.

Figure 3.39: Passenger loading zones at schools must have the proper clear ground space and access to the school entrance.

SUMMARY

The purpose of this chapter is to acquaint designers and facility managers who are involved with primary educational occupancies with some of the principal accessibility issues for schools and their students aged 12 years old and younger. The exception is frequently the rule with regard to children's facility accessibility requirements; the children's standards provisions apply only to facilities to be used specifically by children.

TABLE 3.1: Advisory Specifications for Serving Children Ages 3 through 12

	Ages 3 and 4	Ages 5 through 8	Ages 9 through 12
Forward or Side Reach [Advisory 308.1]			
High (maximum)	36 in. (915 mm)	40 in. (1015 mm)	44 in. (1120 mm)
Low (minimum)	20 in. (510 mm)	18 in. (455 mm)	16 in. (405 mm)
Ramps and Stairs Additional Rail [Advisory 505.4]			
High (maximum)	28 in. (710 mm)	28 in. (710 mm)	28 in. (710 mm)
Vertical Clearance between Rail	9 in. (230 mm)	9 in. (230 mm)	9 in. (230 mm)
Drinking Fountains and Water Coolers [602.2]			
Spout Height (maximum)	30 in. (760 mm)	30 in. (760 mm)	30 in. (760 mm)
Spout from Front Edge	3½ in. (90 mm)	3½ in. (90 mm)	3½ in. (90 mm)
Knee Clearance	parallel approach permitted	parallel approach permitted	parallel approach permitted
Toilet Compartment			
Size [604.8.1.1]			
Depth (minimum)	59 in. (1500 mm)	59 in. (1500 mm)	59 in. (1,500 mm)
Toe Clearance [604.8.1.4]			
High (minimum)	12 in. (305 mm)	12 in. (305 mm)	12 in. (305 mm)
Water Closets			
Centerline [604.9.1]	12 in.(305 mm)	12–15 in. (305–380 mm)	15–18 in. (380–455 mm)
Seat Height [604.9.3]	11–12 in. (280–305 mm)	12–15 in. (305–380 mm)	15–17 in. (380–430 mm)
Grab Bar Height [604.9.4]	18–20 in. (455–510 mm)	20–25 in. (510–635 mm)	25–27 in. (635–685 mm)
Flush Controls Ht. [604.9.5]	36 in. (915 mm) maximum	36 in. (915 mm) maximum	36 in. (915 mm) maximum
Dispenser Height [604.9.6]	14 in. (355 mm)	14–17 in. (355–430 mm)	17–19 in. (430–485 mm)
Lavatories and Sinks			
Rim or Counter Ht[606.2 E4]	Not specified	31 in. (785 mm) maximum[2]	31 in. (785 mm) maximum
Knee Clearance [606.2 E4]	parallel approach permitted[1]	24 in. (610 mm) minimum[2]	24 in. (610 mm) minimum
Mirrors [Advisory 603.3]			
Top of Reflecting Surface	74 in. (1,880 mm) minimum	74 in. (1,880 mm) minimum	74 in. (1,880 mm) minimum
Dressing and Fitting Rooms			
[Advisory 803.1]	Not specified. Permitted	Not specified. Permitted	Not specified. Permitted
Top of Bench	Lower than 17 in. (420 mm)	Lower than 17 in. (420 mm)	Lower than 17 in. (420 mm)
Dining and Work Surfaces			
Knee Clearance [902.4.1]	Not specified where	24 in. (610 mm) minimum	24 in. (610 mm) minimum
Surface Height [902.4.2]	parallel approach provided[1]	26–30 in. (660–760 mm)	26–30 in. (660–760 mm)

[1] by children 5 years and younger [2] by children 6 through 12 years

Reference Sections Chapter 3

The 2010 ADA Standards references several sections for one topic. This reference table assists the designer in finding the pertinent sections pertaining to one specific area. To use the table, find the topic and below are all the different sections that the standards refer to.

Children's Requirements	
ADA Chapter 1: Definitions	
Section Number	**Section Title and Description**
106.5.18	Children's Use.
ADA Chapter 2: Scoping	
Section Number	**Section Title and Description**
234.3	Amusement Rides Minimum Number Exception 2
Advisory 234.3	Minimum Number Exceptions 1 through 3.
Advisory 234.3	Minimum Number Exception 2.
240	Play Areas
240.1	General
Advisory 240.1	General
ADA Chapter 3-10 Technical Standards	
Section Number	**Section Title and Description**
308	Reach Ranges.
Advisory	Children's Reach Ranges.
Advisory 505.4	Height.
	Chapter 6 Plumbing Fixtures
602.2	Clear Floor Space. EXCEPTION
Advisory 603.3	Mirrors.
604.1	General. EXCEPTION
604.8.1.1	Size.
604.8.1.4	Toe Clearance.
604.8.1.4	EXCEPTION:
604.9	Water Closets and Toilet Compartments for Children's Use.
Advisory 604.9	Water Closets and Toilet Compartments for Children's Use.
Advisory	Specifications for Water Closets Serving Children Ages 3 through 12
606.2	Clear Floor Space. EXCEPTION 4
609.4	Position of Grab Bars.
Advisory 803.1	General.
902.1	General. EXCEPTION
902.4	Dining Surfaces and Work Surfaces for Children's Use.
902.4	Dining Surfaces and Work Surfaces for Children's Use. EXCEPTION
Advisory 1008.3	Transfer Systems.
Advisory 1008.3.2.3	Transfer Supports.
1008	Children's Reach Ranges.
Advisory 1008.4.2	Clear Floor or Ground Space.
1008.4.3	Play Tables. EXCEPTION

Secondary and Post-Secondary Education

4

by Wally Tirado, ICC RAS

INTRODUCTION

In Chapter 3, we covered schools handling students through age 12. Depending on jurisdiction or geographic location, the grades or ages covered by secondary education can vary greatly. Students will move to secondary schools between the ages 10 to 14 and finish between the ages of 16 to 19. For the purposes of this chapter, consider the starting age to be after age 12; at that point, accessibility standards no longer specify alternate specifications for heights and clearances, and the standard adult specifications are used.

Postsecondary education is also included in this chapter, because, in terms of accessibility, the types of buildings used for secondary and postsecondary education are difficult to distinguish. Any differences between secondary and postsecondary schools will be identified. Postsecondary schools are considered a third level of education, which typically follows the completion of a secondary education and often occurs at universities, colleges, and vocational schools.

Secondary and postsecondary education contains a variety of multiple buildings and types, which include: classrooms, gymnasiums, libraries, theaters, and dormitories. It is more common now for students with disabilities to further their education by attending institutions of higher learning. Higher educational institutions may have fewer responsibilities in terms of services provided to these students and, in turn, these students must take on more responsibility in their education.

ACCESSIBLE SITES AND PARKING

While at least one accessible route must be provided within the site from other accessible site elements, it's important to remember that each site arrival point must be connected by an accessible route to each of the building's entrances served. Additionally, an accessible route must be provided to connect areas where sport activities occur. Where several sports fields are provided, an accessible route must be provided at each field.

Bus Loading Zones

Access to public transportation is crucial to people with disabilities. The disabled rely on public transportation much more than those without disabilities. Designated bus stops must have areas where these buses can deploy a ramp. Bus loading zones are restricted to use by designated or specified public transportation vehicles. If bus shelters are provided on campus, a clear floor space inside the shelter must also be provided for wheelchairs. This also helps standing students to wait for the bus in inclement weather. These shelters must also be provided on the accessible route to and from the bus stop boarding and alighting area. Furthermore, each transportation facility is required to be on the accessible route as well (see Figures 4.1 and 4.2). See Chapter 3 for more information on passenger loading zones.

Figure 4.1: This figure shows the space required at the bus loading zone for persons with disabilities to board.

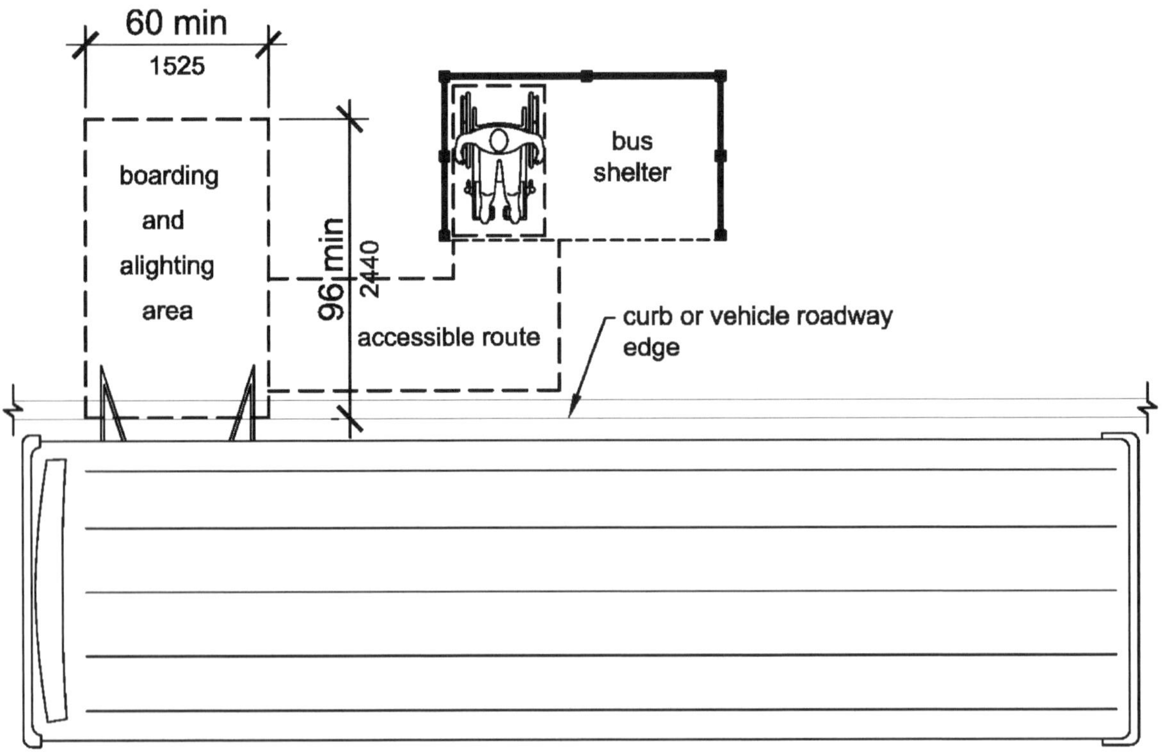

Figure 4.2a: Bus stops on campus should be connected to an accessible route to the rest of the buildings.

Figure 4.2b: A clear floor space inside the bus shelter should be provided for wheelchairs.

Location and Dispersion of Parking

Where parking spaces are provided, accessible parking is to be provided in accordance to each parking facility or lot (see Figure 4.3). Schools often have parking facilities dedicated to specific uses, for example: faculty parking, student parking, bus parking, and public parking. If you have multiple facilities, it is important to realize that each facility's parking is satisfied independently not the aggregate total of all facilities provided on the site or campus.

Parking spaces are still required to be located on the shortest possible route to building entrances and must be dispersed if multiple accessible entrances are provided. If parking facilities do not serve a particular building, provided accessible spaces must be located on the shortest route to the accessible pedestrian route to the facility entrance. If possible, minimize wheelchair travel behind parking vehicles (see Figure 4.4). Although not required, where accessible routes cross traffic, consider marking crossings and minimize travel distances.

Figure 4.3: Parking spaces must be provided for standard cars and for vans. They will each have a size requirement, but the access aisle should be 5 ft 0 in. min. for both.

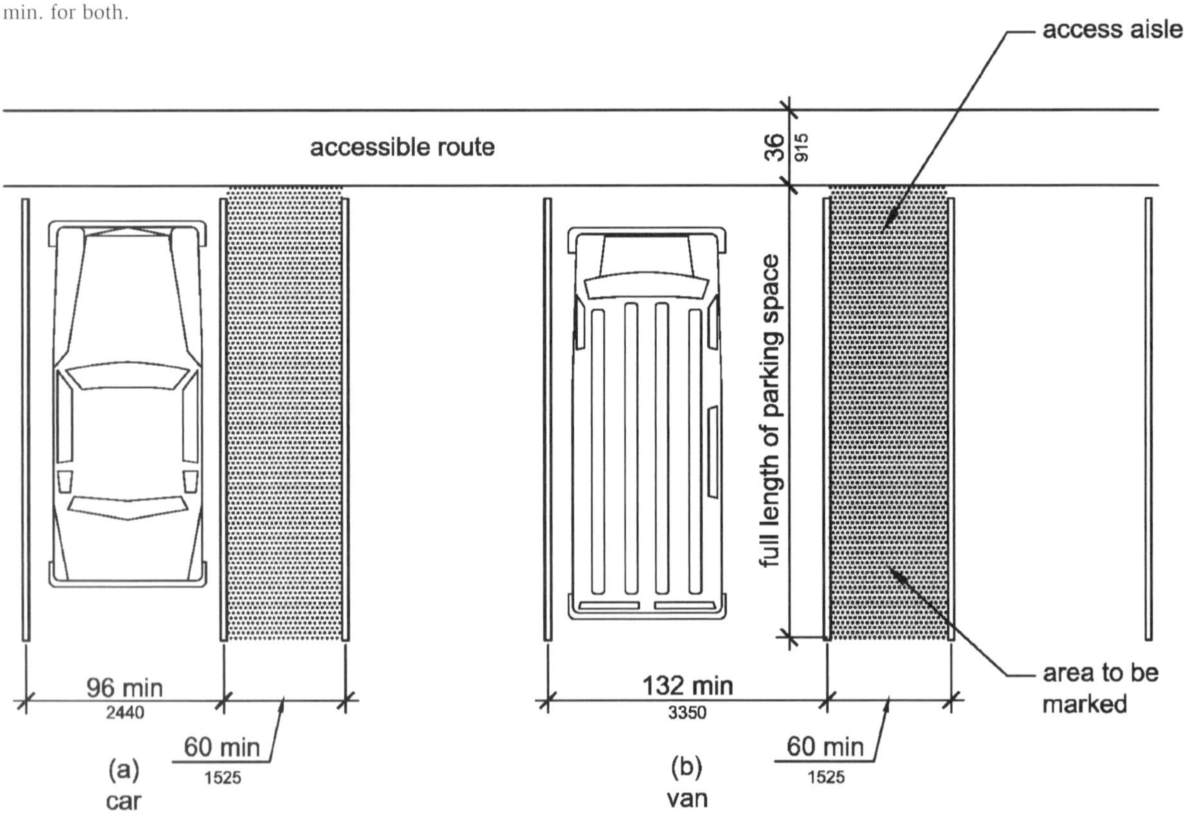

Figure 4.4: Whenever possible, an accessible route in front of the parking spaces should be provided in order to minimize the risk of hazards. Also an access aisle between parking spaces should be provided for exiting.

Leased/Assigned Parking

Parking lots and facilities that are leased or assigned are not exempt from the accessible parking requirements (see Figure 4.5). This is sometimes a difficulty for planning purposes, since most universities have assigned parking lots for students or faculty. The assigning of accessible parking spaces is allowed; however, it is highly discouraged. However, clearly designated accessible parking spaces must be provided and made known to the students and staff with disabilities. Since most of the buildings on campus are accessed by pedestrians and not vehicles, it is not always required that the assigned parking be located closest to one particular building's entrance, unless that parking is assigned to that building.

Figure 4.5: Assigned parking should also have accessible spaces.

Playing Fields and Exterior Athletic Facilities

There are no specific requirements for playing fields other than the general site accessible route requirements of the standards (see Figure 4.6). The accessible areas associated with those facilities, including toilet, shower, locker, and dressing rooms, must be located on an accessible route and designed to be accessible according to applicable standards for each facility type. It is also important to remember that concession stands and ticket booths must be accessible as well.

Grandstands and Bleachers

Grandstand and bleacher requirements are governed by the Assembly Area standards and are discussed later in this chapter. All accessible seating must be connected to an accessible route to all related areas, including the playing field itself, any team and player seating, dressing areas, and locker rooms (see Figures 4.7, 4.8, and 4.9).

Figure 4.6a: A soccer field is exempted from having to be accessible, but an accessible route to the field as well as to any spectator seating is required.

Figure 4.6b: Concession stands are service counters and should meet the requirements for ADA Section 904.

Team or Player Seating

At least one wheelchair space must be provided and comply with the accessibility standards. Wheelchair spaces are to be provided in team or player seating areas serving each sport activity area (see Figure 4.10). When providing the wheelchair space an associated companion space must be provided as well.

Press Boxes

Press boxes in assembly areas shall be on an accessible route. There are some exceptions specified in the standard. An accessible route is not required to press boxes in bleachers if the entry points are at one level and provided that the total area of all press boxes, not just one, is 500 square feet maximum. The other exception specified is that an accessible route is not required to freestanding press boxes that are elevated above a grade of 12 feet minimum provided that the aggregate area of all press boxes is 500 square feet maximum (see Figure 4.11). Where there are multiple assembly areas, the total area of the press boxes at each assembly area is to be calculated separately. This provision reduces the economic impact on smaller sports facilities, like those located at high schools and community colleges.

Figure 4.7: Bleachers located inside the basketball court should have spaces available for wheelchairs.

Figure 4.8: Exterior bleachers and grandstands are required to have wheelchair spaces integrated into the seating.

Figure 4.9: Seating for wheelchairs can be single or double as long as wheelchair seats have companion seats next to them, and they must be part of the regular seating.

Figure 4.10: Team player seating, including baseball dugouts, are required to be accessible and have an accessible route.

Figure 4.11: This press box, even though it is accessed via the bleachers, is bigger than 500 square feet and must have an accessible route.

Luxury Boxes, Club Boxes, and Suites

Each luxury box, club box, and suite within arenas, stadiums, and grandstands is required to have wheelchair spaces and companion spaces. The number of wheelchair spaces required in luxury boxes, club boxes, and suites within an arena, stadium, or grandstand area are calculated according to each type.

Court Sports

In court sports, such as tennis and racquetball, at least one accessible route is required to directly connect both sides of the court (see Figure 4.12).

Entry Gates

Entry gates must comply with the requirements for doors located along the accessible route. An accessible gate must also be provided where turnstiles or revolving gates are provided. An exception is provided where security personnel have sole control doors; however, it is not acceptable for personnel to operate the doors for the disabled when others have independent access (see Figure 4.13).

Figure 4.12: Tennis courts themselves are exempted, but an accessible route is required.

GENERAL ACCESSIBLE AREAS

An accessible route applies to both interior spaces and exterior spaces. Generally, an accessible route must interconnect all accessible features on the entire school campus, from the accessible parking spaces to the building entrances to the classrooms to the sports and playground facilities and other functional spaces.

Figure 4.13: A gate into a sports area must have the proper clearances and door hardware.

Accessible features for those with disabilities must coincide throughout a facility to those for persons without disabilities, allowing people with disabilities the same routes and paths of travel provided for other people. Avoid accessible routes that are provided to alternative secondary entrances.

Security Barriers

Where facilities include security barriers, which include security bollards and security checkpoints, and metal detectors, an accessible route through the security barrier is required. Doors and gates must comply with the standards, including the required minimum approach, width, and hardware. This can often become a problem when designing school libraries and bookstores (see Figure 4.14).

An exception is allowed where certain metal detectors, or other similar devices, cannot comply with the standards. In such cases, the accessible route may be located adjacent to the security screening devices and should allow those passing around security barriers to maintain visual contact with their personal items consistent with fully mobile students' ability to do so.

Figure 4.14: Security barriers at libraries and bookstores have to be accessible and have the proper widths.

Temporary Structures and Facilities

Accessibility standards apply to both temporary and permanent buildings and facilities. Examples of temporary facilities include: reviewing stands, classroom buildings, bleacher areas, stages, platforms, fixed furniture systems, and exhibit areas. Structures and equipment directly associated with the actual construction processes are not required to be accessible.

ASSEMBLY AREAS

Accessibility requirements for educational auditoriums, grandstands, and bleachers are nearly identical with those for any other public-use assembly area. These areas are required to comply with number of wheelchair seating spaces and provide adjacent companion seating. In stadiums, arenas, and grandstands, wheelchair spaces and companion seats should be dispersed to all levels that include seating served by an accessible route.

Accessible routes must also be provided from accessible audience seating areas to performing areas, including stages, stage platforms, dressing and locker rooms, orchestra pits, and other similar performance facilities (see Figure 4.15).

Figure 4.15: Access to the stage from the audience seats is required if there are steps or other means to access the stage from the spectator seats.

Classrooms

A classroom is considered an assembly area and must follow the requirements in ADA Table 221.2.1. Therefore, any classroom with fixed seating must follow this table. Because these are not seats that people purchase to view a performance, it is not necessary to disperse them for choices in "price," but it is a good idea to disperse them for viewing purposes (see Figure 4.16). They also must have companion seating next to them for an able-bodied companion to sit with the disabled person in class. The spaces must be an integral part of the seating and should be in a shoulder-to-shoulder arrangement (see Figures 4.16 and 4.17).

The Department of Justice has been responsive to concerns about unused accessible seating, which does not allow the maximum number of students possible to be seated in a classroom. Accordingly, the department has reduced scoping requirements significantly—by almost half in large assembly areas—and determined that allowing assembly areas to in-fill unused wheelchair spaces with readily removable temporary individual seats appropriately balances the need to address the those concerns and the rights of individuals with disabilities. See section 221.1 of the 2010 Standards (see Figure 4.18).

Figure 4.16: A classroom with stadium seating must have accessible seating. It is best to disperse the seating in order to provide students with different viewing opportunities.

Figure 4.17: Even though a choir or orchestra practice room does not have fixed seats, it is important to provide areas for wheelchairs that are integrated into the stands. This allows students in wheelchairs to feel part of the class and participate like the other students.

Figure 4.18: Classrooms without fixed seating are not required to provide accessible table or seats, but the school or university should provide space for students who require assistance in order to avoid discrimination and to provide program access.

There are times when the classroom has fixed tables and loose seating, and then these will be considered "counters." Because students perform "work," such as experiments, writing, and the like, these furnishings are considered "work counters." In general 5% of fixed work counters must be made accessible and follow ADA section 902, which requires that the counter have a front approach and no higher than 34 inches above finished floor (see Figures 4.19 through 4.21). A work counter might be the desk itself, but it could also be any computer desk or science lab with a sink.

Other Box Seating and Outdoor Seating

Earlier in the chapter we discussed luxury boxes, club boxes, and suites. However, there are provisions for accessible seating in "other boxes." These include tiered box seating provided in facilities such as auditoriums for spatial and acoustical design purposes. The number of wheelchair spaces and companion seating required in these boxes are calculated according to the total number of seats provided in these boxes. The wheelchair spaces must also be located in no fewer than 20% of the boxes and dispersed appropriately.

Figure 4.19a: Computer labs must have 5% of their counters with knee clearance as well as the proper heights.

Figure 4.19b: Labs for students must also have 5% of the counters and at least one sink accessible with the proper knee clearances and heights for the counters.

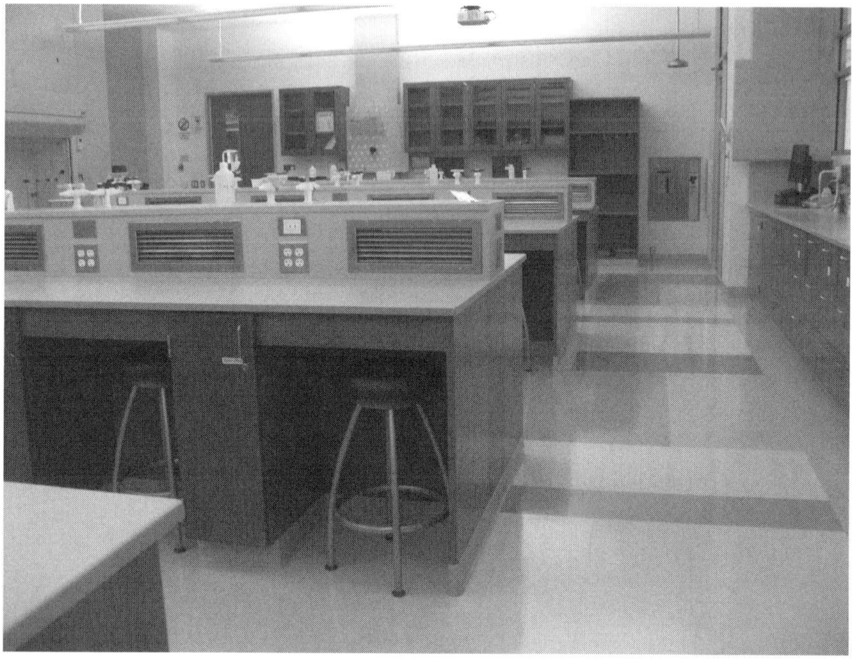

Figure 4.19c: At least one lab counter should be at the accessible height.

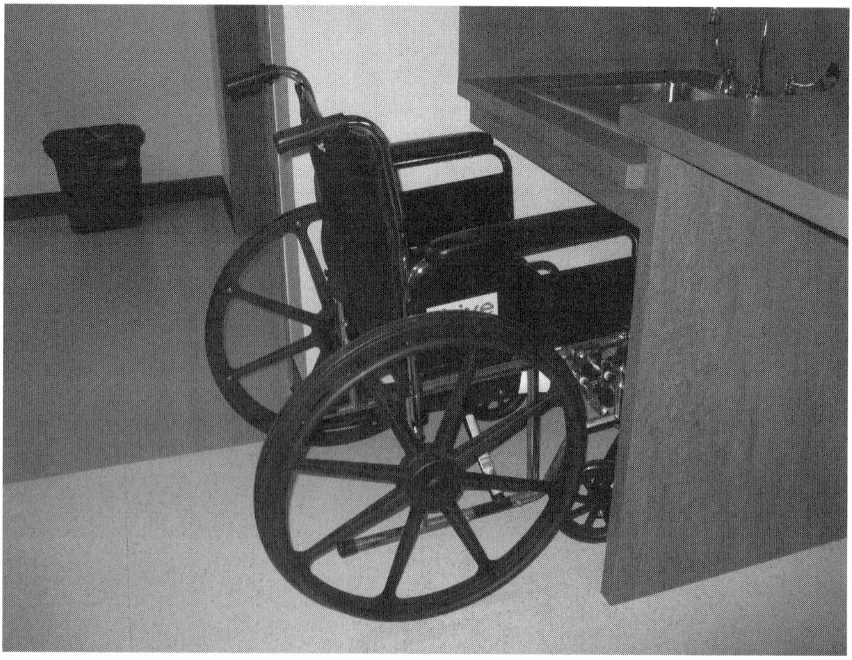

Figure 4.20: A knee clearance for wheelchairs should be provided at classroom sinks.

Figure 4.21: Group seating in science classrooms should allow for a student in a wheelchair to sit at the same table with the rest of the students; 5% of the tables, but no less than one, should be accessible.

Another form of assembly seating is outdoor seating. If there are any outdoor benches, these are not technically scoped in the ADA. The DOJ does allow a designer to provide outdoor benches, using the Public Right of Way Guidelines, but some jurisdictions will see these as "assembly" seating, which must also follow the wheelchair seating table mentioned previously. The designers or building owners should check with their jurisdiction prior to installing these benches to see how they will interpret the rule (see Figure 4.22).

Performance Areas

Colleges and universities have spaces for performances that students put on as part of their curriculum. These performances are typically paid performances and are open to the public (see Figure 4.23). For all intents and purposes, the assembly seating will be designed as in a regular theater with paid customers. The wheelchair and companion seating will follow the same table as the assembly seating we discussed for classrooms. It should also be integrated to the rest of the seating (see Figures 4.24 and 4.25).

The *2010 ADA Guidance* handbook explains further that "Section 4.33.3 of the 1991 Standards and sections 402, 403.5.1, 802.1.4, and 802.1.5 of the 2010 Standards require walkways that are part of an accessible route to have a 36-inch minimum clear width. Section 802.1.5 of the 2010 Standards specifically prohibits accessible routes from overlapping wheelchair spaces. This change is consistent with the technical requirements for accessible routes, since the clear width of accessible routes cannot be obstructed by any object. The 2010 Standards also specifically prohibit wheelchair spaces from overlapping circulation paths. An advisory note clarifies that this prohibition applies only to the circulation path width required by applicable building codes and fire and life safety codes, since the codes prohibit obstructions in the required width of assembly aisles.

Figure 4.22a: An outdoor bench requires access, including an accessible route to the bench.

Figure 4.22b: Box seats that are privately leased throughout the year must also have accessible seating.

Figure 4.23: Theater-style seats must include accessible seating.

Figure 4.24: Wheelchair seating should be arranged so that those who are disabled can have viewing angles in different situations, including seated, standing, and a combination of these.

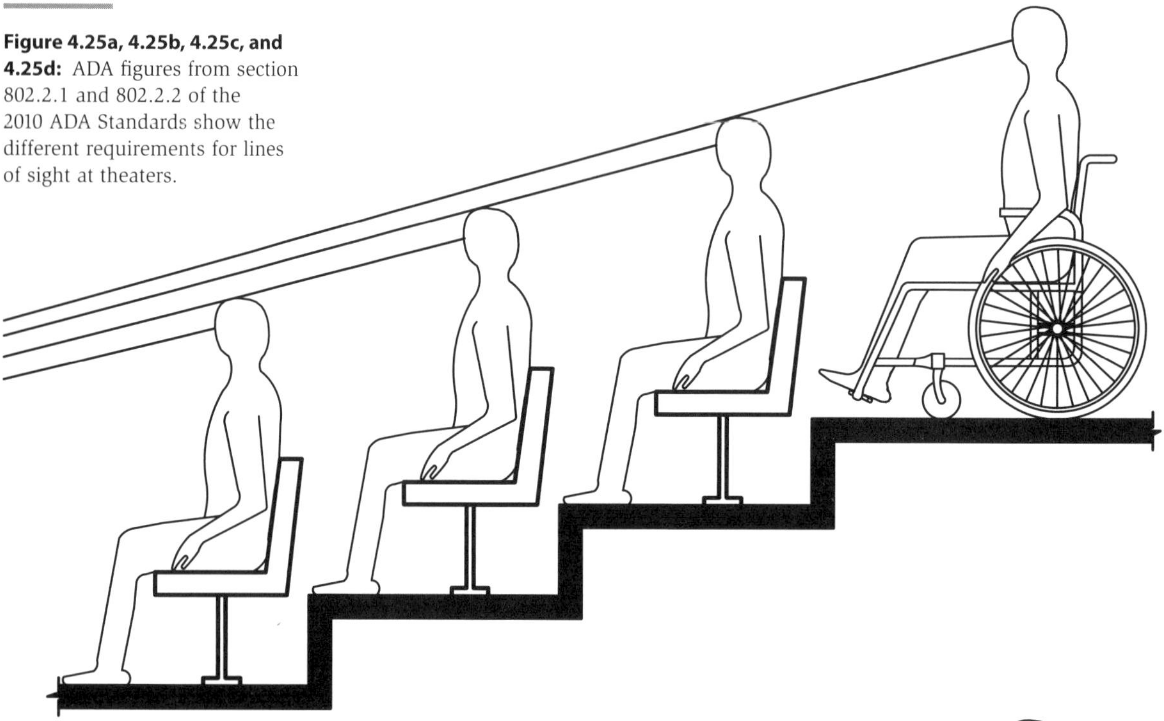

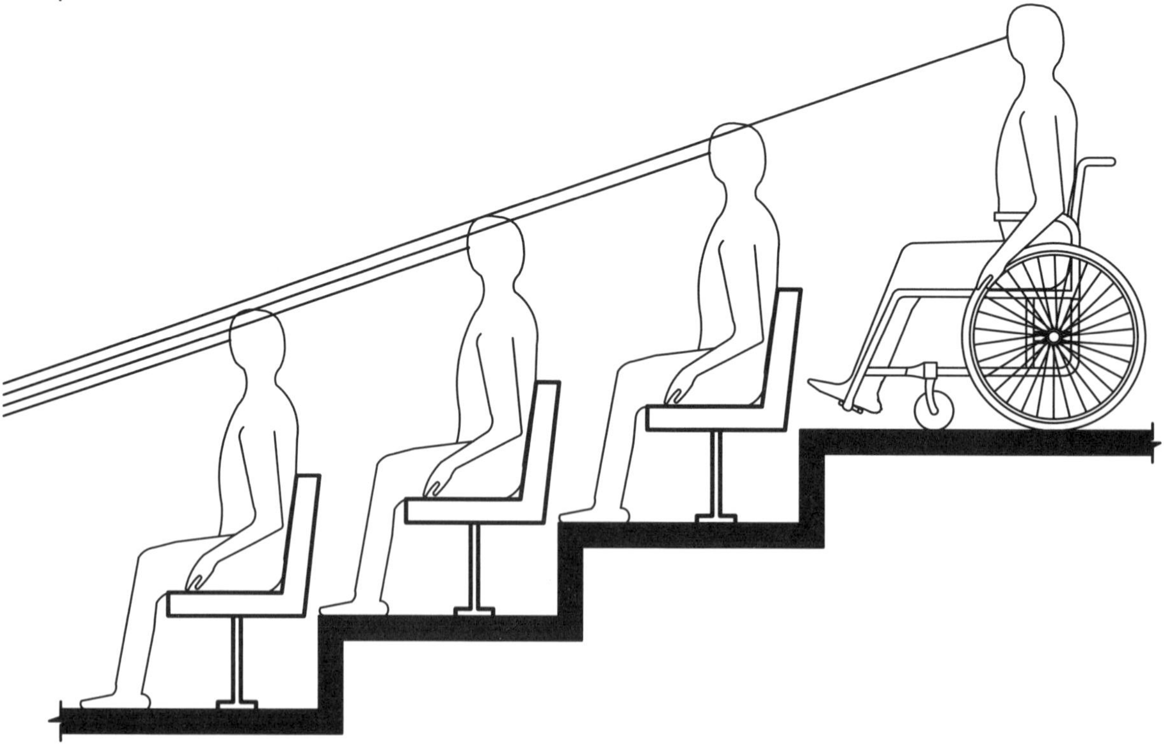

Figure 4.25a, 4.25b, 4.25c, and 4.25d: ADA figures from section 802.2.1 and 802.2.2 of the 2010 ADA Standards show the different requirements for lines of sight at theaters.

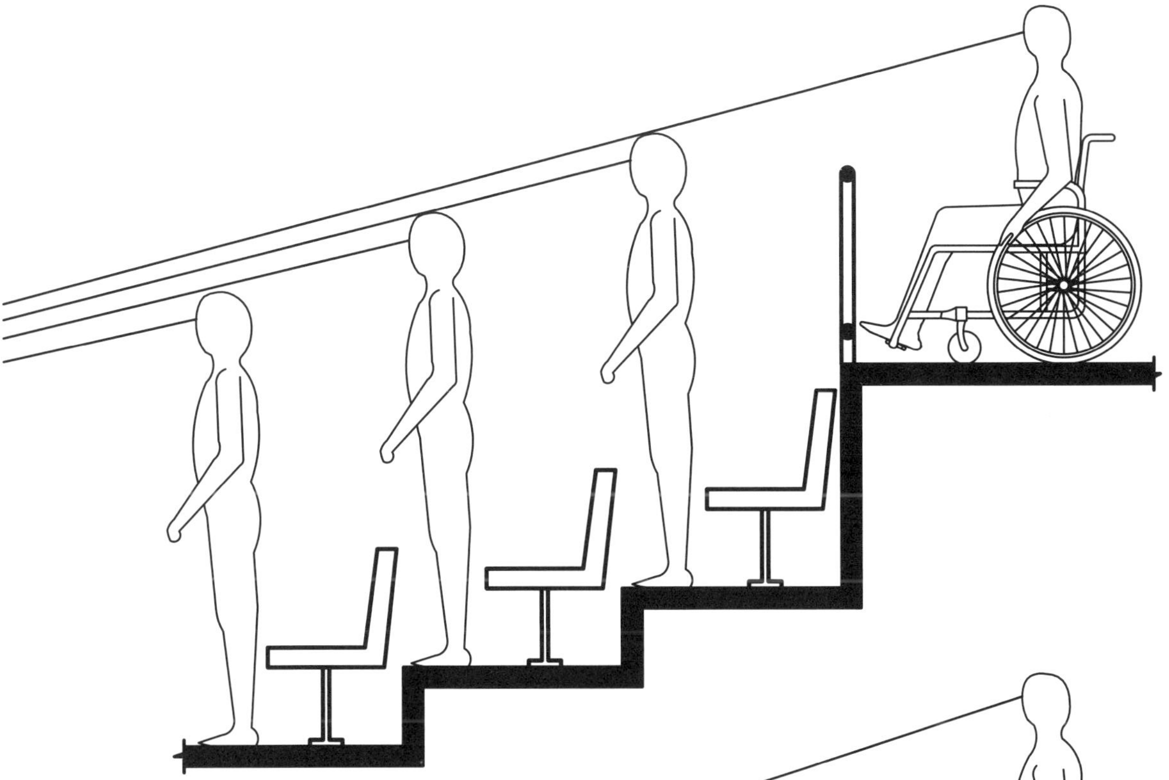

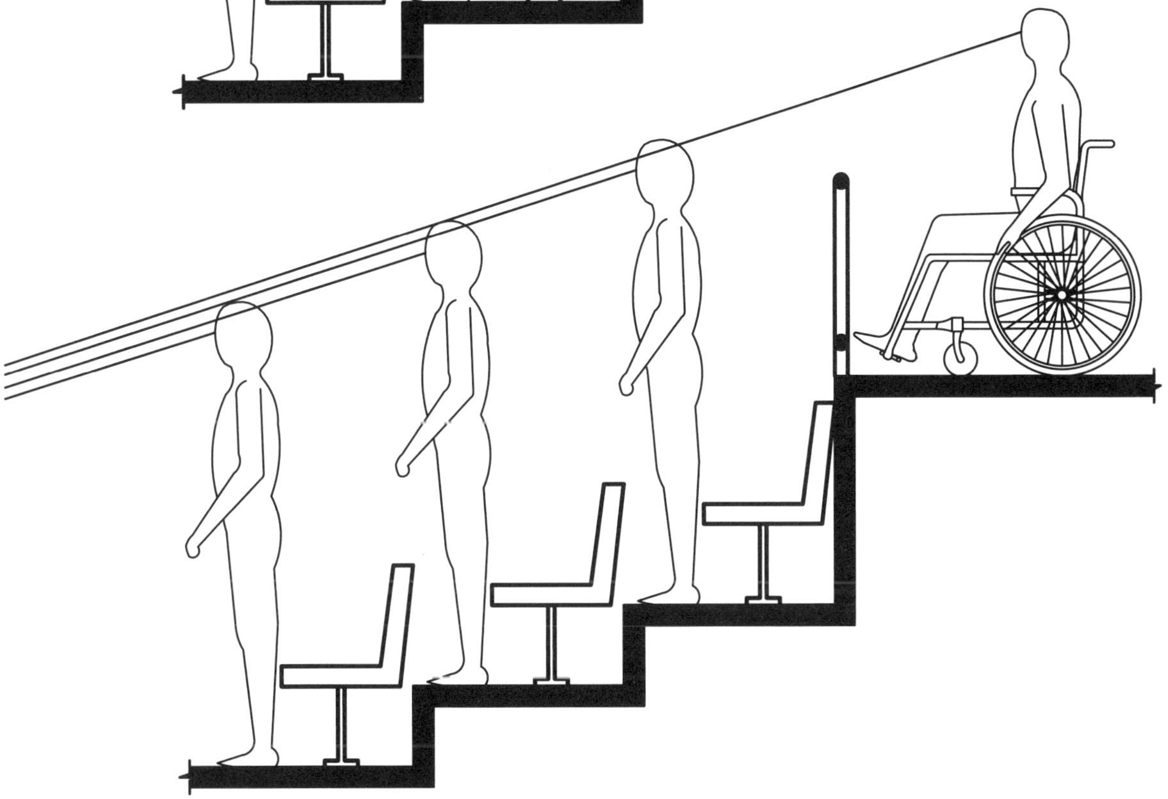

Section 802.1.5 of the 2010 Standards provides that, where a main circulation path is located in front of a row of seats that contains a wheelchair space and the circulation path is wider than required by applicable building codes and fire and life safety codes, the wheelchair space may overlap the "extra" circulation path width. Where a main circulation path is located behind a row of seats that contains a wheelchair space and the wheelchair space is entered from the rear, the aisle in front of the row may need to be wider in order not to block the required circulation path to the other seats in the row, or a mid-row opening may need to be provided to access the required circulation path to the other seats.

The *2010 ADA Guidance* handbook explains that:

> Owners of large assembly areas have historically complained to the Department that the requirement for one percent (1%) of seating to be wheelchair seating is excessive and that wheelchair seats are not being sold. At the same time, advocates have traditionally argued that persons who use wheelchairs will increasingly participate in activities at assembly areas once they become accessible and that at least one percent (1%) of seats should be accessible.
>
> The 1991 Standards, at sections 4.1.3(19)(a) and 4.33.3, require assembly areas to provide wheelchair and companion seats. In assembly areas with a capacity of more than five hundred seats, accessible seating at a ratio of one percent (1%) (plus one seat) of the number of traditional fixed seats must be provided. The 2010 Standards, at in section 221.2, require assembly areas with 501 to 5,000 seats to provide at least six wheelchair spaces and companion seats plus one additional wheelchair space for each additional 150 seats (or fraction thereof) between 501 through 5,000. In assembly areas with more than 5,000 seats at least 36 wheelchair spaces and companion seats plus one additional wheelchair space for each 200 seats (or fraction thereof) more than 5,000 are required. See sections 221.1 and 221.2 of the 2010 Standards. Commenters questioned why scoping requirements for large assembly areas are being reduced. During the development of the 2004 ADAAG, industry providers, particularly those representing larger stadium-style assembly areas, supplied data to the Access Board, demonstrating the current scoping requirements for large assembly areas often exceed the demand. Based on the data provided to the Access Board, the Department believes the reduced scoping requirements will adequately meet the needs of individuals with disabilities, while balancing concerns of the industry. Commenters representing assembly areas supported the reduced scoping. One commenter asked that scoping requirements for larger assembly areas be reduced even further. Although the commenter referenced data demonstrating that wheelchair spaces in larger facilities with seating capacities of 70,000 or more may not be used by individuals with disabilities, the data was not based on actual results, but was calculated at least in part based on probability assumptions. The Department is not convinced that further reductions should be made based upon those projections and that further reductions would not substantially limit accessibility at assembly areas for persons who use wheelchairs.
>
> Section 221.2.1.3 of the 2010 Standards clarifies that the scoping requirements for wheelchair spaces and companion seats are to be applied separately to general seating areas and to each luxury box, club box, and suite in arenas, stadiums, and grandstands. In assembly areas other than arenas, stadiums, and grandstands, the scoping requirements will not be applied separately. Thus, in performing arts facilities with tiered boxes designed for spatial and acoustical purposes, the scoping requirement is to be applied to the seats in the tiered boxes. The requisite number

of wheelchair spaces and companion seats required in the tiered boxes are to be dispersed among at least twenty percent (20%) of the tiered boxes. For example, if a performing arts facility has 20 tiered boxes with 10 fixed seats in each box, for a total of 200 seats, at least five wheelchair spaces and companion seats must be provided in the boxes, and they must be dispersed among at least four of the 20 boxes.

Commenters raised concerns that the 2010 Standards should clarify requirements for scoping of seating areas and that requiring accessible seating in each luxury box, club box, and suite in arenas, stadiums and grandstands could result in no wheelchair and companion spaces available for individuals with disabilities in the general seating area(s). These comments appear to misunderstand the requirements. The 2010 Standards require each luxury box, club box, and suite in an arena, stadium or grandstand to be accessible and to contain wheelchair spaces and companion seats as required by sections 221.2.1.1, 221.2.1.2 and 221.3. In addition, the remaining seating areas not located in boxes must also contain the number of wheelchair and companion seating locations specified in the 2010 Standards based on the total number of seats in the entire facility excluding luxury boxes, club boxes and suites."

Analysis and Commentary on the 2010 ADA Standards page 110 Guidance on the 2010 Standards: Titles II and III

Assistive Listening Systems (ALS)

In each assembly area where audible communication is integral to the use of the space, an assistive listening system is required to be provided. The number of receivers required for an ALS is dictated in the standards by the capacity of seating in an assembly area (see Figure 4.26).

The 2010 Standards add a new exception that allows multiple assembly areas that are in the same building and under the same management, such as theaters in a multiplex cinema and

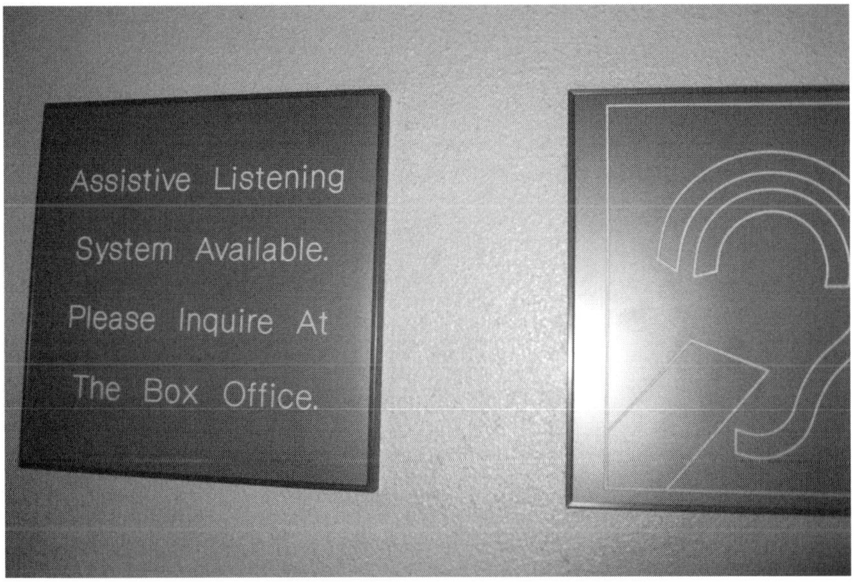

Figure 4.26: When assisted listening devices are provided, a sign should be installed letting hearing impaired spectators that the devices are available and where to find them.

lecture halls in a college building, to calculate the number of receivers required based on the total number of seats in all the assembly areas, instead of in each assembly area separately, as long as the receivers are compatible with the assistive listening systems used in each of the assembly areas.

Ticket Booths and Concession Stands

These facilities are normally staffed by both students and public volunteers. Therefore, both sides of the service counter should be accessible, in addition to meeting the typical accessibility requirements, such as those for maneuvering space, reach, and approach, and operating controls.

LIBRARIES

The 1991 ADAAG has an entire section for libraries. The 2010 ADA Standards eliminated the section, since most of the requirements can be found in other sections that already exist. There are no specific scoping differences or unique requirements for libraries. What is important to note is that an accessible entrance, accessible route into and through the library, and access to service counters and work surfaces must be provided (see Figure 4.27).

The requirements for stacks and book shelves can be found in the Storage section of the 2010 ADA Standards. Scoping for storage facilities are given in section 225. Library stacks are considered self-service shelving. They are not required to be accessible, except for being located on an accessible route (see Figure 4.28).

Figure 4.27: Libraries' stacks and counters are required to be on an accessible route.

Figure 4.28: Library stacks are not required to meet the reach ranges required in the 2010 ADA Standards.

Service counters, such as reference desks, book drops, and checkout desks, are required to follow the guidelines for service counters. They must be no higher than 36 inches and no shorter than 36 inches long (see Figure 4.29). They must have either a forward approach or a parallel approach, depending on the amount of space provided.

Library study spaces should also be accessible, including ones that are located in a mezzanine. If a group of students are studying together, it is recommended that the study spaces all be accessible in order to not discriminate (see Figure 4.30).

PHYSICAL EDUCATION FACILITIES

Gymnasiums must also comply with requirements for accessible seating, including all the requirements for auditoriums and court sports already discussed. Bleachers installed in gymnasiums must comply with applicable requirements and have appropriate protective railings as required.

Exercise Machines and Equipment

Exercise machines and equipment are required to comply with accessibility standards and be on an accessible route. Each type of exercise machine and equipment must have clearance positioned to accommodate transfer of a person seated in a wheelchair (see Figure 4.31). Required clearances at machines and equipment are permitted to overlap and be shared between two pieces of exercise equipment.

Figure 4.29: A portion of service counters at libraries are required to be at an accessible height.

Figure 4.30a: A library with multiple levels should have an accessible route connecting all levels.

Figure 4.30b: Five percent of study carrels must be accessible, since they are work surfaces in libraries.

Figure 4.31: Clear floor space should be provided adjacent to each piece of exercise equipment. An accessible route should also be provided.

Dressing, Fitting, and Locker Rooms

Where dressing rooms, fitting rooms, or locker rooms are provided, at least 5%, but no less than one, of each type in each cluster provided must be accessible and meet the requirements in the ADA Standards. A cluster is defined in the standards as a group of rooms proximate to another. Regardless of the type of facility, dressing, fitting, or locker rooms, the standards require that people with disabilities be provided with facilities that are equal to those provided to others.

A locker room will be considered a dressing room since that is one of its purposes. It will have lockers, which are considered storage facilities, and 5% of them must be along an accessible route, be within reach range of persons in wheelchairs, and have accessible hardware. The locker room will probably also have benches for people to change on, and at least one should be located in the dressing locker room and meet the requirements on ADA Section 903 (see Figures 4.32 and 4.33).

In a dressing room, there will probably be toilet facilities as well. They will follow the guidelines in the ADA Chapter 6, which were explained in Chapter 1 of this book. One unique feature of shower rooms in locker rooms is that they are typically communal showers. If that is the case, a space that has grab bars and accessible controls in the same configuration as a roll in shower should be provided within the communal shower. The shower should also not have a curb along the accessible entrance, in order to allow students to roll in and use the shower (see Figure 4.34).

Figure 4.32: A bench located in a dressing locker room should have a back support.

Figure 4.33: Accessories in a dressing room, such as hand dryers, should be located within the reach range of persons in wheelchairs.

Figure 4.34: Shower rooms in locker rooms should be accessible and follow the requirements for shower compartments.

SWIMMING POOLS

In a university or college, as well as in a high school, there will probably be competitive swimming spaces. Those pools are also required to be accessible and have an accessible means of entry (see Figure 4.35). Chapter 5, which covers hospitality, speaks more about the requirements for pools.

A swimming pool is required to have two means of access if it is larger than 300 linear feet. A pool lift or a sloped entrance must have two means of entry for one of the entrances. The second means of entry could be via a transfer steps, transfer wall, transfer system, or pool steps (see Figures 4.36 and 4.37).

A pool will typically have a shower to rinse off pool water. This type of shower will also require access if provided. A pool shower should have the proper type of controls, clear floor space, and handheld units all within the appropriate reach range. Grab bars should also be provided.

Figure 4.35: Swimming pools at higher education facilities will also have to be accessible.

Figure 4.36: A pool with steps up to it requires at least one means of access.

Figure 4.37: Transfer steps can be one of the secondary means of entry into a pool.

OTHER SPECTATOR SPORTS AREAS

Basketball, indoor soccer, football, baseball, or softball facilities in universities, colleges, and high schools must meet the requirements of assembly areas. If fixed seating is provided, it will have to follow the requirements described previously. Indoor or outdoor bleachers will also have to have wheelchair spaces with companion seats, as well accessible routes to the field (see figures 4.38 and 4.39). Stadium seating and lawn seats for certain sports will also be required to comply with the standards.

Figure 4.38: Bleachers for baseball games require access up to the seating.

Figure 4.39: Bleachers in a basketball court require wheelchair spaces.

DINING FACILITIES

The requirements of reach ranges and dining surfaces generally apply to dining, vending, and food-serving areas. Kitchen areas where food is prepared are considered employee work areas and must comply only with minimal accessibility requirements, which cover the ability to approach the kitchen, enter it, and exit. However, in the event a food preparation employee becomes disabled or an employee with a disability is hired, the work areas for that employee must then be made accessible. This would also apply to food storage facilities, including dry storage rooms and walk-in coolers and refrigerators. Any other facilities used only by staff would be subject only to employee work area requirements. If there are common-use areas within the kitchen, such an employee restroom, locker room, or break room, those will have to be accessible and be on an accessible route.

Students will be dining in cafeterias, and the counters they will be using are considered "dining counters." They should meet the requirements in Section 902 of the 2010 ADA Standards. "Dining counter" applies to fixed tables located within a dining area in a cafeteria and even a picnic area outside of the building (see Figures 4.40 and 4.41). Five percent of dining surfaces must be 34 inches high maximum and have a forward approach that is 30 inches wide minimum with a clear floor space that is a minimum of 17 inches deep, just as ADA Section 306 requires.

Figure 4.40: A fixed table and chairs will require a wheelchair space positioned for forward approach. The table pictured does not have a wheelchair space.

Figure 4.41: Exterior picnic tables must also have a wheelchair space.

Dish return and dish-washing areas are not specified in particular; however, the counter height at any pass-through openings from the public or common use side must comply with typical approach and reach requirements.

ADMINISTRATIVE AREAS

Administrative areas are both work spaces and a component of public spaces. Students use administrative spaces to register, sign up for classes, or get counseling with school advisors. Even though the offices in the administration will be private, they also are used for meeting and conferences with students. Therefore, the work area exemption cannot be taken for those offices. Service counters for students must be provided. Five percent of the counters must be accessible and at the proper service counter height. Some counters are used to fill out forms and register. Those are considered work surfaces, which require a forward approach and must be between 28 inches and 34 inches in height (see Figure 4.42).

Figure 4.42: Registrar's registration counters are considered "work surfaces" and must be accessible.

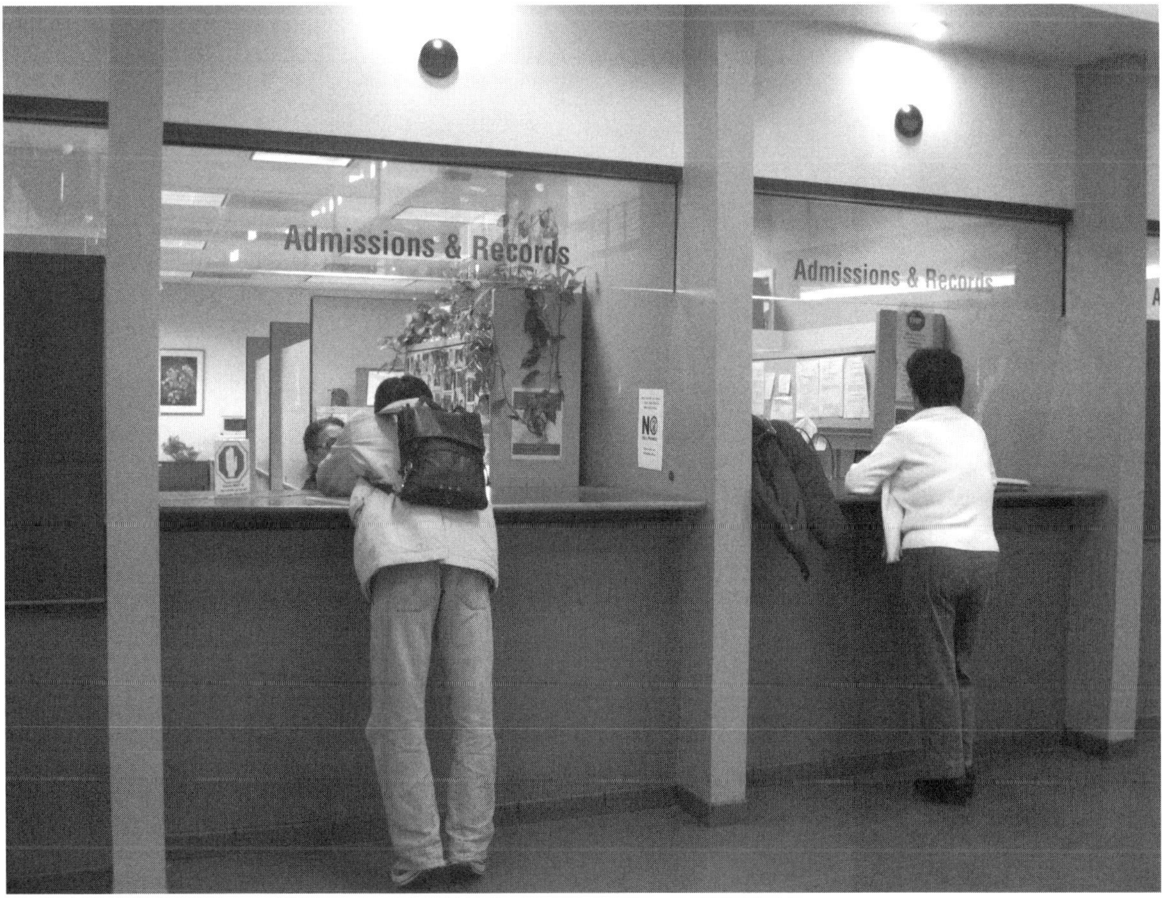

Service counters, such as information or security desks, must be 36 inches high, and a portion of the main counter must be 36 inches in length (see Figure 4.43).

The employee work areas, as mentioned before, are exempted except for the ability to approach them, enter them, and exit. However, an employee break room or restroom is not exempt and will have to comply. If the kitchenette in a break room has a cooktop, the sink will have to have a knee space (see Figure 4.44). Otherwise a parallel approach is allowed.

Permanent rooms must have signage with Braille and raised text. A private office is not considered a permanent room, since it can be changed for use for another function, such as conference room or even storage, in the future. If a common-use room is located within the work area, it will require signage; since common-use spaces are considered permanent (see Figure 4.45).

Some universities and colleges also have police stations and holding cells, which are required to be accessible. One of each type of cell must have enough room for a turning space, and if a bench is provided, it must be 42 inches long with a back support as well as a 30 inches x 48 inches clear floor space adjacent to the short side of the bench (see Figure 4.46).

Figure 4.43: An information desk is considered a service counter.

Figure 4.44: This kitchenette requires a knee space at the sink, since there is a cooktop in the break room.

Figure 4.45: This service sink is located in front of the sign to the employee restroom. This does not comply with the requirement to have an 18 inch x 18 inch unobstructed standing space in front of the sign so that a person can read it.

Figure 4.46: Holding cells in university police stations must comply with the ADA Standards.

Staff and student lockers that are provided on campus must be on an accessible route as well as within reach ranges and with the proper hardware. The minimum number required is 5% but no less than one (see Figure 4.47).

A loading dock or trash dumpster is also considered an extension of a work area and is not required to have access beyond the minimum required for work areas (see Figure 4.48).

Other amenities in administration areas might be public or service telephones or schedulers for conference rooms. Those have to be within appropriate reach ranges and include clear floor space for a parallel approach (see Figure 4.49).

Figure 4.47: Lockers are storage facilities and must comply with the standards.

Figure 4.48: Loading docks are not required to be accessible, since they are work areas.

Figure 4.49: The telephone and room scheduler are not within the proper reach range heights required.

HOUSING AT A PLACE OF EDUCATION

Housing at a place of education is required to comply with the accessibility standards applicable to that of transient lodging. When applying the transient lodging standards, the term "sleeping room" is intended to be used interchangeably with the term "guest room."

Secondary educational housing typically provides lodging for up to one academic year. While these institutions may be closed during vacation periods, they may be used for short-term stays during this time. Graduate and faculty housing is often provided year round in the form of townhouses or apartments. The accessibility standards contain provisions to address housing of each type.

In addition to rooms with mobility features, rooms with communication features are required. Review Chapter 5 for specific accessibility requirements for transient lodging.

Kitchens

Kitchens provided within housing units containing accessible sleeping rooms with mobility features or on floors containing accessible sleeping rooms with mobility features are required to comply with the accessibility standards. Turning spaces and clearances positioned for front approach must be provided at kitchen work surfaces (see Figure 4.50). Additionally, a 30-inch-wide work surface, no more than 34 inches above the finished floor, is required. In addition, 50% of the storage shelves must be provided within an accessible reach range. These requirements are discussed in more detail in Chapter 9.

Multi-Bedroom

Multi-bedroom housing units containing accessible sleeping rooms with mobility features must have an accessible route throughout the unit. If there is only one accessible route, it is not allowed to pass through bathrooms, closets, or similar spaces. Transient lodging units, including the ones that are not for disabled students, are required to have a minimum of 32-inch-wide opening at entry doorways.

Apartment or Townhouse Facilities

Housing that is leased on a year-round basis exclusively to graduate students or faculty and that does not contain any public-use or common-use areas available for educational uses is not subject to the transient lodging standards and does not have to comply with the requirements for residential facilities.

Public universities and schools that receive federal financial assistance are also subject to Section 504 of the Rehabilitation Act of 1973, in addition to Title II of the ADA. The Fair Housing Act requires new multifamily housing to be accessible and incorporate certain adaptable design features. Title II of the ADA requires that all programs be made available and accessible to persons disabled with disabilities. These entities have stricter requirements than the private sector.

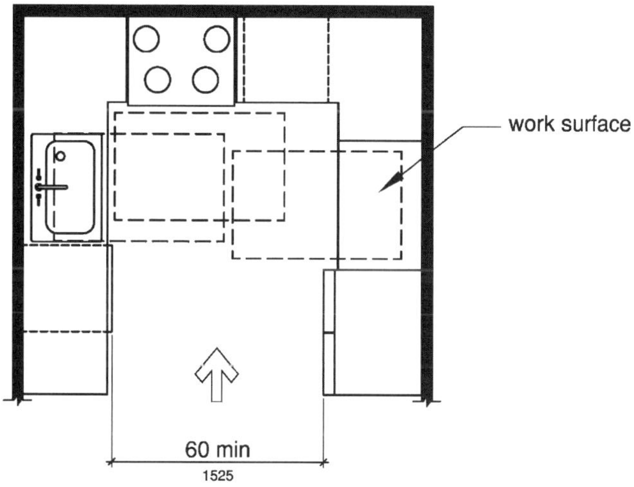

Figure 4.50: Clear floor spaces inside a kitchen are required at appliances.

SUMMARY

In using Chapter 3, in tandem with this chapter, the majority of typical educational spaces have been reviewed. This chapter was written to summarize the accessibility requirements in educational occupancies of secondary and postsecondary education for students over age 12 and those of adults. As a result of addressing the needs of students with disabilities, all students benefit from higher-quality educational facilities.

Reference Sections Chapter 4

The 2010 ADA Standards reference several sections for one topic. This reference table assists the designer in finding the pertinent sections pertaining to one specific area. To use the table, find the topic and below are all the different sections that the standards refer.

DOJ § 35.151 New construction and alterations	
Section Number	**Section Title and Description**
(g)	Assembly areas
(g)(2)	Wheelchair space
DOJ § 36.406 Standards for new construction and alterations	
Section Number	**Section Title and Description**
(f)	Assembly Areas
(f)(2)	Wheelchair space
ADA Chapter 1: Definitions	
Section Number	**Section Title and Description**
Definition	Assembly Area
Definition	Space
ADA Chapter 2: Scoping	
Section Number	**Section Title and Description**
206.2.4	EXCEPTIONS: (2)
206.2.7	Press Boxes
206.2.7	ADVISORY: Press Boxes Exception 2
210.1	General: EXCEPTIONS: (3)
216.1	General: EXCEPTIONS: (1)
216.10	Assistive Listening Systems
216.10	Assistive Listening systems: EXCEPTION: ticket windows
219.2	Required Systems
219.3	Receivers
219.3	Receivers: EXCEPTIONS: (1)
219.3	Receivers: EXCEPTIONS: (2)
Table 219.3	Receivers for Assisted Listening Systems
221	Assembly Areas
221.1	General
221.2	Wheelchair spaces
Table 221.2.1.1	Number of Wheelchair Spaces in Assembly Areas
221.2.2	ADVISORY: Integration
221.2.3.1	Horizontal Dispersion: EXCEPTIONS: (1)
221.2.3.2	Vertical Dispersion: EXCEPTIONS: (1)
221.4	ADVISORY: Designated Aisle Seats

ADA Chapters 3-10: Technical	
Section Number	**Section Title and Description**
405.1	Ramps: General: EXCEPTION
505.2	Handrails: Where Required: EXCEPTION
505.3	Handrails: Continuity: EXCEPTION
505.10	Handrail Extensions: EXCEPTIONS: (2)
706.1	Assistive Listening Systems: General
Chapter 2: Scoping	
209.2.2	**Bus Loading Zones**
209.2.2	ADVISORY: Bus Loading Zones
§ 35.151 New construction and alterations	
(g)(2)	**Assembly Areas and Wheelchair spaces**
§ 36.406 Standards for new construction and alterations	
(f)(2)	**Assembly Areas and wheelchair spaces**
Chapter 2: Scoping	
206.2.6	Performance Areas
206.7.1	**Platform Lifts**
221.2.3.2	Vertical Dispersion (Wheelchair Spaces)
221.2.3.1	ADVISORY: Horizontal Dispersion (wheelchair spaces)
Chapter 3-10: Technical Standards	
802.2	Lines of sight

Hospitality

5

by Jeromy Murphy, AIA RAS

INTRODUCTION

Hotels are the original mixed-use facility, combining entertainment, dining, business, and retail facilities with guest sleeping rooms. The hospitality industry is constantly innovating to provide an improved or unique experience for their guests.

Each of the different areas of a transient lodging facility is subject to its applicable section of the ADA Standards. For instance, a restaurant within a hotel is treated no differently from a standalone restaurant; a sundry shop in the lobby is treated like any other convenience store.

What is transient lodging? Transient lodging includes hotels, motels, boarding houses, and other facilities where short-term sleeping accommodations are provided. Facilities that provide long-term housing, such as apartments or retirement communities, are not considered to be transient lodging. The definition also excludes hospitals, prisons, and small facilities such as a bed & breakfasts if they are occupied by the proprietor and have no more than five rooms. Hospitals, prisons, and residential facilities are covered by other sections of the standards and other chapters of this book. Unlike residential facilities where alterations can be made to accommodate a specific resident with a disability within a specific apartment at the time the dwelling unit is occupied, transient lodging facilities must provide accessible guest rooms in anticipation of the need.

Dormitories at a university should be regarded as transient lodging. While the length of stay at a dormitory is typically much longer than at a hotel, it is not long enough to justify making expensive alterations for access at the time accommodations are required. Dormitories are also subject to the design requirements of the Fair Housing Act:

> *106.5.71* **Transient Lodging.** A building or facility containing one or more guest room(s) for sleeping that provides accommodations that are primarily short-term in nature. Transient lodging does not include residential dwelling units intended to be used as a residence, inpatient medical care facilities, licensed long-term care facilities, detention or correctional facilities, or private buildings or facilities that contain not more than five rooms for rent or hire and that are actually occupied by the proprietor as the residence of such proprietor.

New Construction

For new construction, all guest areas of the facility are required to be accessible. Because people with disabilities are entitled to equal enjoyment of the goods and services, if an amenity is provided, accessible amenities are required. Employee-only areas are also required to be accessible in newly constructed facilities. Work areas are not required to be accessible, but areas such as back-of-house employee-only toilet rooms, locker/shower rooms, or break areas are required to be fully accessible.

Existing Facilities

Any existing facility constructed after July 26, 1992, and prior to March 15, 2012, was subject to the 1991 ADA Standards. Facilities constructed prior to July 26, 1992 are only required to be made accessible when an alteration is made or when it is readily achievable to do so. The ADA defines readily achievable as easily accomplishable and able to be carried out without much difficulty or expense.

Any individual element that is altered or newly constructed is required to be made accessible. For instance, as part of an interiors package, the carpet and wall sconces are replaced in a hotel corridor. While this alteration would not require that the whole facility be brought into compliance, the installed carpet and the wall sconces would be required to meet the requirements for new construction, including ADA section 305 Ground Surface and 307 Protruding Object.

If the alteration affects the usability or access to an area containing a primary function (meeting rooms, restaurant and guest rooms are all primary functions of a hotel), the path of travel to the altered area is required to be made accessible including elements such as restrooms, drinking fountains, and public telephones located along the path of travel.

Public and Guest Areas

Site Access and Access to Public Transportation

If public sidewalks or public transportation stops are located on the perimeter of the site, an accessible route is required to connect from those facilities to the accessible building entrance. The exception is for facilities where the buildings are remote from the public right-of-way and the primary access is vehicular.

Parking and Passenger Loading Zones

It is perplexing that architects ever designed hotels where it was necessary to drag luggage up a flight of stairs. For modern hotels, providing access for wheelchair users and other people with mobility impairments is as simple as designing to accommodate rolling luggage.

If parking is provided, accessible parking is required based on the total number of parking spaces provided. Accessible parking is required even if the parking area is valet only or employee only. The exception in Section 208.1 applies only to parking areas for buses, trucks, delivery vehicles, law enforcement vehicles, or vehicular impound.

Accessible parking spaces are required to be on the shortest route to an accessible entrance. Essentially, the best parking spaces should be made accessible parking spaces.

The 1991 ADA Standards had an exception for valet-only facilities. This exception was not included in the 2010 ADA Standards. If valet parking is offered, an accessible passenger loading zone is required.

The front entrance of many modern hotels includes a passenger loading zone that provides a convenient covered vehicle pull-up space and unloading area. An accessible passenger loading zone will include

- A vehicle pull-up space that is 8 ft. 0 in. wide and 20 ft. 0 in. long minimum
- A 5 ft. 0 in. wide access aisle the same length and at the same level as the vehicle pull-up space
- A vertical clearance of 9 ft. 6 in.

Access aisles are required to be marked to discourage parking within the aisle. This does not necessarily mean that signs are required or that the aisle must be striped. Changes in floor materials or bollards at the front and back of the aisle can be used to identify the location of the access aisle in lieu of pavement striping. Note that bollards should never be placed between the access aisle and the required vehicle pull-up space, because this might restrict use; provide a minimum clearance of 20 feet between any obstructions.

The access aisle and the vehicle pull-up space are required to be level. In order to be considered level, the slope within the required areas cannot exceed 1:48 or 1/4 inches per foot. A common violation occurs when the horizontal distance between the access aisle and the entry doors is not long enough to provide an accessible route. If the slope between the access aisle and the required level landing at the entry doors is greater than 1:20 (5%) a ramp will be required. A best practice is to raise the grade of the vehicle pull-up space so that a ramp is not required.

Where curbs are provided within passenger loading zones, curb ramps shall be provided. The curb ramp shall connect to the access aisle.

When covered passenger loading zones are provided, the required vehicle pull-up space, access aisle, and accessible route to the entrance are also required to be covered (see Figure 5.1). It is not acceptable to require wheelchair users to maneuver within the rain if the convenience of shelter is provided for others.

Registration and Guest Services

The front desk gives the first impression of the quality of service to be expected. If guests are inconvenienced at the front desk, why would they assume the rest of their visit will be any different?

To accommodate guests who are shorter or wheelchair users, a counter that is at least 36 inches wide and no higher than 36 inches is required. There is no need to provide knee and toe clearance under the guest side of the counter. The accessible portion of the counter

Figure 5.1: Passenger loading zone.

needs to extend the full depth as the whole counter to facilitate assistance from and interaction with the staff.

Consider providing convenient access through or around the counter so that staff can move to the public side of the counter to help guests who need additional assistance. Avoid cluttering the accessible portion of the counter with brochures, computer monitors, or decorations. If a separate concierge desk or other service counters are provided, one of each type, in each area is required to be accessible.

For existing facilities where it is not readily achievable to modify an existing counter, a flip-up counter can be used (see Figure 5.2). Flip-up counters are not an acceptable option for new construction.

Sundry Shop/Retail

A minimum clearance of 36 inches is required between all shelves. Retail goods are not required to be within accessible reach ranges, but assistance should always be available. The service/sales counter needs to be at least 36 inches wide and no higher than 36 inches per ADA section 904. The sales counter can be a part of the registration counter.

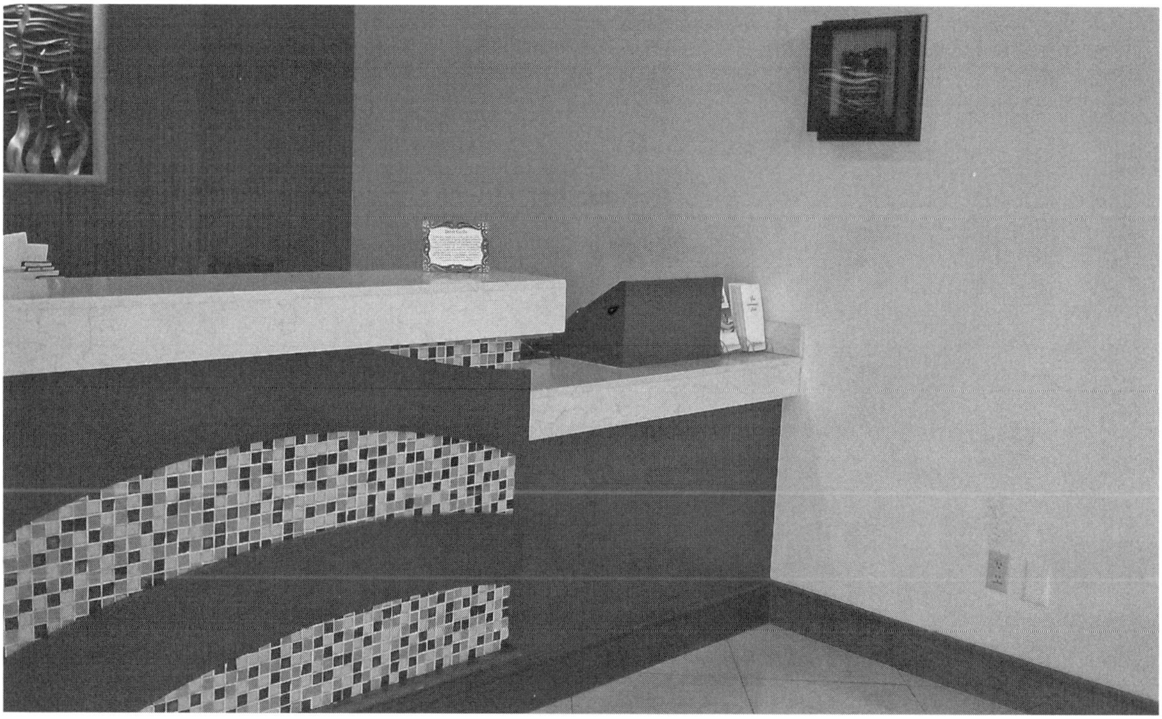

Figure 5.2: Registration counter—avoid cluttering the accessible counter.Sundry Shop/Retail

Business Center

At least one of each type of equipment needs to be on an accessible route and placed within accessible reach ranges. Different types of equipment might include computers dedicated for printing or Internet access, printers, scanners, or telephones. There are no requirements for the operation of the equipment, except that it should be placed within accessible reach ranges.

If desks or work counters are provided, at least 5% of each type is required to be accessible per ADA Section 902. A typical sit-down desk will usually satisfy the requirements for an accessible desk. If keyboard trays are used, they should not reduce the knee clearance below 27 inches.

Meeting Rooms/Conference Areas

All meeting rooms are required to be on an accessible route and have an accessible entry. In facilities served by fire alarm systems, visual appliances (strobes) are required in all meeting rooms. If a meeting room can be divided by temporary partitions, the visual appliances are required in each divisible area.

If audio/visual (A/V) controls are provided, they must be located on an accessible route and be placed within the appropriate reach ranges, no higher than 48 inches. A/V controls that are used only by hotel staff are not required to be accessible since they are considered part of a work area.

In larger meeting rooms where audio amplification is provided, assistive listening systems are required. The total number of receivers is based on the capacity of seating, both fixed and movable, within each assembly room. For hotels and conference centers that have several meeting rooms that require assistive listening systems, the required number of receivers can be based on the total seating of all assembly areas combined rather than on a room-by-room basis. Although this reduces the total number of receivers available, management is able to provide the receivers where they are needed. In this case, all assembly rooms must use compatible systems.

Restaurant/Bar

In new construction, all dining areas, raised or sunken, are required to be accessible. There is an exception for mezzanines within dining areas, but the mezzanine cannot include services, décor, or experiences that are not also provided on accessible levels. This could include different views or outdoor vs. indoor spaces.

In existing facilities, access is not required to existing raised or sunken dining areas provided that all of the same services are provided in accessible dining areas.

Where bars or other dining counters are provided, 5% of the counters are required to be accessible with a maximum height of 34 inches and knee and toe clearance. The accessible dining surfaces should be dispersed throughout all of the dining areas.

The 1991 Standards did not require accessible seating at bars if service was provided at accessible tables in the same area as the bar. This is no longer an option. When fixed dining counters are provided, fixed accessible dining counters are also required.

The ADA Standards apply to the fixed or built-in elements, but do not include provisions for furniture. This does not imply that accessible tables are not required. In order to provide equal and enjoyment of the goods and services for guests with disabilities, loose tables should be provided that accommodate wheelchair users. Center-post tables do not provide sufficient clear floor space for wheelchairs unless there is 17 inches minimum clearance provided from the counter edge to the post.

A food service line is required to provide sufficient width and clearances to permit passage of a wheelchair. The minimum width is 36 inches, but additional clearances are required where a 180° switchback is provided (see Figure 5.3).

Fifty percent, but no less than one of each type of self-service shelves and dispensers are required to be within accessible reach ranges. The maximum height of operable parts of dispensers is 48 inches. This maximum height is reduced if the user must reach over an obstruction such as a base cabinet or tray slide. Self-service items should not be placed more than 24 inches beyond the front of shelves or cabinets (see Figure 5.4).

At food service counters or snack bars, where customers might order or pick up food, an accessible counter is required for each type of counter. If the order counter is separate from the pick-up counter, an accessible counter is required at each location. The accessible counter is permitted to be 36 inches high and does not require knee clearance if it is at least 36 inches wide. Service counters (order/pick-up) should not be confused with food service counters such as a bar, where the food is consumed at the counter.

Temporary dining areas or food service lines, such as those set up for a Sunday brunch, are required to meet the same requirements as permanent facilities.

Fitness Center

A common misconception is that people with disabilities are incapable of using exercise equipment. However, exercise is no less important, and in some cases is more important, for

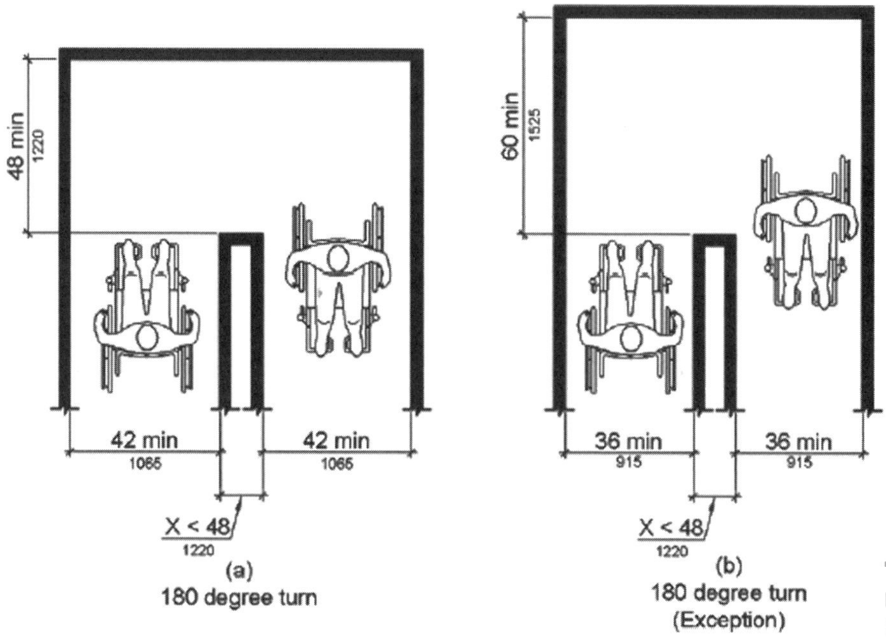

Figure 5.3: Clear width at a turn (ADA Standards Figure 403.5.2).

people with disabilities. While it may not seem logical that a wheelchair user would have use for some equipment, disabilities come in many varieties, and it is possible that a person may have limited mobility in their legs and would benefit from exercise on a bike or treadmill even if they are incapable of walking without assistance.

Blocked access to equipment and overly crowded fitness rooms are a common complaint of wheelchair users. The 2010 ADA Standards require a clear floor space positioned for transfer or for use by an individual seated in a wheelchair at one of each type of equipment. Examples of different types include free weights, treadmills, stationary bikes, and bench machines. One full unobstructed side of each clear floor space shall adjoin a 36-inch-wide accessible route. A single clear floor space can serve more than one machine.

Because there were no previous requirements in the 1991 ADA Standards, existing fitness centers are not protected by the safe harbor covering existing facilities that complied with

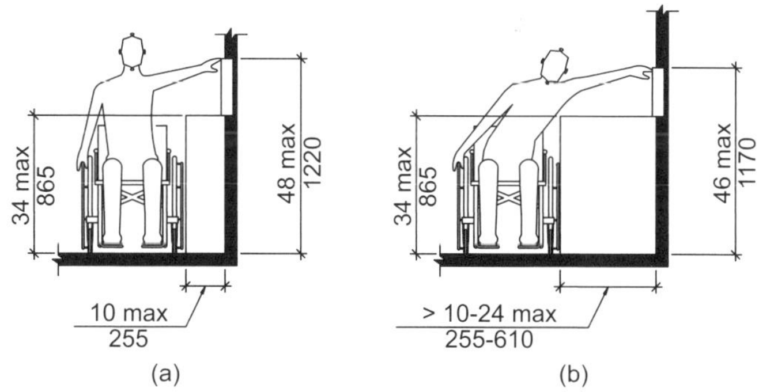

Figure 5.4: Obstructed high reach (ADA Standards Fig 308.3.2).

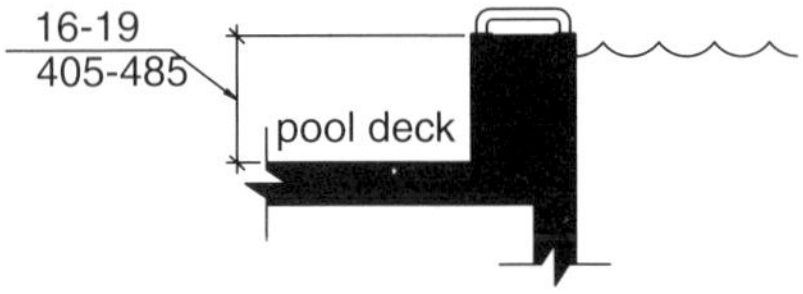

Figure 5.5: Transfer wall (ADA Standards Figure 1009.4.2).

the 1991 Standards (refer to Chapter 1 General Guidelines). Therefore, equipment within existing fitness centers should be rearranged to comply when it is readily achievable to do so.

Other items within a fitness center required to be accessible:

- Towel racks
- Hair driers
- 5% of lockers
- Dressing rooms
- Toilet/shower rooms
- Drinking fountains
- Courtesy phones
- TV controls, if TVs are available to guests

Swimming Pool/Spa/Sauna

Requirements for swimming pools, saunas, and spas were added in the 2010 ADA Standards. For pools that were constructed after March 15, 2012, accessible means of entry and exit are required and may be either a permanently installed lift or ramp. Swimming pools with 300 feet or greater of perimeter are required to have at least two accessible means of entry. At least one shall be a lift or ramp and the other entry may be a lift, ramp, transfer wall, or transfer system, and pool stairs meeting certain requirements.

Spas, such as hot tubs and jacuzzis, shall have at least one accessible means of entry. Accessible means of entry may include lifts, transfer walls, or transfer systems. If more than one spa is provided, only 5% of the spas in each cluster are required to have accessible means of entry (see Figures 5.5 and 5.6).

Because the requirements for swimming pools were not included in the 1991 ADA Standards, existing facilities are not able to claim a safe harbor for existing swimming pools that do not include accessible means of entry and exit.

An existing swimming pool that is not being altered is not required to be equipped with a lift or other accessible means of entry unless it is considered "readily achievable" to do so.

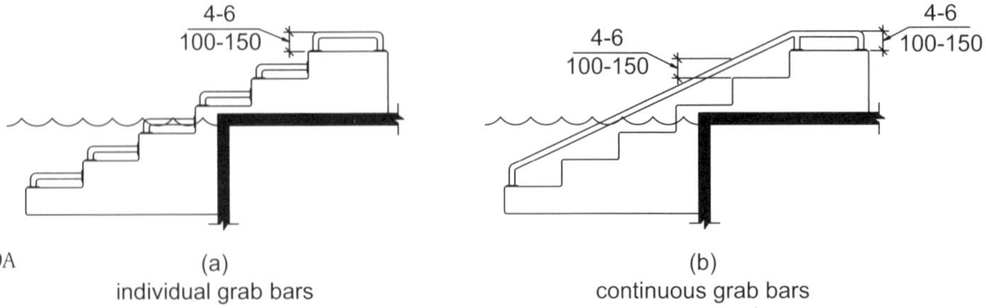

Figure 5.6: Transfer system (ADA Standards Figure 1009.5.7).

Determinations of readily achievable barrier removal are dependent on the nature of the existing facility and the resources available to the owner. Concerns about equipment use and safety should not be used as excuses for not providing access. Where permanent lifts or ramps are not feasible, provision of portable lifts, transfer walls, or transfer systems should be considered.

Alterations to an existing swimming pool can trigger the requirement to provide accessible means of entry. The *Guidance on the 2010 ADA Standards*, published by the DOJ, provides some clarification on the requirements for existing swimming pools:

> A physical change to a swimming pool which affects or could affect the usability of the pool is considered to be an alteration. Changes to the mechanical and electrical systems, such as filtration and chlorination systems, are not alterations. Exception 2 to section 202.3 permits an altered swimming pool to comply with applicable requirements to the maximum extent feasible if full compliance is technically infeasible. "Technically infeasible" is also defined in section 106.5 of the 2010 Standards.

In addition to pools and spas there are also requirements for saunas and steam rooms. Saunas shall include turning space and accessible benches if seating is provided. If more than one sauna is provided, only 5% of each cluster is required to be accessible.

Play Areas/Recreation

Some hotels will include activity centers for children. Accommodation should be made to include children with disabilities in each of the activities. At least 5% of counters or computer stations provided within these are required to be accessible and meet the requirements for ADA Section 902. Where children are the primary users, the dimensions for children should be used.

The 2010 ADA Standards includes requirements for playgrounds, including accessible routes and a certain number of pieces of ground-level play equipment accessible by transfer systems or ramps (see Figures 5.7 and 5.8a).

Guest Laundry Facilities/Ice Machines/Vending Machines

At least one of each type, in each location of vending machines or other self-service equipment provided for guest use is required to be on an accessible route and have controls within accessible reach ranges.

If laundry facilities are provided for guest use, at least one washer and one dryer shall be accessible. If more than three of each are provided, at least two of each, washer and dryer, are required to be accessible. The requirement in the ADA Section 611 requires a clear floor space for the washer and dryer as well as controls within reach range.

Employee-Only Work Areas

In new construction, employee work areas shall be designed for approach, entry, and exit only. There is no requirement for work areas, such as commercial kitchens, laundry facilities, or work rooms, to be equipped with accessible features.

Employee work areas are different from employee-only areas. Employee only toilet rooms, lockers, showers, and break rooms are required to be accessible.

Figure 5.7: Temporary facilities must comply with the same requirements for new permanent construction.

Figure 5.8a: Activities for children should be inclusive.

For an existing facility, in regard to barrier removal within employee-only areas, including restrooms and locker rooms, these are only required to be made accessible if an alteration is made to those areas or if access is required as an accommodation for an employee.

Guest Rooms with Mobility Features or Communications Features

Transient lodging facilities are required to provide guest rooms that include mobility features for guests with physical disabilities and communication features for guests with hearing impairments.

MOBILITY FEATURES INCLUDE:

- Accessible routes into and through the room, including patios, terraces, and balconies
- Clear floor space adjacent to beds
- At least one accessible bathroom
- When provided, accessible kitchens and kitchenettes
- Wheelchair turning space within the guest room
- Storage and clothes rods within appropriate reach ranges
- Operable controls, outlets, light switches, thermostats, and television
- If operable windows are provided, at least one in each space

COMMUNICATION FEATURES INCLUDE:

- Visual and audible alarms
- Visible notifications for doorbell and telephone
- Telephone volume controls
- Outlet near the phone to accommodate a text telephone (TTY = teletypewriter).

In new construction, the total number of rooms with mobility or communications features is determined by the total number of guests rooms provided, as shown in Tables 224.2 and 224.4 of the standards. These are included in the following sections for easy reference.

For rooms with mobility features, Table 224.2 lists, by brackets, the number of rooms required to have roll-in showers and the number required without roll-in showers. The required rooms without roll-in showers are permitted to have either an accessible bathtub or an accessible shower, including any of the acceptable shower designs.

The Standards require that a bench be provided in a transfer shower, since a person with mobility impairments will transfer from the wheelchair into the shower and onto the bench. A roll-in shower, on the other hand, does not require a bench to transfer to, except in transient lodging such as hotels, motels, or places of lodging in places of education. A roll-in shower in a hotel will require a fixed but foldable bench or seat in the shower in case a guest requires transferring (see Figure 5.8b).

When a bench is provided in the shower, the controls should be placed close to the seat, since that is where persons with disabilities will be using the controls. This essentially becomes a transfer shower. ADA figure 608.5.2 shows the distance from the back wall of the seat to where the controls should be located (see Figure 5.8c).

Under the 1991 Standards, each of the required accessible rooms was also required to be equipped with communications features, and separate rooms were required to have only the communication features.

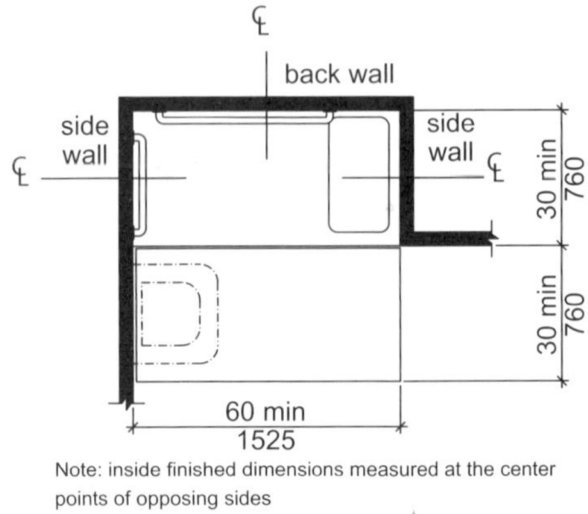

Figure 5.8b: A roll-in shower in a guest room of a hotel requires a bench to be provided. The ADA Figure 608.2.2 shows a possible layout for roll-in showers with benches.

The 2010 Standards takes a different approach. Because it is rare that a person would require both mobility features and communication features, only 10% of the rooms with mobility features are allowed to be equipped with communications features to also satisfy the required number of rooms with communication features. As part of the dispersion requirements found in section 224.5 of the ADA standards, at least one room with mobility features must also include communication features.

In a bunk room or other guest accommodation with more than 25 beds, 5% of the beds shall have the required clear floor space adjacent to the bed. (See Tables 5.1 and 5.2.)

So that guests with disabilities have the same options as other guests, rooms with mobility features and rooms with communications features must be dispersed among the various classes of rooms. In some facilities, there will be more room options than the required number of rooms with mobility or communication features. In this situation, the required rooms should be dispersed to give an equivalent range of options.

Examples of classes or amenities that should be considered include, but are not limited to: room size, bed size, cost, view, bathroom fixtures such as hot tubs and spas, smoking and nonsmoking designations, and the number of rooms provided.

A good rule of thumb for determining what factors to consider is to identify those amenities that are often requested by guests. A hotel that faces a busy street may need to consider the

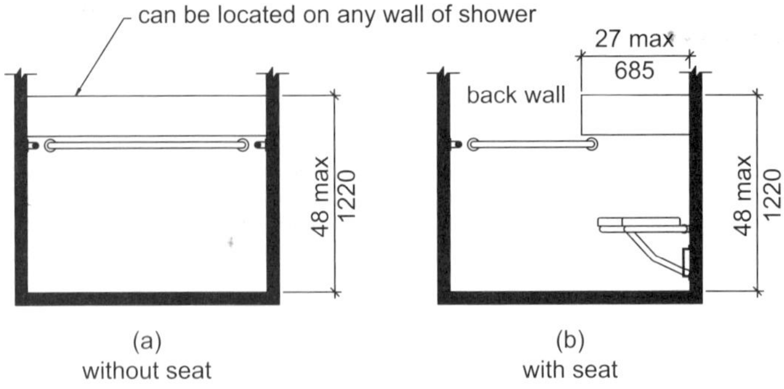

Figure 5.8c: The controls for a roll-in shower with a seat are required to be close to the seat.

TABLE 5.1: Guest Rooms with Mobility Features

Total Number of Guest Rooms Provided	Minimum Number of Required Rooms Without Roll-In Showers	Minimum Number of Required Rooms With Roll-In Showers	Total Number of Required Rooms
1 to 25	1	0	1
26 to 50	2	0	2
51 to 75	3	1	4
76 to 100	4	1	5
101 to 150	5	2	7
151 to 200	6	2	8
201 to 300	7	3	10
301 to 400	8	4	12
401 to 500	9	4	13
501 to 1000	2 percent of total	1 percent of total	3 percent of total
1001 and over	20, plus 1 for each 100, or fraction thereof, over 1000	10, plus 1 for each 100, or fraction thereof, over 1000	30, plus 2 for each 100, or fraction thereof, over 1000

Table 224.2 Guest Rooms with Mobility Features (2010 ADA Standards Table)

noise from the street as factor for dispersing accessible guest rooms. If an amenity is advertised, it should be made available for people with disabilities.

An elevator is not required in a multistory hotel where all of the accessible rooms are located on the ground floor. This does not limit the requirement to provide equivalent views or amenities (see Figure 5.9). A multistory hotel that advertises views from upper floors may still be required to provide an elevator to provide equal enjoyment of the facilities.

TABLE 5.2: Guest Rooms with Communication Features

Total Number of Guest Rooms Provided	Minimum Number of Required Guest Rooms With Communication Features
2 to 25	2
26 to 50	4
51 to 75	7
76 to 100	9
101 to 150	12
151 to 200	14
201 to 300	17
301 to 400	20
401 to 500	22
501 to 1000	5 percent of total
1001 and over	50, plus 3 for each 100 over 1000

Table 224.4 Guest Rooms with Communication Features (2010 ADA Standards Table)

Figure 5.9: Two-story motel.

Portable kits are not an option under the 2010 ADA Standards to satisfy the requirement for rooms with communication features. A facility that was constructed prior to July 26, 1992, can use portable kits when it is not readily achievable to provide permanent accommodations. Visible alarms are not required in existing facilities unless the existing alarm system is upgraded or replaced or a new system is installed (see Figures 5.10 and 5.11).

Common violations within rooms with mobility features include:

- A high threshold at patios or sliding exterior doors
- Thermostats placed too high or blocked by furniture
- Not providing coat rods within accessible reach ranges
- Hair dryer or iron placed in inaccessible locations
- Controls on window units that are too high or blocked by furniture
- Providing less than 36 inches between beds or on both sides when only one bed is provided
- Providing less than 36 inches clearance between furniture or not providing turning space

- Providing insufficient maneuvering clearance at the entry door
- Latches or chains on the door that are too high
- Controls for lamps.

Examples

All names have been changed to protect the guilty.

Hotel Isabel

Hotel Isabel is an example of new construction of a 254-room hotel/conference center.

The construction documents were submitted to the city for permit after March 15, 2012, therefore, this facility is subject to the 2010 ADA Standards for Accessible Design. All public and common-use areas and employee restrooms, locker rooms, and break areas are required to be accessible. Exceptions for compliance are limited to the rare instances where existing site constraints may limit access.

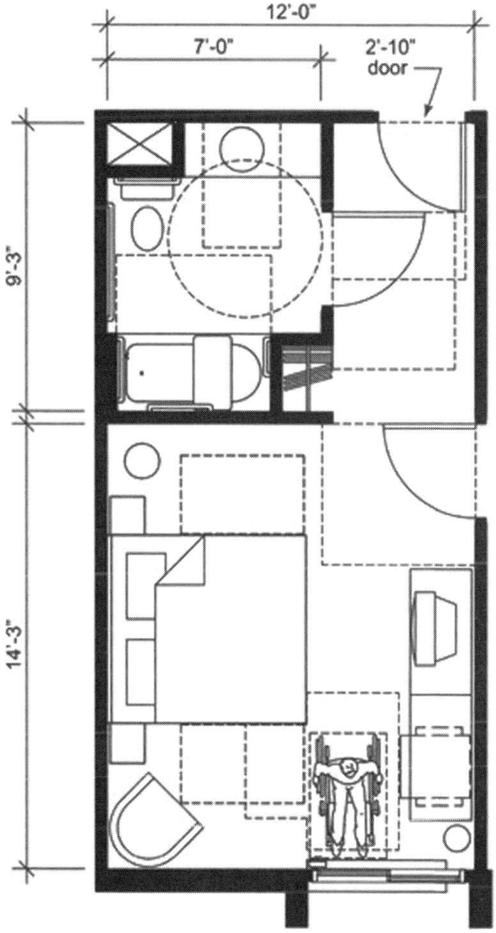

Figure 5.10: Twelve-foot-wide room with king bed and bathtub.

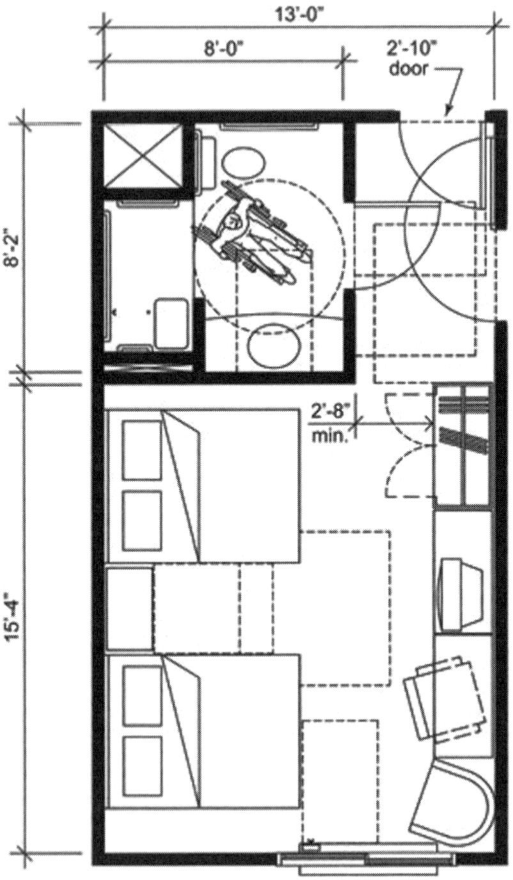

Figure 5.11: Thirteen-foot wide room with two beds and roll-in shower.

Willow's Fork Resort

Willow's Fork Resort is a 220-room country resort constructed in 1997 and currently undergoing an extensive remodel and addition.

Because this facility was constructed for first occupancy after January 26, 1993, existing elements are required to comply with the 1991 ADA Standards (28 CFR§36.401(a)(1); there is no provision for grandfathering. Unlike older facilities, which are required to remove architectural barriers only when it is deemed to be "readily achievable," compliance with the standards is required.

The existing facilities and elements of the hotel are covered under a safe harbor if they complied with the 1991 Standards. The altered areas and the addition will be subject to the 2010 ADA Standards.

The Beth Lorraine

The Beth Lorraine is a historic hotel constructed in 1880, renovated and altered several times throughout its history. The hotel is currently undergoing a renovation of the lobby and restaurant.

The altered areas are subject to compliance with the 2010 Standards. These alterations will trigger compliance for the path of travel serving the altered areas. The path of travel includes accessible routes, restrooms, drinking fountains, and public telephones that serve the altered area. If the guest rooms are outside the scope of work, they will not be required to comply as a result of the alterations to the lobby and restaurant but will still be subject to the readily achievable barrier removal requirement.

The Grant Motel

Built in the 1950s, this small drive-in has never been renovated except for sporadic replacement of paint and carpet and occasional repairs. The owner was recently named in a lawsuit alleging failure to comply with Title III of the Americans with Disabilities Act.

The owner was under the assumption that the motel was "grandfathered" and did not need to be made accessible. There is no grandfather provision in the ADA. Instead, public accommodations constructed prior to January 26, 1993, are obligated to make a facility accessible when it is readily achievable to do so. Barrier removal is considered readily achievable if it is easily accomplishable and can be carried out without much difficulty or expense. Determinations of readily achievable corrections are determined on a case-by-case basis and are dependent of the nature and cost of the problem and the resources available to the owner/operator.

SUMMARY

To say an architect specializes in hospitality is to say he or she specializes in everything. A new resort must comply with new standards while providing enough enjoyment to meet guest expectations. A historic hotel must respect its historic integrity and at the same time provide equal enjoyment for disabled guests. The designer and operators of transient lodging have a complicated challenge. Dividing the multitude of functions into smaller components and applying the standards to each component will make compliance achievable in even the biggest of facilities.

Reference Sections Chapter 5

The 2010 ADA Standards reference several sections for one topic. This reference table assists the designer in finding the pertinent sections pertaining to one specific area. To use the table, find the topic and below are all the different sections that the standards refers to.

Chapter 5 Section References	
ADA Chapter 1: Definitions	
Section Number	**Section Title and Description**
106.5	Residential Dwelling Unit
106.5	Transient Lodging
DOJ 35.151 New construction and alterations.	
Section Number	**Section Title and Description**
(f)	Housing at a place of education.
(f)(3)	Apartments or townhouse facilities
DOJ 36.406 Standards for new construction and alterations	
Section Number	**Section Title and Description**
(c)	**Places of lodging**
(c)(1)	Guest Rooms
(c)(3)	Facilities with residential units and transient lodging units.
(e)	Housing at a place of education.
(e)(3)	Apartments or townhouse facilities
ADA Chapter 2: Scoping: Transient Lodging	
Section Number	**Section Title and Description**
106	Definition
206.2.3	Accessible Route in multi-story buildings Exception (5)
206.5.3	Transient Lodging Facilities
206.2.5	Entrances and doorway to non-mobility rooms
206.7.6	Platform lifts
215.4	Fire Alarms
224	Transient Lodging Facilities and Guest Rooms
224.1	EXCEPTIONS: 1. Facilities with Residential Units and Transient Lodging Units.
Advisory 224.1	General
224.2	Guest Rooms with Mobility Features.
224.4	Guest Rooms with Communication Features
224.6	Housing at a Place of Education
224.6	EXCEPTION 3
241	Saunas and Steam Rooms
242	Swimming Pools, Wading Pools, and Spas
Advisory 242.2	Swimming Pools.

Advisory 242.2	Swimming Pools Exception 1.
242.3	Wading Pools.
242.4	Spas.

ADA Chapters 3-10 Technical Standards	
Section Number	**Section Title and Description**
608.4	Shower Seats
612	Saunas and Steam Rooms
608.6	EXCEPTION: fixed shower head
Advisory 801.1	Scope
806	Transient Lodging Guest Rooms
806.1	General
	1009 Swimming Pools, Wading Pools, and Spas

Healthcare and Senior Living Communities

6

by Greg Hunteman, AIA RAS

INTRODUCTION

Before passage of the Hospital Survey and Construction Act (also known as the Hill-Burton Act) in 1946, hospitals were typically institutions for indigent care, usually places where the poorest went toward the end of life. Following World War II, President Truman proposed federal funding to improve the national hospital system, and the Hill-Burton program began to address inequity of care. The Americans with Disabilities Act and subsequent updates focus on improving access to care and continue improving quality of life for Americans.

Healthcare and long-term care facilities serve the broadest array of visitors and occupants, ranging from the multigenerational members of a newborn's family to the assortment of visitors to the bedside of an ailing nursing home resident. The baby boom that ended in the 1960s will ultimately result in a corresponding elder boom and increased construction to meet demand for services. This demand will enable designers to update existing facilities and create new facilities that better serve patients, residents, visitors, and staff throughout their lives (see Figure 6.1).

Different Types of Healthcare

Healthcare and senior living facilities are defined as licensed medical care and long-term care facilities where the period of stay exceeds 24 hours. Healthcare facilities include hospitals, rehabilitation facilities, psychiatric facilities, and detoxification facilities and are designed to offer services not specifically isolated to issues of mobility. Healthcare facilities that specialize in rehabilitation require a greater amount of accessible resident sleeping rooms.

Figure 6.1: Wellness center with indoor pool and exercise areas, Dallas, Texas.

(Pi Architects Inc.).

Long-term care facilities are primarily nursing homes and assisted living communities but can also include hospice and other forms of specialty services. The long term nature of most resident stays dictates the integration of home-like amenities and expanded accessibility.

Alterations to Existing Healthcare and Long-Term Care Facilities

Much of the existing healthcare infrastructure, especially nursing homes, was built prior to accessibility regulations and does not meet the needs of healthcare and long-term care users. Innovations in care, technological advancements, lack of accessibility, and changing attitudes about care have rendered existing buildings technically outmoded and socially undesirable. Updating existing buildings and campuses to meet current standards is especially critical for both improving the delivery of care to patients and residents and empowering disabled individuals who desire greater independence.

As owners update existing buildings, the scope of work required for alterations is dependent on the type of areas being renovated. If the areas of primary function are being altered, then additional areas serving the primary function may need to be updated also (see Figure 6.2).

A primary function area is defined by the major activity which the building was designed to serve. Patient care is the primary function of a hospital and a nursing home. For example,

Figure 6.2: Alteration to a primary function area.

(Pi Architects Inc.)

primary function areas would include the lobby, administration, exam and treatment rooms, resident sleeping rooms, and employee work areas. Mechanical rooms, boiler rooms, supply and storage rooms, employee lounges or locker rooms, janitorial closets, entrances, corridors, and restrooms are not considered primary function areas.

If the primary function of a building is being altered, then accessibility of features along the path to that altered area, including telephones, restrooms, and drinking fountains (if provided) must be included in the scope of the renovation. In such areas where it would be technically infeasible to provide an accessible toilet or bathing room, there is an exception that may allow a unisex toilet room or bathing room that is fully accessible in the same area and on the same floor. Check with your local regulatory officials.

When updating individual elements within a space, not required as a scope of primary function renovation, the individual element or fixture will need to be brought into compliance as much as possible. An example is replacing the sink or toilet in a bathroom. Although the desired clear floor space may not be achievable, the sink and toilet would need to be set at the correct heights.

The standards note that it is not the intention of the ADA that costs of updating the accessible path should impede necessary alterations to the primary function area. If the costs to provide an accessible path to the altered area exceed 20% of the cost of alteration to the primary function area, full compliance would be disproportionate. This is further clarified in Advisory 202.4:

> "An area of a building or facility containing a major activity for which the building or facility is intended is a primary function area. Department of Justice ADA regulations state, "Alterations made to provide an accessible path of travel to the altered area will be deemed disproportionate to the overall alteration when the cost exceeds 20% of the cost of the alteration to the primary function area." (28 CFR 36.403 (f)(1)). See also Department of Transportation ADA regulations, which use similar concepts in the context of public sector transportation facilities (49 CFR 37.43 (e)(1)).

There can be multiple areas containing a primary function in a single building. Primary function areas are not limited to public use areas. For example, both a bank lobby and the bank's employee areas such as the teller areas and walk-in safe are primary function areas.

Also, mixed use facilities may include numerous primary function areas for each use. Areas containing a primary function do not include: mechanical rooms, boiler rooms, supply storage rooms, employee lounges or locker rooms, janitorial closets, entrances, corridors, or restrooms.

2010 ADA Standards Advisory 202.4

GENERAL GUIDELINES

Healthcare and senior living facilities share many of the common use elements and areas with other building types. This chapter will first review the basic building elements then examine the individual rooms that are most common in healthcare and senior living projects.

Accessible Routes

ADA section 206 defines where accessible routes are required at the exterior and interior of buildings. Accessible routes within the site are required from accessible parking and passenger loading zones to accessible entrances. Multiple arrival points must be connected by an accessible route to accessible entrances. If there is pedestrian access between buildings within a site at least one accessible route connecting all accessible spaces, arrival points and buildings has to be provided.

Licensed healthcare or long-term care facilities where the stay is anticipated to exceed 24 hours are required to have an accessible passenger loading zone at one of the accessible entrances. Earlier standards also required the passenger loading zone to be covered, but this provision has been eliminated. However, if covered drop-offs are included, either as a desired feature or because of local state licensing standards, the covered drop-off must have a vertical clearance of at least 114 inches.

The standards only require 60% of the entrances be accessible per ADA section 206.4. However, given the nature of the population served, typically all entry points used by the public and staff are designed to be accessible.

The accessible route continues through the interior, providing entrance, turn around, and exit through the majority of rooms in the building. Doors are included as part of the accessible route and can make mobility a challenge for the most disabled residents. Where doors are required, but are to remain open all the time, provide hold-opens that allow the door to remain open the majority of the time and close when the fire alarm is actuated. Automatic door openers are also a good option, especially when providing access at main entries and to exterior activity areas (see Figures 6.3 and 6.4).

Because elderly residents of long-term care facilities will generally have issues associated with impaired vision, it is highly recommended that a path be provided that offers safe transition from the indoors to bright sunlight. An ideal transition is a series of seating areas where

Figure 6.3: Activity and physical therapy courtyard at Crown Point Health Suites, Lubbock, Texas.

(Pi Architects Inc.)

elders can sit and allow their eyes to adjust to the changing light. Consider providing seating inside adjacent to the door, on an exterior porch, and then along the outdoor path.

Parking Spaces

Accessible parking spaces should be dispersed throughout the parking facility and located adjacent to the shortest accessible route to accessible entrances. The minimum number of

Figure 6.4: Accessible raised planter for residents at Cartmell Home, Palestine, Texas.

(Pi Architects Inc.)

accessible parking spaces per parking facility is given in ADA Table 208.2 (see Chapter 1, Figure 1.16), and includes parking lots and parking garages. Both parking lots and parking garages are considered parking facilities. If there were a combination of lots and garages serving a healthcare building, then each would be considered a unique parking facility, obligated to comply with the minimums set forth in Table 208.2.

There are additional parking requirements unique for outpatient and rehabilitation healthcare facilities. Ten percent of parking spaces for outpatient facilities that provide regular medical treatment, but not overnight stays, and are located inside of hospitals, shall be accessible. Facilities that provide similar treatment, but are not located inside a hospital, are not defined as outpatient facilities by the ADA standards.

Twenty percent of parking spaces for rehabilitation facilities and outpatient physical therapy facilities that specialize in treating conditions affecting mobility and outpatient physical therapy shall be accessible. Conditions that specifically affect mobility would require use of an appliance, such as a brace, cane, crutch, wheelchair, or numerous other items as described in Advisory 208.2.2:

> "Conditions that affect mobility include conditions requiring the use or assistance of a brace, cane, crutch, prosthetic device, wheelchair, or powered mobility aid; arthritic, neurological, or orthopedic conditions that severely limit one's ability to walk; respiratory diseases and other conditions which may require the use of portable oxygen; and cardiac conditions that impose significant functional limitations."
>
> 2010 ADA Standards Advisory 208.2.2

Public Restrooms

In a long-term care facility, it is advisable to distribute public-use restrooms with special attention given to proximity to activity areas. Incontinence or general urgency of bodily functions can be more common with advanced age, and easy access to restrooms will encourage the use of activity areas and community rooms. Lack of access to a nearby bathroom is an impediment to an otherwise good multipurpose area. When unisex restrooms are clustered, 50% of the restrooms shall be accessible. All plumbing fixtures must be compliant, as should the various heights of water closets and lavatories, per ADA section 604. However, if a toilet room provides only one urinal, that urinal is not required to be accessible.

Washing Machines and Clothes Dryers

The new standards have added washing machines and clothes dryers. When washing machines and clothes dryers are provided for resident and visitor use, they must be accessible. The standards go into detail on clear floor space and reach range requirements.

Fire Alarm Systems

Fire alarm systems have an exception in healthcare and long-term care facilities that permit the fire alarm system to be placed in accordance with industry practice. NFPA and state licensing regulations define local requirements. In most circumstances, a fire alarm is not required in resident rooms, since the device can scare the occupant and cause agitation among residents, especially in Alzheimer's communities.

Dressing Rooms

Dressing rooms have been updated in the new standards requiring additional clearances. When dressing rooms are provided, 5% and no less than one of each type of dressing room, fitting room, or locker room shall be accessible. Dressing rooms are considered any area where a patient or resident is required to dress or undress. If dressing benches are provided along with shower facilities, accessible dressing benches are required.

Dining Rooms

Special attention should be paid to built-in elements of dining rooms, which include dining surfaces, work surfaces, and service counters. These elements offer great opportunities for design but can become more challenging for accessibility. Accessible dining surfaces, such as bars, tables, and booths, and work surfaces such as writing surfaces, study carrels, or fixtures for personal grooming should be provided per ADA section 902. In addition, 5% of dining seating (sitting and standing), as well as work surfaces not intended as employee work areas, must be accessible and dispersed throughout (see Figure 6.5).

Service counters are provided in many ways throughout healthcare and long-term care facilities. Key points from ADA section 904 to keep in mind while designing include

- Accessible countertop must extend the same depth as the main service countertop.
- Parallel approaches to the portion of the accessible counter shall be a minimum of 36 inches long and 36 inches above the finished floor. If the counter is less than 36 inches long, then the entire counter surface shall be 36 inches above finish floor.
- Forward approaches require a portion of the counter to be 30 inches wide and 36 inches above the finished floor, with allowance for knee and toe space per section 306.

Figure 6.5: Dining facility and bistro at Silverado Senior Living — Onion Creek, Austin, Texas.

(Pi Architects Inc.)

Lines for food service and drink stations are also well defined in the standards. See ADA section 904 for requirements for patient and visitor access.

If vending machines are provided, at least one of each type of vending machine must have operable parts complying with ADA section 309.

Individual Spaces

Employee Work Areas

Employee work areas are spaces where employees are being paid to perform functions of their job, for example, nurses' station, labs, or storage. Work areas are not required to be accessible, and wheelchair-turning space is not required, but the standard expectations for accessible approach, entry, and exit do apply. In this instance, although accessibility with Title III of the ADA is not required, it would be best practice to make reasonable accommodations for disabled employees since these are required by Title I of the ADA which states that one cannot discriminate against a disabled person if they want to work there. Designing for accessibility in the initial phase could save costly retrofits down the road if current employees become temporarily or permanently disabled. ADA Advisory 203.9 encourages this precaution, and directs the designer or business owner to be aware of implications of the Equal Employment Opportunity Commission on their workplace design.

Areas where employees are not performing work duties need to be fully accessible. Employee restrooms and break areas need to be fully accessible.

Exam Rooms

Exam rooms are required to have the basic requirements of approach, entry, turn around, and exit. Generally, the casework would be for employee use and would not be required to be accessible. There is no specific requirement for accessible equipment but Access to Medical Care for Individuals with Mobility Disabilities published by the Access Board, provides additional information on exam rooms and provides recommendations. In addition to accessible-height exam tables, it also recommends providing transfer equipment such as portable and ceiling-mounted lifts in exam and treatment areas. Additional space should be provided for equipment and clear floor spaces (see Figures 6.6 and 6.7).

Physical and occupational therapy suites contain spaces that are intentionally inaccessible. These therapy areas can include inaccessible bedrooms, bathrooms with tubs, and kitchens for the purpose of training patients to return to their own homes, which are typically not accessible. In some states, occupational therapy areas are considered employee work areas, since staff are present for the purpose of assisting patients with their therapy program. However, some states require a variance to allow the inaccessible areas.

Shower Rooms

Shower rooms are required to have one of each type of fixture accessible. This will include all the plumbing fixtures such as sink, toilet, and shower. Freestanding whirlpool tubs are considered medical equipment and are exempt from specific requirements. The upcoming section on resident and patient room bathrooms goes into more detail on the individual plumbing fixture requirements (see Figure 6.8).

In addition, a bench is required if patients or residents will be undressing and dressing in the room. The bench requirements have been revised to provide greater access. The clear floor space is now at the end of the bench parallel with the short axis. Bench size has also

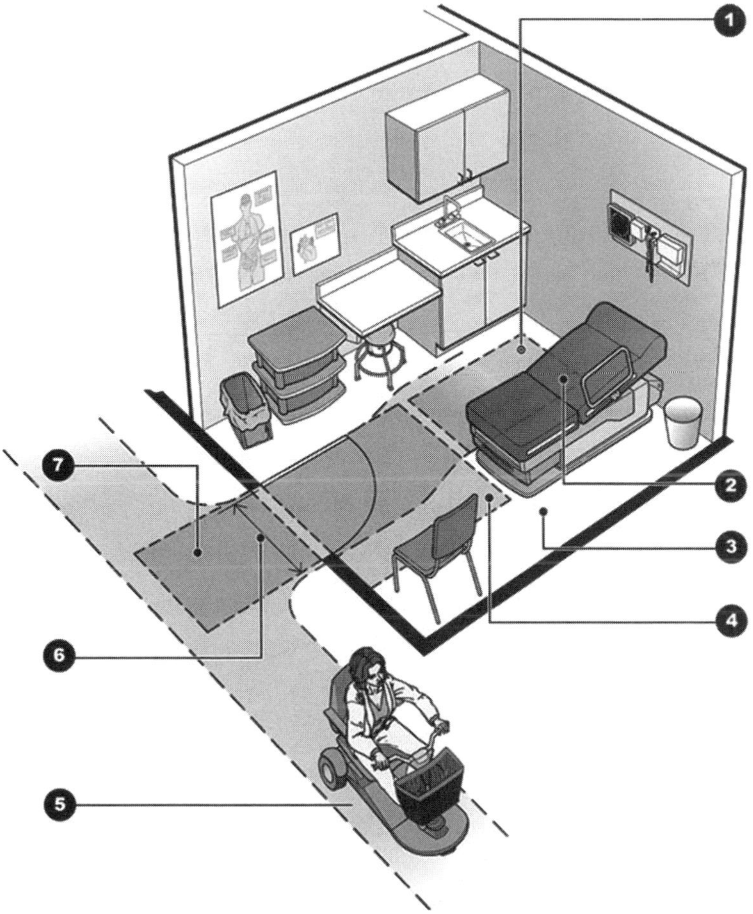

1. A clear floor space, 30" X 48" minimum, adjacent to the exam table and adjoining accessible route make it possible to do a side transfer.
2. Adjustable height accessible exam table lowers for transfers.
3. Providing space between table and wall allows staff to assist with patient transfers and positioning. When additional space is provided, transfers may be made from both sides.
4. Amount of floor space needed beside and at end of exam table will vary depending on method of patient transfer and lift equipment size.
5. Accessible route connects to other accessible public and common use spaces.
6. Accessible entry door has 32" minimum clear opening width with door open 90 degrees.
7. Maneuvering clearances are needed at the door to the room.

Note: Additional clear floor space can be provided by moving or relocating chairs, trash cans, carts, and other items.

Figure 6.6: Features of an accessible exam room.

(Department of Justice; ADA, Access to Medical Care for Individuals with Mobility Disabilities [2010]).

decreased to 42 inches long, 20 to 24 inches deep, and a height of 17 to 19 inches above finished floor. Any benches provided in wet conditions should have a slip-resistant surface that does not accumulate water.

Patient and Resident Sleeping Rooms

The major regulatory differences between healthcare facilities and long-term care facilities, as defined earlier in the chapter, is the required percentage of accessible sleeping rooms. These sleeping rooms can be private and semiprivate rooms, as are often found in hospitals and nursing homes. Assisted living communities will also have one- and two-bedroom apartments.

When designing a conventional healthcare facility, a minimum of 10% of each type of sleeping room should be accessible. Designers may want to consider a larger percentage of

Figure 6.7: Occupational therapy kitchen to provide rehabilitative training in a residential setting, Crown Point Health Suites, Lubbock, TX

(Pi Architects Inc.)

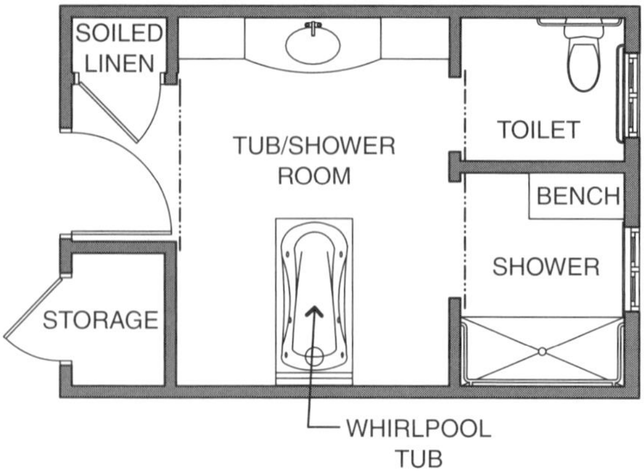

Figure 6.8: An example of a tub/shower room with accessible lavatory, toilet, shower, and dressing areas.

(Pi Architects Inc.)

accessible rooms, or alternatively, creating universal rooms for a variety of levels of care. ICUs and CCUs are not required to have accessible sleeping rooms, since patients typically don't do things independently without assistance.

Patient sleeping rooms in a healthcare facility that specializes in treating conditions affecting mobility must be 100% ADA compliant. For clarification, ADA Advisory 223.2.2 defines conditions that affect mobility as conditions that require the use of an assisting device. Examples given of such devices include wheelchairs, canes, crutches, and prosthetic devices.

Long-term care facilities are required to have a minimum of 50% of sleeping rooms be accessible. As with healthcare facilities, one of each room type must be included in that percentage. Because of high levels of resident mobility challenges and residents aging in place, most communities strive, where possible, to provide accessibility in 100% of sleeping rooms. This preventative measure makes admissions much easier and enables residents to age in place by eliminating the potential need to relocate residents. Review local state regulations for potential additional requirements, since each state may have its own interpretations of and additions to the federal requirements (see Figure 6.9).

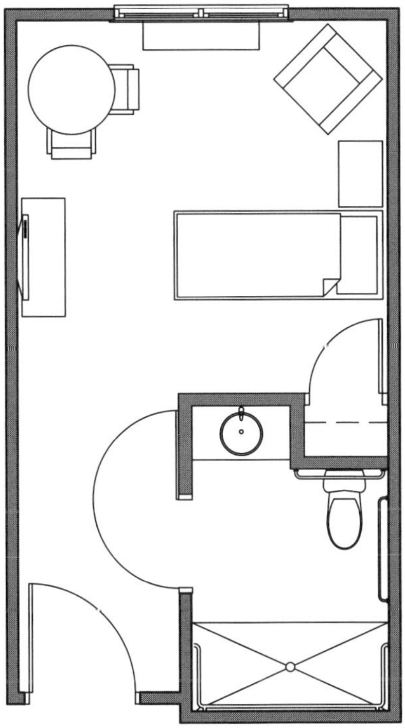

Figure 6.9: Resident sleeping room with roll-in shower.

(Pi Architects Inc.)

There is not a requirement for dispersion of accessible rooms throughout facilities, which is discussed in ADA Advisory 223.1. The advisory acknowledges that medical facilities often reconfigure spaces to reflect changes in specialties and does not mandate specific dispersion of accessible rooms. It does recommend that accessible rooms be concentrated in core areas that are less likely to be reconfigured or rededicated.

While the requirement for dispersion allows for flexibility in renovations and additions, designers must still provide an equal percentage of accessible room types. That number is based on total sleeping rooms added or altered, not the total sleeping rooms in that facility. ADA Advisory 223.1.1 recommends that rooms being brought up to meet accessibility standards be dispersed throughout the facility and located in different departments.

Accessible Sleeping Rooms

Entry doors in hospitals and long-term facilities have different entry door requirements. Long-term care sleeping rooms are required to have the required maneuvering clearances at entry doors. Hospital patient rooms are not required to provide the clearance beyond the latch site of door (within the room). A turnaround and 30-inch access on each side of the bed is required within the room. This is a reduction from the 36-inch clearance provided from the floor to the underside of the bed. The new requirements also allow the turning space to extend under the bed 6 inches where there is a minimum of 9 inches clearance from the floor to the underside of the bed.

Another addition to the standards is that at least one operable window, if provided in resident rooms, be accessible. This requires the latches be placed within one of the accessible reach ranges, be operable with a closed fist, and include appropriate clear floor space.

Where closets are provided, hanging bars and shelves are required within the accessible reach ranges. The ranges have been revised to be a maximum of 48 inches high for both the side and forward approach. If the resident is anticipated to be reaching across obstructions, height ranges are decreased. See ADA section 308 for more information (see Figure 6.10).

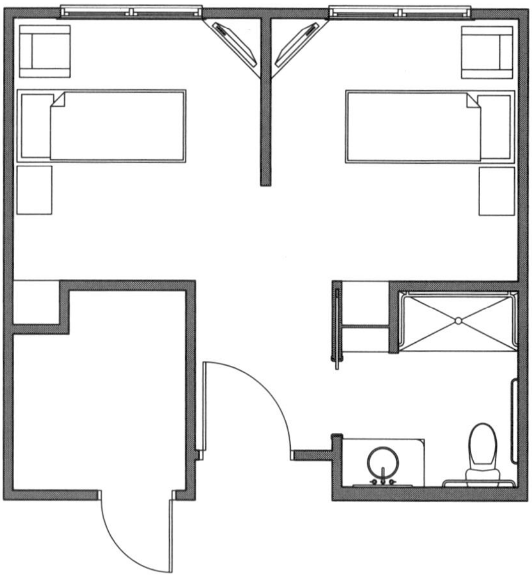

Figure 6.10: Semiprivate sleeping room.

(Pi Architects Inc.)

Resident Room Bathrooms

Bathrooms are one of the most complex areas to design. It is a puzzle of overlapping clearance, transfer, and reach range requirements that start with the door. Doors in hospitals and nursing homes open out of the bathrooms to allow staff access in case of an emergency. Most states will also allow the use of a surface-mounted, barn door style sliding door on the outside face of the wall. Assisted living communities typically do not have mandates that prohibit the door from opening into the bathroom.

ADA section 404 outlines the maneuvering clearances at doors with several options, depending on the door approach. Make note that it does not only depend on the push or pull side of the door but also on the direction of travel. Maneuvering clearances range from 42 to 48 inches perpendicular to the door and 0 to 24 inches on either side of the door. Since these are single-user toilets, the door can overlap maneuvering clearances of plumbing fixtures but not the plumbing fixture themselves.

Clear floor space at toilets has been updated with the new requirements to more closely match other codes that do not allow the lavatory to overlap the toilet clear floor space. New considerations to look for include a 16- to 18-inch clearance for the water closet from the sidewall, and 60-inch-wide clear floor space. An optional, alternative back grab bar layout for a 24-inch-long grab bar has been added to permit a reduction from the previous standard of a 36-inch length. This alternative may be used only where wall space is insufficient because of recessed fixtures adjacent to the water closet. Refer to Figure 6.9.

Toilet paper dispensers have been updated to include greater detail on the location. The centerline of the dispenser has to be 7 to 9 inches from the front of the toilet on the sidewall, and the outlet must be 15 to 48 inches above the finished floor. ADA advisory 604.7 also notes that when toilet paper dispensers are located above grab bars, the outlet must be 48 inches above the finished floor.

Sinks in resident room bathrooms are described in ADA section 606, which references ADA sections 305 and 306 for clearance heights and depths, as well as the clear floor space. Mirrors at lavatories or counters should be placed a maximum of 40 inches to the bottom of the reflecting surface above the finished floor. If not placed over a lavatory or countertop, such as on an adjacent wall, mirrors are required to be 35 inches maximum to the reflecting surface from the finished floor. Minimum height requirements to the top of the mirror have been removed from the standards, although ADA advisory 603.3 noted that the top edge of mirrors should be 74 inches above finished floor to accommodate a variety of people (see Figure 6.11).

Soap and towel dispensers must be installed within the specified reach ranges. If they are deeper than 4 inches, they should be located over a sink or counter so that they do not create an obstruction that impedes circulation of vision-impaired persons.

Shelves and coat hooks in the bathrooms are required to be placed a maximum of 48 inches above the finished floor, and clear of obstructions per ADA section 305 which describes reach ranges. Shelves are described in greater detail and shall be located from 40 inches to 48 inches above the finished floor. Storage is typically not allowed above the toilet, which would protrude into maneuvering clearance and not be within resident's reach ranges.

Shower compartment layout options are delineated in ADA section 608. Roll-in showers are the most utilized in healthcare and senior living facilities, since they allow the greatest flexibility in caring for patients and residents. Transfer showers, with their required 36 inch wide x 36 inches deep clearances, can be more difficult to use for patients with greater mobility impairments or when assisted by staff. An alternative roll-in shower, combining the benefits of transfer and roll-in showers, has been added using ADA figure 608.5.3 and is a good option. The layout adds a wing wall and increased the depth to 36 inches.

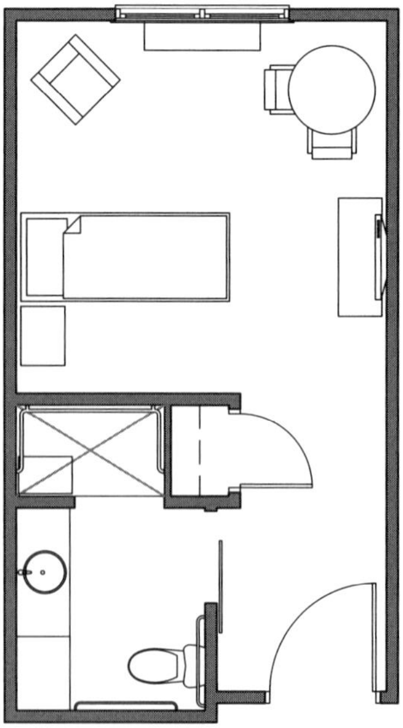

Figure 6.11: Resident sleeping room with alternate roll-in shower.

(Pi Architects Inc.)

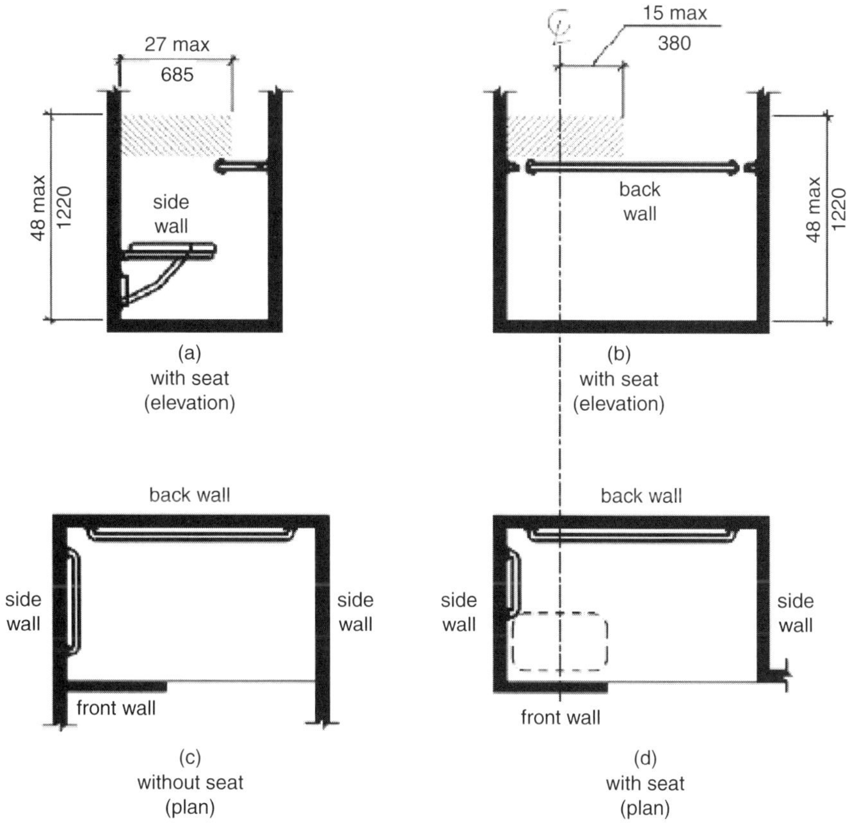

Figure 6.11a: ADA Figure 608.5.3 Alternate Roll-In Type shower compartment

Maneuvering clearances at showers are dependent on the type and layout of the shower. Transfer showers require the clear floor space to extend 12 inches past the seat side of the shower for patient transfers. A standard roll-in shower requires 30 inches to be clear along the shower opening, which may be shared with a lavatory. The alternate roll-in shower does not have specific clearance requirements but requires a 36-inch minimum entry.

Shower controls, grab bars, and seats are located according to the type of shower. Shower controls are also placed according to the nature of a seat, if provided, to allow appropriate reach ranges. Grab bar sizes and sections have been amended to provide more options for both circular cross sections and noncircular cross sections. Shower seats can be either rectangular or L-shaped and are sized according to the type of shower.

Thresholds at showers have been amended in the new standards. Thresholds can be a maximum of ½ inch and are required to be beveled in roll-in showers per ADA section 303 if they are greater than ¼ inch. The new allowance for thresholds in roll-in showers provide for a better control of water but can be a greater challenge for residents. Transfer showers are allowed to have a ½-inch vertical threshold without a bevel and can be as high as 2 inches in existing facilities, where a ½-inch threshold would disturb the structural reinforcement of the floor slab. Check with your local authorities to determine when this is allowed.

As a final precaution when designing accessible toilet and bathing rooms, make sure that the toilets and lavatories specified, and ultimately installed, do fit within the provided clearances and turnaround. This can be especially challenging when toilets are located across from showers, which require 30 inches clear floor space.

SUMMARY

Healthcare and long-term care facilities are among the most complex types of buildings. They serve the greatest variety of users and touch the lives of everyone (see Figure 6.12). Hospitals are a critical part of our healthcare system and have enabled us to live longer and fuller lives. Long-term care communities provide care to residents who can no longer live in their homes and need daily care. Designers have an opportunity to integrate accessibility standards and good design practices to create facilities and homes that create access to care and improve the quality of life for our most fragile population.

Figure 6.12: MyHouse™ nursing and assisted living prototype, a new model of resident centered care. Shown, courtyard and living room

(Pi Architects Inc.)

Reference Sections Chapter 6

The 2010 ADA Standards reference several sections for one topic. This reference table assists the designer in finding the pertinent sections pertaining to one specific area. To use the table, find the topic and below are all the different sections that the standards refer to.

CHAPTER 6 REFERENCE SECTIONS	
DOJ § 35.151 New construction and alterations.	
Section Number	**Section Title and Description**
(h)	Medical care facilities.
(k)(2)(iii)	Alterations to detention and correctional facilities.
(k)(3)	Medical and long-term care facilities in jails, prisons, and other detention and correctional facilities
DOJ § 36.406 Standards for new construction and alterations.	
Section Number	**Section Title and Description**
(g)	Medical Care Facilities
ADA Chapter 2: Scoping	
Section Number	**Section Title and Description**
Advisory 201.1	Scope.
208.2.1	Hospital Outpatient Facilities.
Advisory 208.2.1	Hospital Outpatient Facilities.
209.3	Medical Care and Long-Term Care Facilities.
217.4.6	Hospitals.
223	Medical Care and Long-Term Care Facilities
223.2	Hospitals, Rehabilitation Facilities, Psychiatric Facilities and Detoxification Facilities.
232.3	Special Holding Cells and Special Housing Cells.

ADA Chapters 3-10:Technical Standards	
Section Number	**Section Title and Description**
608.6	Shower Spray Unit and Water. EXCEPTION
702	Fire Alarm Systems EXCEPTION
805	Medical Care and Long-Term Care Facilities

Amusement Parks and Play Areas

7

by Marcela Abadi Rhoads, AIA RAS

Before the 2010 ADA design standards was published and adopted by the Department of Justice as civil rights law of the land for the disabled, children were ignored. Everything was designed for adults, and all the heights and maneuvering guidelines were only for adults. Disabled children didn't have guidelines for restrooms that were suitable for their heights or drinking fountains that they could reach. Not only were they not taken into account for building elements, but they weren't considered when creating places to recreate. Spaces such as playgrounds, amusement parks, and swimming pools were not part of the scope of the ADA when it was originally written. *The 2010 ADA Standards for Accessible Design* includes in the requirements scoping for recreation facilities, and they also have requirements for children. Chapter 10 of the *ADA Standards for Accessible Design* deals with recreational facilities, which include requirements for children also.

In order to explain how to apply the ADA to these recreation facilities, we will showcase the world's first ultra-accessible family fun park specifically designed with special needs individuals, Morgan's Wonderland located in San Antonio, Texas. The unique and colorful 25-acre park is the brainchild of Gordon Hartman and began in 2009 before the 2010 ADA Standards were adopted and required access to amusement rides and play areas for children in wheelchairs.

> *"Morgan's Wonderland is a special place where anyone can have fun," said philanthropist Hartman, president and CEO of The Gordon Hartman Family Foundation, "but it was created with special needs individuals in mind. We've taken an abandoned rock quarry in Northeast San Antonio and transformed it into an outdoor recreation oasis for those with cognitive and physical challenges."*
>
> *"Unfortunately, countless children and adults with special needs do not have access to facilities that can help them fully enjoy outdoor recreation. We truly hope Morgan's Wonderland will begin to change that."*
>
> Gordon Hartman

The inspiration for the park came from Hartman's 18-year-old daughter Morgan. Her soaring spirit, despite cognitive and physical challenges, sparked within Hartman a deep desire to create a haven not only for those with special needs but also for their families, caregivers, invited friends, and the public at large. "Inclusion is the overarching objective for Morgan's Wonderland," he explained. "Our vision is to play an instrumental role in helping establish more ultra-accessible family fun parks throughout the nation and the world."

Morgan's Wonderland, which is completely wheelchair accessible, features more than 25 elements and attractions, including rides, playgrounds, gardens, an 8-acre catch-and-release fishing lake, 18,000-square-foot special events center, a 575-seat amphitheater, picnic area, and rest areas throughout the park. On March 3, 2010, Morgan's Wonderland became a reality, and since its grand opening it has attracted approximately 200,000 guests from all 50 states and almost 40 other countries.

SITE ARRIVAL

The park was designed by Luna Architecture and Design of San Antonio, Texas. The first thing people notice when they arrive is the number of parking spaces for the disabled (see Figure 7.1). There are many more than what the ADA Design Guidelines recommend. People are greeted

Figure 7.1: Parking spaces.

with a large, colorful sign and open canopy that welcomes everyone and guides them to the entrance (see Figure 7.2). In the lobby, guests can be equipped with a radio-frequency identifying wrist band, which enables them to know exactly where all members of the group are at all times. After the guests register and check in, they are free to use any and all of the park at their leisure. Just as any facility is required to have the minimum required amenities for the disabled; Morgan's Wonderland does as well. It has 18 accessible restrooms, curb ramps, and accessible drinking fountains and tables. What makes this park so special, however, is what happens beyond the minimum. All the rides and amenities are designed so that any individual with any type of ability or disability can feel comfortable and independent.

Once you are inside the park itself, it is such a well-designed, universal place that every able-bodied as well as disabled patron can enjoy it and locate something that they find entertaining. In the park's first two years of operation, they had children with autism, orthopedic impairments, visual impairments, cognitive disorders, and cerebral palsy all playing together in the same park. There is a bright-colored butterfly-themed play area, which features a double-ramp system wide enough for two wheelchairs to pass each other for extra freedom of movement. All playground equipment was carefully designed for individuals with cognitive and physical special needs. The play area is shaded and has a rubberized surface for comfort and safety, too.

Figure 7.2a: Passenger loading zone. A bus shelter inside the facility allows for different ways of arriving at the amusement park.

Figure 7.2b: Accessible entrance. The entrance to the amusement park is inviting and accessible.

PLAY AREAS

In the ADA Standards, play areas that are not in home-based family child care facilities, must be accessible. Play areas are defined by the ADA as a portion of the site containing play components. Play components are elements used to play, socialize, or learn (see Figure 7.3). Play components are either ground level, which can be accessed directly from the ground, or elevated components, which are mounted and accessed above the ground and require that a person leave the ground to access them. The number of play components is used to determine how many must be accessible and what method of access will be required. One of each type of ground-level play components should be made accessible, as well as each type of play areas. So, if a site has multiple play areas and they are for different activities, then each one must be made accessible. This also applies to interior play areas. The advisory of the ADA Standards explains that:

> When designing the play components for accessibility, one must consider the general experience provided by each play component. For example, a spiral

Figure 7.3a: Accessible play areas help children with different abilities to play together.

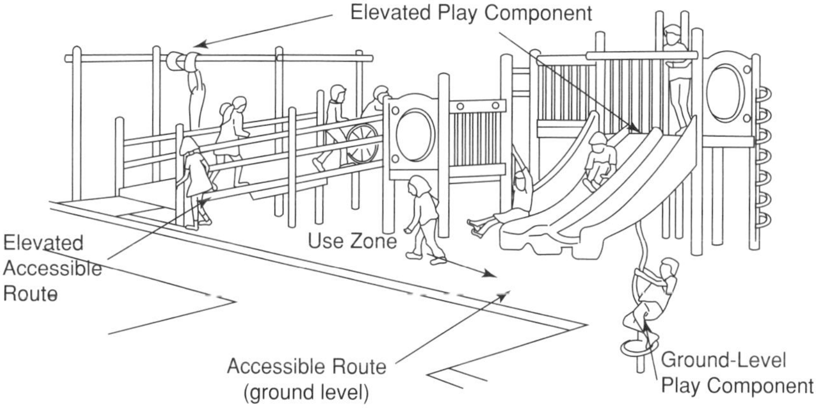

Figure 7.3b: This diagram shows the different terms in the play area mentioned in ADA Section number 1008.

slide may provide a different experience than a straight one. Ground level play components accessed by children with disabilities must be integrated into the play areas. Designers should consider the optimal layout of ground level play components accessed by children with disabilities to foster interaction and socialization among all children. Grouping all ground level components accessed by children with disabilities in one location is not considered integrated.

2010 ADA Standards Advisory 240.2.1

Hence the requirements in the standards say that if two required play components are provided, they must be dispersed.

Ground Play Components

Some examples of ground-level components are spring rockers, swings, diggers, and standalone slides (see Figure 7.4).

Figure 7.4: Swings are considered ground-level play components because they are accessed from the ground. This swing at Morgan's Wonderland was designed for children who do not have upper body mobility and cannot hold themselves up. The back support is recommended for play components when it can be incorporated.

Where a standalone slide is provided, an accessible route must connect the base of the stairs at the entry point to the exit point of the slide. A ramp or transfer system to the top of the slide is not required. Where a sandbox is provided, an accessible route must connect to the border of the sandbox (see Figure 7.5). Accessibility to the sandbox would be enhanced by providing a transfer system into the sand or by providing a raised sand table with knee clearance complying with ADA 1008.4.3.

The play components must have turning spaces and clear ground space inside the play components for children in wheelchairs to maneuver. Clear floor or ground spaces, turning spaces, and accessible routes are permitted to overlap within play areas. Each play component may require that the spaces be placed in a unique location. Where play components include a seat or entry point, designs that provide for an obstructed transfer from a wheelchair or other mobility device are recommended. This will enhance the ability of children with disabilities to independently use the play component. When designing play components with manipulative or interactive features, consider appropriate reach ranges for children seated in wheelchairs (see Figure 7.6).

Figure 7.5a: Sandbox play component. An accessible route must connect to the border of a sandbox, but not access to the inside the sandbox. This photograph shows four areas where sandbox play components are located and an accessible route leading into them.

Figure 7.5b: Children with disabilities other than mobility issues can enjoy the sandbox.

Figure 7.6: The interactive features next to the slide in this play component are not within a reach range for a child who is seated. Some of them are too high for them to reach.

CHILDREN'S REACH RANGES- ADVISORY			
FORWARD OR SIDE REACH	Ages 3 and 4	Ages 5 through 8	Ages 9 through 12
High (maximum)	36" (915 mm)	40" (1015 mm)	44" (1120 mm)
Low (minimum)	20" (210 mm)	18" (455 mm)	16" (405 mm)

Figure 7.7: Table for Children's reach ranges.

Figure 7.7 is a table that provides guidance on reach ranges for children seated in wheelchairs. These dimensions apply to either forward or side reaches. The reach ranges are appropriate for use with those play components that children seated in wheelchairs may access and reach. Where transfer systems provide access to elevated play components, the reach ranges are not appropriate.

Elevated Play Components

According to the 2010 ADA Section 106 Definitions, an elevated play component is:

> "106.5…a play component that is approached above or below grade that is part of a composite play structure consisting of two or more play components attached or functionally linked to create an integrated unit providing more than one play activity" (see Figure 7.8).

Figure 7.8: Elevated play components are also required to be accessible and on an accessible route.

Play components that are attached to a composite play structure and that can be approached from a platform or deck area are also considered elevated play components. The number of elevated play components in a playground will determine how many and what types of accessible routes are required to be provided.

Accessible Route

An accessible route is a pathway specifically designed to provide access for individuals with disabilities, including children who use wheelchairs and other mobility features. Play components must have an accessible route to them even if they are elevated. There are two requirements that determine how many ground-level components must be on an accessible route:

- One of each type
- Ground-level requirements based on the number of elevated components

The intent for these requirements is to provide a variety of experiences at the play area.

Where the accessible route serves ground-level play components, it should be clear from obstructions up to 80 inches above the ground. The width for an accessible route connecting play components at a ground level shall be 60 inches minimum. This is different from the requirement of a regular accessible route, which is typically 36 inches minimum. In smaller play areas, if they are less than 1,000 square feet then the accessible route is required to be only 44 inches in width, but only if there is a 60-inch turning space within the space and it is not more than 30 feet away from the play components. In soft contained play structures, such as those at an indoor shopping center, the transfer system itself can be used as part of the accessible route. The route on the ground can narrow to 36 inches for a distance of 60 inches (1,525 mm). This permits flexibility to work around site design features like existing equipment or trees (see Figure 7.9).

Figure 7.9: A jog on the accessible route around the tree is acceptable as long as the route is not reduced to less than 36 inch in width and only for 60 inches in length.

Where elevated play components are provided in the same playground as the ground-level play components, Table 240.2.1.2 of the ADA Standards is used to determine how many will be required to be accessible, but it should always be no less than 50%.

ADA Table 240.2.1.2 Number and Types of Ground Level Play Components Required to Be on Accessible Routes

Number of Elevated Play Components Provided	Minimum Number of Ground Level Components Required to Be on an Accessible Route	Minimum Number of Different Types of Ground-Level Play Components Required to Be on an Accessible Route
1	Not Applicable	Not Applicable
2 to 4	1	1
5 to 7	2	2
8 to 10	3	3
11 to 13	4	3
14 to 16	5	3
17 to 19	6	3
20 to 22	7	4
23 to 25	8	4
26 and over	8, plus 1 for each additional 3, or fraction thereof, over 25	5

2010 ADA Standards Section 240.2.1.2

2010 ADA Standards for Accessible Design

The table explains how many ground-level play components must be on an accessible route and, therefore, must have either ramps or transfer systems to access them. If at least 50% of the elevated play components are connected by a ramp and at least three of the elevated play components are of different types, then designers are not required to use the table to determine access.

Composite play structures are those that have multiple elevated play components in combination (see Figure 7.10). Where a large play area includes two or more composite play structures designed for the same age group, the total number of elevated play components on all the composite play structures must be added to determine the additional number and types of ground-level play components that must be provided on an accessible route. A double or triple slide that is part of a composite play structure is one elevated play component. Ramps, transfer systems, steps, decks, and roofs are not considered elevated play components. Although socialization and pretend play can occur on these elements, they are not primarily intended for play.

Some play components that are attached to a composite play structure can be approached or exited at the ground level or above grade from a platform or deck. For example, a climber attached to a composite play structure can be approached or exited at the ground level or above grade from a platform or deck on a composite play structure. Play components that are attached to a composite play structure and can be approached from a platform or deck (e.g., climbers and overhead play components) are considered elevated play components. These play components are not considered ground-level play components and do not count toward the requirements in ADA Table 240.2.1.2 regarding the number of ground-level play components that must be located on an accessible route.

Figure 7.10: This is a composite play structure with a double slide. The number of individuals who can play on a play component at once does not determine the quantity of play components provided in a play area. A play component can hold many children but is considered one type of play experience, or one play component in a play area. While a double slide may provide one experience, a spiral slide would provide a different experience, but they are both the same "type."

Two acceptable methods to connect the play components are ramps and transfer systems. Ramps are preferred over transfer systems, since not all children who use wheelchairs or other mobility devices may be able to use, or may choose to use, transfer systems (see Figure 7.11). A transfer system is allowed to connect ground-level and elevated play components, except if there are 20 or more components. In that case, 25% of them can be accessed via a transfer system.

A transfer system is one that allows for the child to get out of his or her wheelchair and climb onto the play component using other means of mobility. Transfer systems are either platforms or steps. Where transfer systems are provided, consideration should be given to the distance

Figure 7.11: Ramps connecting ground-level play components to elevated components is one method of connection.

between the transfer system and the elevated play components. Moving between a transfer platform (see Figure 7.12) and a series of transfer steps requires extensive exertion for some children. Designers should minimize the distance between the points where a child transfers from a wheelchair or mobility device and where the elevated play components are located. There should also be at least one means of support for transferring such as rails. Transfer systems themselves can be 24 inches wide.

Transfer steps are shallower and shorter than transfer platforms, but still allow for access to the elevated play components (see Figure 7.13). Transfer supports are required on transfer platforms and transfer steps to assist children when transferring. Some examples of supports include a rope loop, a loop type handle, a slot in the edge of a flat horizontal or vertical member, poles, or bars, or D rings on the corner posts.

There are several requirements for ramps that connect elevated play components that are different from regular ramps (see Figure 7.14):

- The maximum rise of any ramp run is limited to 12 inches (305 mm).
- The maximum slope of a ramp connecting play components is 1:16. Where possible, designers and operators are encouraged to provide ramps with a slope less than 1:12.

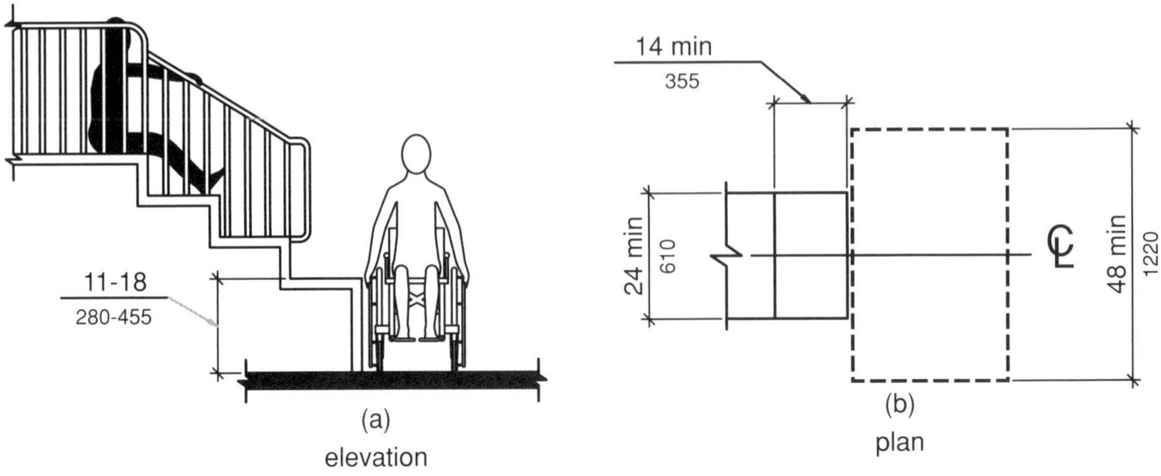

Figure 7.12a: ADA Figure 1008.3.1 Transfer Platforms.

- Handrails are required at both sides of ramps connecting play components, except within ground-level use zones.
- Handrail extensions are not required at the top or bottom of the ramps.
- Handrails height shall be 20 inches minimum to 28 inches maximum.
- The gripping surface shall be between .95 inches and 1.55 inches outside diameter.

Figure 7.12b: Transfer platforms are another method of access for elevated play components.

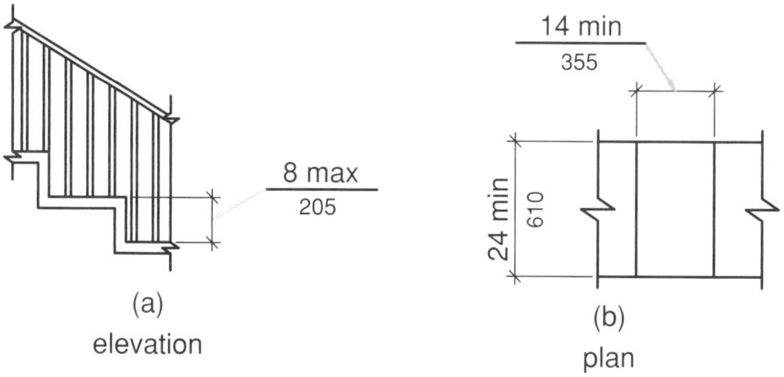

Figure 7.13a: ADA Figure 1008.3.2 Transfer Steps.

Figure 7.13b: Transfer steps allow children with different abilities to use play components together.

Figure 7.14: Ramps are one way to enter elevated components.

Ground surfaces along accessible routes, clear floor or ground spaces, and maneuvering spaces, must comply with the American Society for Testing and Materials (ASTM) F 1951-99 Standard Specification for Determination of Accessibility to Surface Systems Under and Around Playground Equipment. This standard assesses the accessibility of a surface by measuring the work an individual must exert to propel a wheelchair across the surface. The standard includes tests of effort for both straight-ahead and turning movements, using a force wheel on a rehabilitation wheelchair as the measuring device. To meet the standard, the force required must be less than that which is required to propel the wheelchair up a ramp with a slope of 1:14. When selecting ground surfaces, designer should request information about compliance with the ASTM F 1951-99 standard.

Use zones ground surfaces shall comply with ASTM F 1292-04 Standard Specification for Impact Attenuation of Surface Systems under and around Playground Equipment. A use zone is the area where a child enters or exits the play component. Accessible and non-accessible surfaces can be combined to provide variety and excitement in play areas. An engineered wood fiber surface can be used as the accessible ground surface but will require maintenance to comply with ASTM F1202-4.

Clear floor or ground spaces, turning spaces, and accessible routes are permitted to overlap within play areas. A specific location has not been designated for the clear or ground spaces or turning spaces, except for swings (see Figure 7. 15), because each play component may require that the spaces be placed in a unique location.

Entry Points and Seats

Where play components include a seat or entry point, a design that provides for an unobstructed transfer from a wheelchair or other mobility device is recommended. This will enhance the ability of children with disabilities to independently use the play component (Advisory 1008.4.2).

An entry point or seat directly next to play components to enter should be a minimum of 11 inches or 24 inches maximum height, respectively. A midlevel height of 18 inches is recommended. Play tables, such as sand or water tables, counters with toys, or music tables, should also be made accessible and have the proper knee clearances (see Figure 7.16). Play tables should have knee clearance that are 17 inches deep minimum and 30 inches wide minimum shall be provided. The tops of rims, curbs, or other obstructions shall be 31 inches high maximum. Play tables designed and constructed primarily for children 5 years and younger are not required to provide knee clearance, and a parallel approach can be provided.

Play for Visually and Hearing Impaired

At Morgan's Wonderland, the play areas are equipped with features for the mobility impaired, but also provide play components and attractions for children who are visually, hearing impaired, and even cognitively impaired, which do not have special requirements in the ADA. The Sensory Village is a cluster of themed spaces that wrap around an indoor streetscape. The Village has interactive videos, areas for creating music, designing a custom car, and going for a simulated test drive through San Antonio, where this park is located. The Village Market grocery store is full of fun, colorful groceries, perfect for imaginative play, and a pretend TV station allows guests to do the weather forecast and see themselves on TV! Each one of these themed environments not only inspires imaginative play, but also offers interactive sensory stimulation through the use of colors, lights, sounds, and textures (see Figure 7.17). Sensory stimulation is important for everyone, but it's especially significant for individuals with special needs.

Amusement Rides

Morgan's Wonderland is also a real amusement park, which offers rides for all. The ADA section 1002 lists requirements for amusement rides. Morgan's Wonderland incorporates all the minimum requirements and provides opportunities for guests with many different abilities to enjoy.

Figure 7.15a, 7.15b: Swings for disabled children can take many forms. This one allows a wheelchair to be strapped inside in order for the child to swing while he is in his wheelchair.

Figure 7.15c: A father of a disabled child who uses a wheelchair told Morgan's Wonderland that, the first time he put his child in that swing, it brought tears to his eyes "It was the first time I was able to swing him like a normal kid."

The amusement ride standards apply to newly designed and constructed amusement rides and attractions. The standards do not apply to temporary amusement parks, such as traveling carnivals and fairs that are only set up for short periods of time. Amusement rides that are required to be accessible by the ADA Standards must have accessible routes to them and have a loading and unloading area (see Figure 7.18).

Figure 7.16a: ADA requirements for play tables.

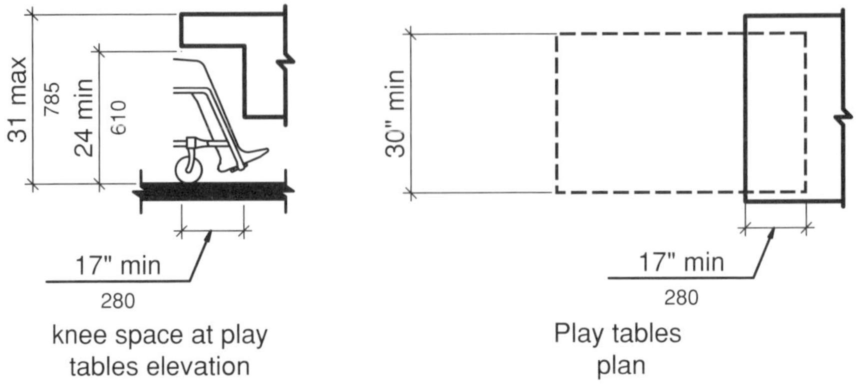

Figure 7.16b: This water table will require a knee space and clearances for children who use wheelchairs.

Figure 7.16c: Music tables are also required to have knee clearances and reach ranges.

When existing amusement rides are altered, more than just maintenance or resurfacing, a loading and unloading area must be added if one does not already exist. Some existing conditions do not allow for a 1:12 slope to be used and the standards allow for a ramp no steeper than 1:8 to be used instead. A turning space at the loading and unloading zone will also have to be provided.

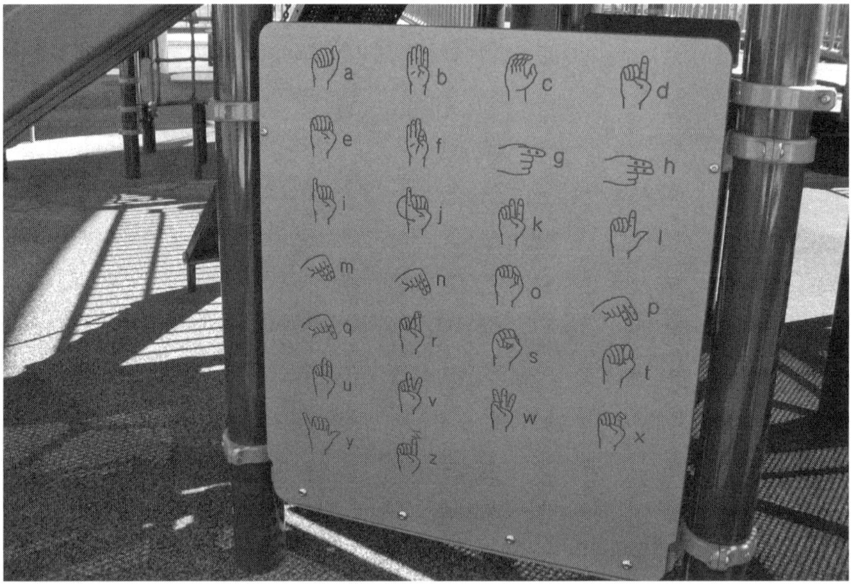

Figure 7.17a, 7.17b, and 7.17c: The Sensory Village at Morgan's Wonderland allows for many different experiences that are geared toward engaging children with special needs.

Most of the same requirements for wheelchairs listed in Chapter 1 will also be required for accessible amusement rides, such as ground floor surfaces, openings along the accessible route, and accessible route. Some amusement rides or routes to amusement rides are meant to be rustic or adventurous, and gaps along the route may be difficult to make smaller. The ADA Standards also allow designers to use the requirements listed in the ADA Accessibility Guidelines for Transportation Vehicles – Light Rail vehicles and systems—Mobility Aid Accessibility, which is found at U.S. Access Board's website (www.access-board.gov).

At least one amusement ride seat shall be designed for transfer or have a space that a wheelchair user can ride. The proximity of the clear floor or ground space next to an element and the height of the element one is transferring to are both critical for a safe and independent transfer. Providing additional clear floor or ground space both in front of and diagonal to the element will provide flexibility and will increase usability for a more diverse population of individuals with disabilities.

Transfer devices for use with amusement rides should permit individuals to make independent transfers to and from their wheelchairs or mobility devices. There are a variety of transfer devices available that could be adapted to provide access onto an amusement ride. Examples of devices

Figure 7.18a, 7.18b: This amusement ride has a transfer platform, where a person in a wheelchair can transfer onto the ride.

that may provide for transfers include transfer systems, lifts, mechanized seats, and custom-designed systems. Operators and designers have flexibility in developing designs that will facilitate individuals in transferring onto amusement rides. These systems or devices should be designed to be reliable and sturdy. Designs that limit the number of transfers required from a wheelchair or mobility device to the ride seat are encouraged. When using a transfer device to access an amusement ride, the least number of transfers and the shortest distance is most usable. Where possible, designers are encouraged to locate the transfer device seat no higher than 17 to 19 inches (430 to 485 mm) above the loading and unloading surface. Where greater distances are required for transfers, providing gripping surfaces, seat padding, and avoiding sharp objects in the path of transfer will facilitate the transfer. Where a series of transfers is required to reach the amusement ride seat, each vertical transfer should not exceed 8 inches (205 mm).

Not all amusement rides or attractions require accessibility. Rides such as the ones that are controlled by the rider or designed for children who are assisted on and off the ride, and amusement rides that do not provide seats are not required to have loading and unloading spaces. Even though these rides do not require loading and unloading, an accessible route should still be provided. The ones that provide loading and unloading on the side must have sufficient maneuvering clearance for individuals using wheelchairs (see Figure 7.19). The amount of clear space needed within the ride and the size and position of the opening are interrelated. A 32-inches (815-mm) clear opening will not provide sufficient width when entered through a turn into an amusement ride. Additional space for maneuvering and a wider door will be needed where a side opening is centered on the ride. For example, where a 42- inch (1065-mm) opening is provided, a minimum clear space of 60 inches (1525 mm) in length and 36 inches (915 mm) in depth is needed to ensure adequate space for maneuvering.

The standards also allow objects to project along the front of the wheelchair space in an amusement ride if these are necessary for the ride (see Figure 7.20).

Figure 7.19: A wider door and a spacious cab allow a person in a wheelchair to enjoy this amusement ride.

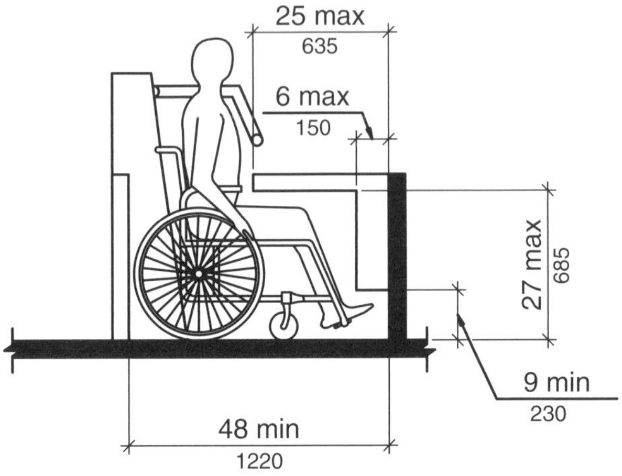

Figure 7.20: ADA Figure 1002.4.4.3.

Rides themselves also have requirements. A ride entry, just like all other accessible entrances, must be 32 inches wide minimum (see Figure 7.21). One side of the wheelchair space shall adjoin an accessible route when in the loading and unloading position. If the width inside the ride is more than 53 inches, which allows more than one rider, and the wheelchair is not required to be centered in the amusement ride, then an able-bodied companion seat shall be provided for each wheelchair space. The only rides on which a companion seat is not required are those where shoulder-to-shoulder seating is not required.

Figure 7.21: This ramp entry onto a ride is larger than 32 inches wide, which allows many different people, including wheelchair users to ride.

Morgan's Wonderland also has a one-of-a-kind carousel, which is designed to allow children and adults of different abilities to fully experience the fun of a merry-go-round (see Figure 7.22). Morgan's Wonderland worked closely with the ride's engineers to create adaptive animals that serve as special seats for guests incapable of sitting upright. Unique benches allow a special-needs guest to be safely secured and sit next to a friend or caregiver, and guests in wheelchairs can enjoy the experience with custom chariots that go up and down just like the carousel's other creatures.

Autistic children, who have a hard time relating to others or experiencing new things, might feel intimidated or scared to climb on the carousel or other rides. The designers thought of that and decided to create stationary rides throughout the park, which resemble the toys on the ride (see Figure 7.23). For example, there is a freestanding carousel horse (see Figure 7.23), which children can climb and experience until they are used to the feeling, and then when they were comfortable enough to ride the real carousel, they can do it without fear. The park also has stationary cars that resemble one of the rides, which again children can climb on and experience so that they can get used to the real ride.

Figure 7.22: This carousel has different types of features, including some with back supports and some for wheelchair users to transfer on.

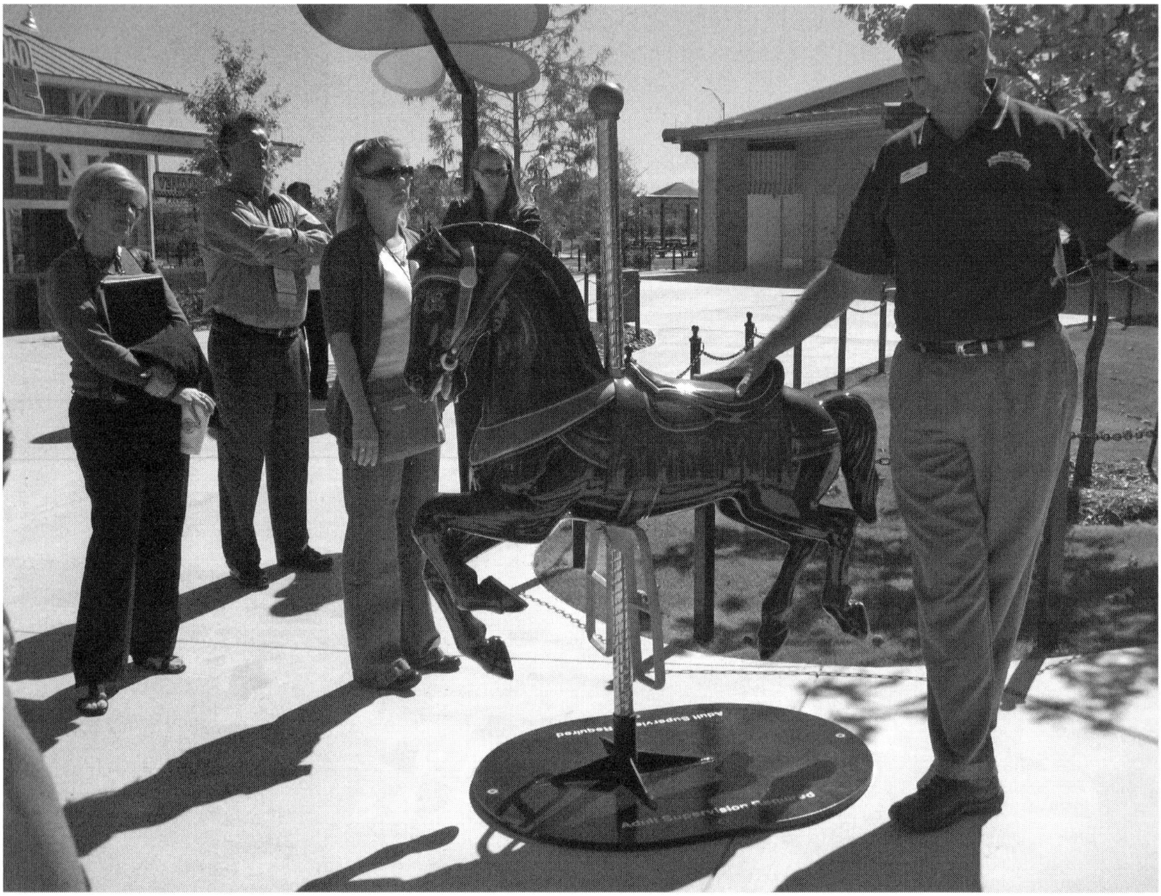

Figure 7.23: This stationary horse is next to the carousel so that kids can climb and get comfortable with the seat before they ride the carousel.

The designers and owners worked together to develop different experiences for children and adults with different disabilities (see Figure 7.24). The Water Works play is an interactive array of water-related play elements, such as squirting pipes and spinning water wheels, plus special dams that control water flow. All of it is specially designed with many sensory activities involving lights, sound, and tactile features, and of course it provides full wheelchair access to all the amenities. At water parks, the ground surface is not required to be slip resistant.

The Sand Circle was created with four wide pathways leading into the center of the circle. A raised sand table in the middle offers hands-on play, while accessible "diggers" around the perimeter enable those in wheelchairs to fully take part in the fun (see Figure 7.5b). The park also provides nine large, shaded outdoor instruments along a winding garden path combining for a great sensory experience involving the visual beauty of the garden, the smells of the flowers, and the sounds of music. The instruments are easily accessible from wheelchairs and produce pleasing melodies when played alone or in a group. They're designed so that anyone can experience the joy of making music (see Figure 7.16c).

Figure 7.24: Morgan's Wonderland has different experiences for all types of special needs children and adults.

Fishing Piers

As part of any themed amusement park, Morgan's Wonderland also has areas that transport guests through their imagination to other parts of the world. They have a wharf where guests can fish. The fishing pier itself has different height rails to allow for wheelchair users to safely enjoy the fishing experience (see Figure 7.25).

The ADA also has requirements and specifications for fishing piers. They are located in Section 1005 of the 2010 ADA Standards (see Figure 7.26). Each fishing pier has to be on an accessible route, except in floating fishing piers and platforms. Twenty-five percent of the railings should be at 34 inches, and they should be dispersed so that, if it is a large pier, wheelchair users can experience different locations. The edge of the pier should also have edge protection with either a curb barrier or extended ground or deck surface. The pier should also have a clear floor space so that a wheelchair user can have access to the rail. A turning space at the pier is also required.

Figure 7.25: The fishing pier at Morgan's Wonderland is designed for all types of users.

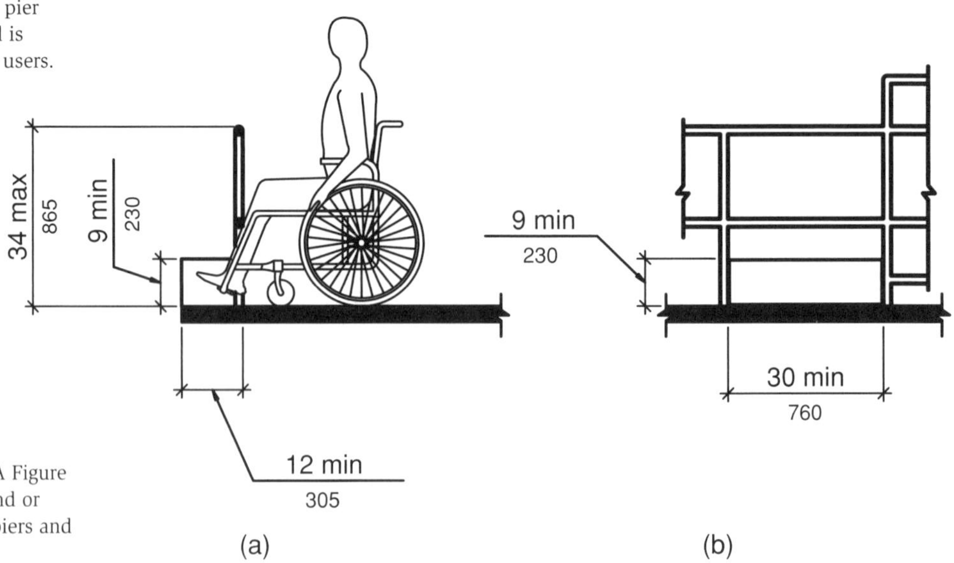

Figure 7.26: This is ADA Figure 1005.3.2 Extended ground or deck surface at fishing piers and platforms.

The park also has a pirate-themed island playground and an area called "Around the World" with rest areas reminiscent of Africa, Germany, Japan, Mexico, Italy, and the Caribbean.

In 2011, Morgan's Wonderland was awarded the First Annual Accessibility Professionals Association/TRASA Accessibility Awards for Design Excellence by the Texas Governor's Committee on People with Disabilities, in partnership with the Texas Association of Accessibility Professionals.

"This award recognizes businesses and organizations that have gone above and beyond legal requirements to provide both physical and service accessibility to people with disabilities."

SUMMARY

The founder's vision at Morgan's Wonderland, as well as the people who wrote the ADA Standards, was to establish a special place where smiles and laughter make wonderful memories with family members, caregivers, and friends. Where the common element of play creates an atmosphere of inclusion for those with and without disabilities, so everyone can gain a greater understanding of one another. It is Morgan's fervent hope that everyone with special needs— young and old, healthy or ailing, introspective or outgoing—will be touched in a very special way by this park (see Figure 7.27).

Figure 7.27: Morgan's Wonderland is a wonderland for all.

Reference Sections Chapter 7 Amusement Parks and Play Areas

The 2010 ADA Standards reference several sections for one topic. This reference table assists the designer in finding the pertinent sections pertaining to one specific area. To use the table, find the topic and below are all the different sections that the standards refer to.

ADA Chapter 1: Definitions	
Section Number	**Section Title and Description**
106.5	Defined Terms: Amusement Attraction
106.5	Defined Terms: Amusement Ride
106.5	Defined Terms: Amusement Ride Seat
106.5	Defined Terms: Transfer Device
ADA Chapter 2: Scoping	
Section Number	**Section Title and Description**
206.2.9	Amusement Rides
206.2.9.2	Wheelchair Spaces, Ride Seats Designed for Transfer, and Transfer Devices.
206.7.7	Platform Lifts
216.12	Signs
216.12	Signs: **ADVISORY:** Amusement rides
234	Amusement Rides (entire section)
240.1	Play Areas: General: EXCEPTIONS (3)
ADA Chapters 3-10: Technical	
Section Number	**Section Title and Description**
1002	Amusement Rides (entire section)

Amusement (Rides) and Play Areas

ADA Chapter 2: Scoping	
Section Number	**Section Title and Description**
105.2.3 ASTM.	**ADVISORY**
204.1	EXCEPTIONS (2)
206.2.17	Play Areas
206.2.17.1	Ground Level and Elevated Play Components
206.7.8	Platform Lifts
233.1	**ADVISORY:** General
240	Play Areas
240.1	General
240.1	EXCEPTIONS (1)
240.1	EXCEPTIONS (2)
240.1.1	Additions
240.1	**ADVISORY:** General

ADA Chapter 2: Scoping	
Section Number	**Section Title and Description**
240.1.1	**ADVISORY:** Additions
240.2.1	Ground Level Play Components
240.2.1	**ADVISORY:** Ground Level Play Components (continued)
240.2.1.2	Additional Numbers and Types EXCEPTION
240.2.1.2	**ADVISORY:** Additional Numbers and Types
ADA Chapter 1: Definitions	
Section Number	**Section Title and Description**
Definitions	Play area
ADA Chapter 3-10: Technical	
Section Number	**Section Title and Description**
1008	Play Area
1008.1	General
1008.2	Accessible routes
1008.2.4.1	Ground Level EXCEPTIONS (1)
1008.2.5	Ramps
1008.2.6	**ADVISORY:** Ground Surfaces
1008.4.2	**ADVISORY:** Clear floor or ground space

Historic Preservation and Remodels

8

by Marcela Abadi Rhoads, AIA RAS

There is a misconception in the building industry that existing buildings that were built before the ADA was enacted don't have to be accessible. Because the ADA is not a construction law, but a civil rights law, existing buildings, including historic facilities registered with the historic landmark commission, according to Title III of the ADA, are not exempt from having to be accessible. Therefore, any building that was built pre-ADA is not "grandfathered" in and must be accessible to the disabled community. The Department of Justice (DOJ) wrote in its 1991 Title III regulations:

> Existing facilities that are subject to the ADA (i.e. commercial facilities and places of public accommodations) would require to be brought up to ADA compliance as it was "readily achievable."

What the DOJ meant by "readily achievable" is that when there was enough money and did not require much effort, then the building owner would be required to bring his building up to compliance. Even though this is still vague, it gives a directive that existing buildings are not exempt or grandfathered from having to comply. Many states have accessibility guidelines, but many are only applicable if there is a construction project, whereas the ADA requires accessibility even if there is no construction currently being done in the facility. Since the new standards included new sections that were not in place in 1991 when the ADAAG was passed, these will be treated the same way as the new standards when the ADA was first published. Therefore, the new standards must be implemented in existing building and facilities, as they are readily achievable. For example, an existing playground will have to be made accessible even though this was never required prior to 2010.

There are certain times, when a facility is temporary and it would be difficult to bring things up to compliance and to provide access. The DOJ requires those facilities be made accessible to the "maximum extent feasible." This phrase, as used in this section, applies to the occasional case where the nature of an existing facility makes it virtually impossible to comply fully with applicable accessibility standards through a planned alteration. In these circumstances, the alteration shall provide the maximum physical accessibility feasible. Any altered features of the facility that can be made accessible shall be made accessible. If providing accessibility in conformance with this section to individuals with certain disabilities (e.g., those who use wheelchairs) would not be feasible, the facility shall be made accessible to persons with other types of disabilities (e.g., those who use crutches, those who have impaired vision or hearing, or those who have other impairments).

By implementing the standards to existing facilities, the owner of the building engages in barrier removal, more specifically elimination of architectural barriers. Architectural barriers are any element that prevents a disabled person from using the building or facility as it was intended. Therefore, in order to eliminate the barrier, typically construction must occur and an "alteration" will take place.

ALTERATIONS

The ADA defines alteration as:

> A change to a place of public accommodation or a commercial facility that affects or could affect the usability of the building or facility or any part thereof.

Any type of remodeling, renovation, rehabilitation, reconstruction, historic restoration, changes or rearrangement in structural parts or elements, and changes or rearrangement in the plan configuration of walls and full-height partitions, if they affect accessibility, will be considered an alteration. Normal maintenance, reroofing, painting or wallpapering, asbestos removal, or changes to mechanical and electrical systems are not alterations unless they affect the usability of the building or facility. Notice that the list does not exempt changes in plumbing systems such as replacing toilets, lavatories, and sinks. Those might be considered alterations if they are not changed for maintenance reasons.

In the ADA Standards there are two types of alterations described: one in an area that is of a primary function and one in an area where there is no primary function. A "primary function" is a major activity for which the facility is intended. Depending on the facility, different spaces would be considered primary. As an example, an office in an office building is a primary function space, but a restroom or break room would not be. Mechanical rooms, boiler rooms, supply storage rooms, employee locker rooms, janitorial closets, entrances, and corridors are not areas containing a primary function. Restrooms are not areas containing a primary function unless they are located at a rest stop, where going to the restroom would be a primary activity. Also, alterations to windows, hardware, controls, electrical outlets, and signage are not alterations that affect the usability of or access to an area containing a primary function, even if they are located in a major activity space. They are still alterations and must be compliant if provided.

If the alteration occurs in an area that is not primary, then only the elements that are getting remodeled or altered will have to comply. Therefore, if an element such as a feminine napkin dispenser in a restroom is installed, then that dispenser should be located at the proper height for reaching it and have the proper operating mechanism (see Figure 8.1).

If an entire restroom is getting remodeled, all the new elements must be made accessible. Sometimes there are elements inside the existing space that do not comply. Those elements may remain as long as they do not affect the usability of the new element. For example, in a restroom remodel, there may be existing paper towel dispensers that are considered protruding objects because they are mounted higher than 27 inches and also project onto the circulation path more than 4 inches (see Figure 8.2). This would affect access to the new fixtures since it will be considered a protruding object. This obstruction will have to be resolved. When existing elements are not compliant, it is not always required that they be replaced with new ones. It might be as simple as adding cane detection, such as a permanent object mounted below the existing one which is detectable to a blind person who uses a cane for wayfinding.

Figure 8.1: A new vending machine installed in an existing restroom will have to comply with the guidelines for reach ranges as well as for operating mechanisms. This vending machine does not have the proper operating mechanism.

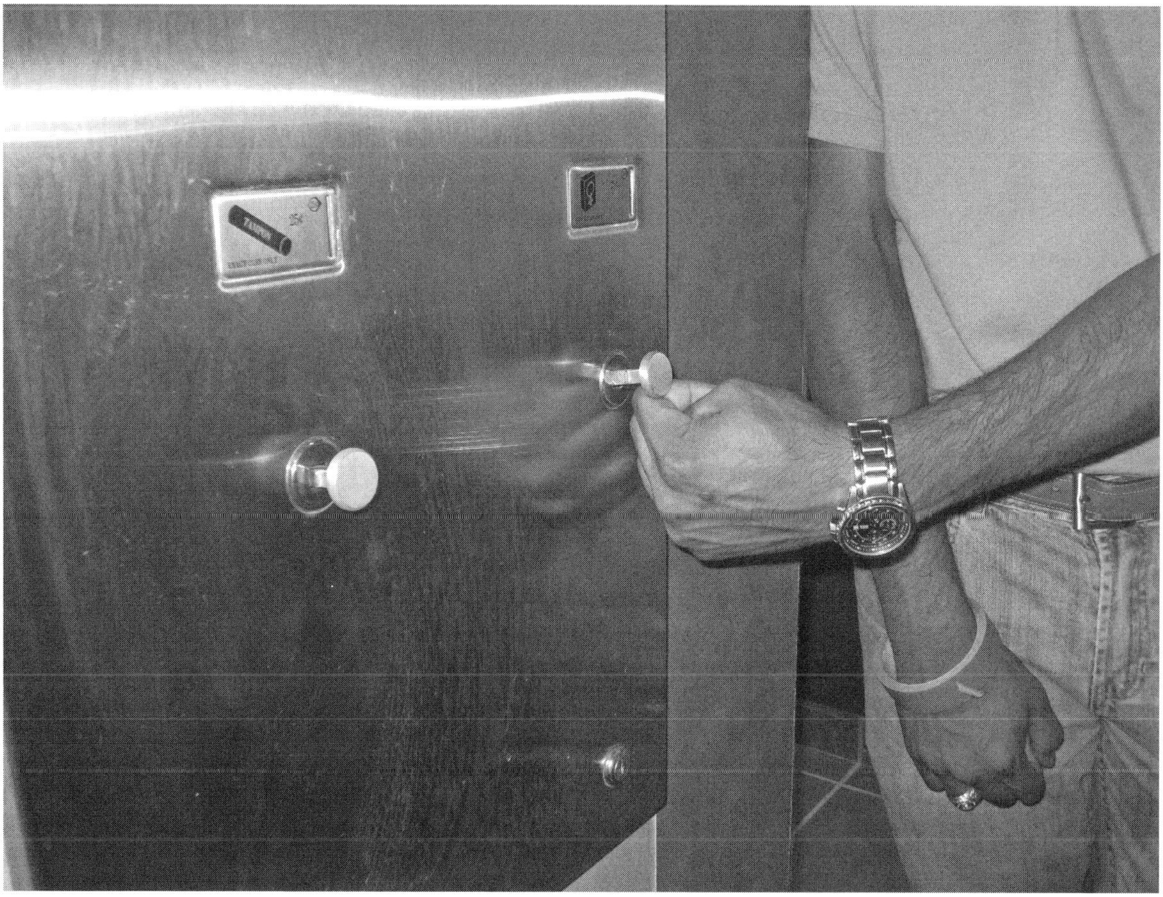

Figure 8.2: This existing paper towel dispenser was a protruding object until the permanent waste paper basket was installed below it.

If an element is altered but the accessible route to that element was not intended to be updated or brought up to compliance, the route will not have to be altered, since the element is not a primary function, even if it's an entire space like a restroom. For example, if a restroom is located on a different level than the corridor, the interior of the restroom will have to be accessible, but the route to the restroom would not have to be upgraded (see Figure 8.3).

Although building owners are permitted to limit the scope of an alteration to individual elements, the alteration of multiple elements within a room or space may provide a

Figure 8.3: This restroom has one step up to it, but because the restroom is not a primary function, it will not require an accessible route to it.

cost-effective opportunity to make the entire room or space accessible. By the same token, an alteration cannot decrease access or require greater access once it is finished (see Figure 8.4).

If the area that is getting altered is an area that contains a primary function, then not only must the new elements comply, but also the path of travel to the altered area, including the restrooms, drinking fountains, and telephones located along the path of travel and serving the altered area, have to be brought up to compliance.

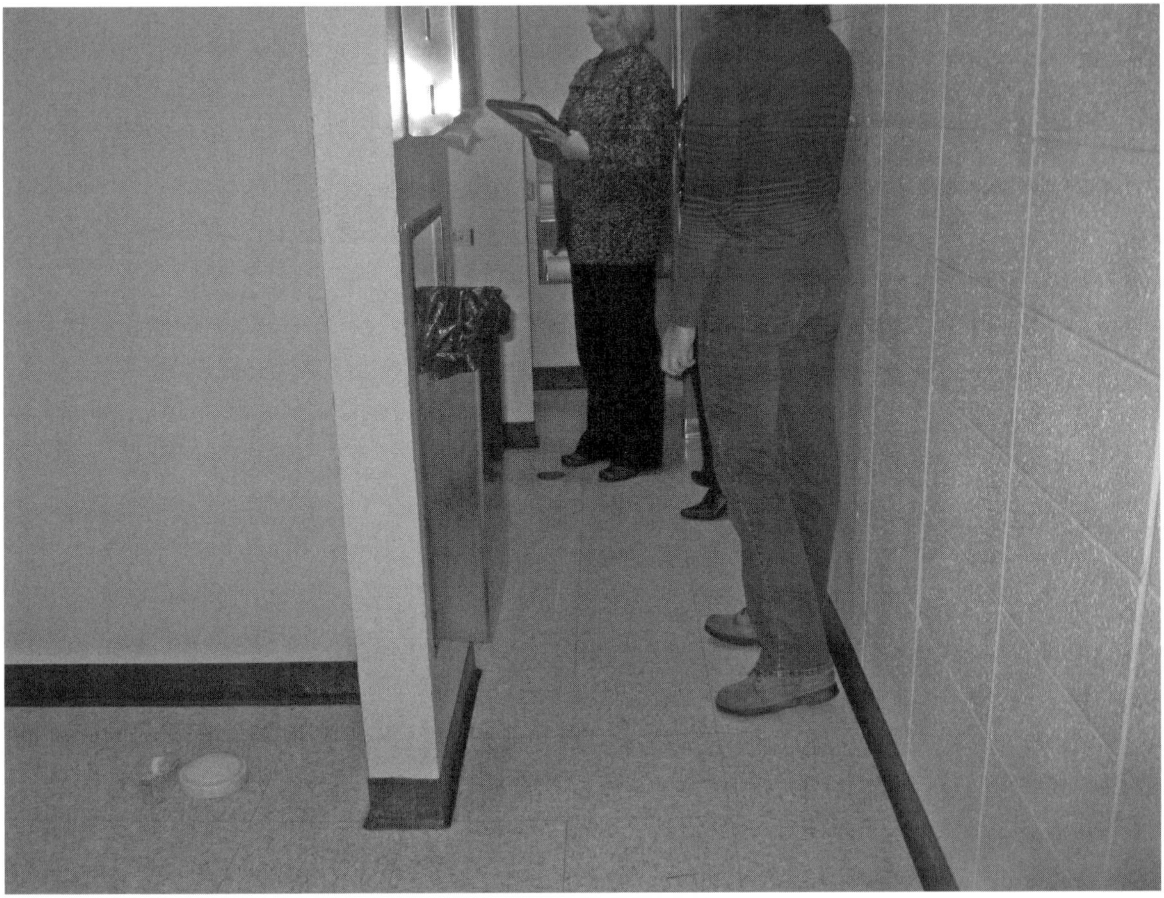

Figure 8.4: This new paper towel dispenser reduced the accessible route width to the toilet compartment.

According to the DOJ a "path of travel includes a continuous, unobstructed way of pedestrian passage by means of which the altered area may be approached, entered, and exited, and which connects the altered area with an exterior approach including sidewalks, streets, and parking areas, an entrance to the facility, and other parts of the facility."

Therefore, if the existing facility where an alteration of an area containing a primary function is being done, the path of travel will begin at the site arrival. If the facility has a bus stop nearby, the path of travel will begin there and will be required to take it to the entrance of the altered area. However, a path of travel is not required to the public right of way if the only means of arriving to the site is through a vehicle. At that point, the path of travel begins at the parking space or passenger drop-off.

Since the ADA Standards give parameters for alterations, the first place designers begin when remodeling and altering an existing space for accessibility is by looking at the existing conditions and seeing if the space's function is primary or not. The second place they look is in the scooping ADA chapters, Chapters 1 and 2, and then at the technical standards, ADA Chapter 3–10. If the designer begins in the technical chapters, he or she will miss some important information about what is truly required. For the purpose of this chapter, we will assume an alteration of an area containing a primary function is being done.

In an alteration project, a designer will begin with the scoped space and then move out to the path of travel elements. The path of travel, as mentioned before, might begin at the site arrival point, which can be either the public street or the parking space. The designer would begin his or her investigations at the site arrival and find the accessible route to the entrance of the altered space. Any element that is located along that accessible route, such as a curb ramp, protruding objects along the path, and the entrance itself, would also be part of the alteration project. Existing elements that meet the 1991 ADAAG are allowed to remain as they are as long as the element is not being altered. A curb ramp that is located along the path of travel from the site arrival to the entrance of the altered area, which does not have a landing at the top, is allowed to have flared sides at 1:12 so that a person in a wheelchair can exit the ramp and get onto the accessible route using the flared sides (see Figure 8.5).

Figure 8.5: This curb ramp does not have a landing at the top, and it is closer than 36 inches to the building, but since it is an existing ramp, it is acceptable because the wheelchair user can exit the ramp using the flared sides, which are 1:12.

ENTRANCES

If the alteration is an alteration to an entrance, and the building or facility has another entrance that is compliant and is on an accessible route, the altered entrance is not required to comply as well. Only one accessible entrance is required to be provided in an existing building. All new accessible entrances will have to be a 32-inch clear minimum width. For new construction, that width should be clear without any projections lower than 34 inches a.f.f., but alterations of doors may have a projection lower than 34 inches for the latch side stop but only for ⅝ inch (see Figure 8.6).

ACCESSIBLE ROUTE

Once inside the building, the path of travel to the altered space might take you to different floors, depending on where the alteration is located. If the building is not a shopping center, office of a healthcare provider, or a transportation facility, and has less than three stories or less than 3,000 square feet per story, an accessible route will not be required to the upper floors. This is called the Elevator exception. Even though the DOJ does not require an elevator or an accessible route, it does require that the elements on the upper levels be accessible and compliant with the standards. This is so that in the future, when it is readily achievable to add an elevator, the other elements will be able to be used by the disabled community. If a new stair or escalator is provided inside the space, an accessible route will also be required. This may include an elevator if the building doesn't already have one. The new standards also require that any stair that serves as a means of egress comply with ADA Chapter 5, except in an alteration project. If there is an existing stair and there is another means of access, either via elevator or ramp, then the stairs do not have to comply or be brought up to compliance. If a ramp is required to connect levels in an

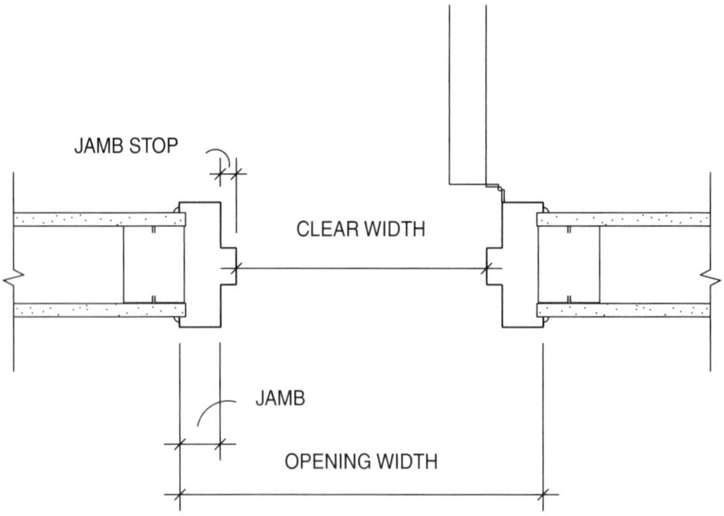

Figure 8.6: This plan shows an existing door and the clearances required for access.

existing building, the ramp must comply with the new construction standards. These include adding landings at the top and bottom of the runs, and adding handrails that extend 12 inches on the top and bottom of the ramp if the handrails are not continuous. However, in an alteration, if extending the rails 12 inches might be a hazard, then full extensions are not required (see Figure 8.7).

PATH OF TRAVEL ELEMENTS

As the person travels to the altered space, he or she will probably encounter restrooms, drinking fountains, or even public or service telephones. Only those found along the path of travel that serves the altered area must be brought up to compliance. If restrooms that serve the altered area do not comply with the standards and making them compliant would be technically infeasible, a different solution can be provided. Technically infeasible is defined by the ADA as:

Figure 8.7: This handrail extension is turned before the 12-inch extension is achieved because it is an existing ramp and the extension would be a hazard.

> With respect to an alteration of a building or a facility, something that has little likelihood of being accomplished because existing structural conditions would require removing or altering a load-bearing member that is an essential part of the structural frame; or because other existing physical or site constraints prohibit modification or addition of elements, spaces, or features that are in full and strict compliance with the minimum requirements.

For example, if the only way to make the restrooms comply is to remove fixtures in order to make the compartments wider, and the plumbing code will not allow fewer fixtures, then ADA 213.2 Exception 1 in the standards allow a single-user restroom that is accessible to be used instead. A sign leading them to the accessible restroom should be located at the one that is not accessible. This is also true of historic preservation projects with registered historic buildings. If the renovation would jeopardize the historic standing, then designers can also take the exception and provide a unisex restroom. Unisex toilet rooms benefit people who use opposite sex personal care assistants. For this reason, it is advantageous to install unisex toilet rooms in addition to accessible single-sex toilet rooms in new facilities.

Drinking fountains and public telephones are also required to be brought up to compliance, but only if provided and if they are the ones that serve the altered area. In the new standard, a drinking fountain for a standing person is required as well as a drinking fountain for a wheelchair user. Since the 1991 ADAAG did not require this, an existing drinking fountain that only has a wheelchair-height unit is considered a safe harbor, and it is not required to be brought up to compliance with the 2010 ADA Standards. In the 1991 ADAAG, a drinking fountain was allowed to have a parallel approach. The 2010 ADA Standards only allows drinking fountains with a front approach and required knee clearances. Therefore a drinking fountain that has a parallel approach, even though it does not meet the new requirements, will not have to be replaced with one that has knee clearances (see Figure 8.8). However, if the existing drinking fountain doesn't even meet the 1991 ADAAG, it will need to be brought up to compliance with the 2010 ADA Standards.

TENANT FINISH-OUTS

When an alteration occurs inside a space that is being leased from a building owner, and the new tenant is paying for the entire finish-out, then the rules pertaining to the path of travel will not apply. If the landlord owns the path of travel and all the elements along the path of travel leading to the new tenant's space, then it will not be required to be in compliance or be brought up to compliance as part of the tenant alteration unless it is part of the construction plan. Only the altered space will have to be in compliance. Of course, even if the landlord is not required to upgrade any item in his building that is not in compliance, this does not mean that he or she is meeting the intent of the ADA civil rights law. The ADA still requires access to the spaces in the building and at a certain point, when it is readily achievable, the path of travel will have to be upgraded to comply.

There are specific requirements for new medical care facilities patient rooms, transient lodging sleeping rooms, holding cells, and residential dwelling units that are exempted when alterations occur. In general, the requirements for new construction don't always apply to

Figure 8.8: This existing parallel-approach drinking fountain is a safe harbor and will not be required to be replaced with a drinking fountain that has a front approach.

existing facilities that deal with sleeping accommodations. Also, some existing facilities are exempted when maintenance of the facility would require that construction be done. An example of this is repainting the exterior of the building when, in order to do so, some demolition or resurfacing might occur. Because this type of remodel does not affect accessibility, it is not considered an "alteration."

ALTERATIONS OF MEDICAL CARE FACILITIES' PATIENT ROOMS

In long term medical care facilities, where patient sleeping rooms are being remodeled, the new rooms or remodeled rooms will have to be in compliance and provided in the amount specified in the ADA Standards (see Chapter 6 of this book for specific standards for new construction of medical care facilities).

> **223.1.1 Alterations.** Where sleeping rooms are *altered* or *added*, the requirements of 223 shall apply only to the sleeping rooms being *altered* or *added* until the number of sleeping rooms complies with the minimum number required for new construction.

If the existing hospital did not have sufficient accessible patient rooms prior to the alteration or addition, it does not have to be brought up to compliance with the 2010 ADA Standards. Only the new or added rooms will have to comply and count for compliance.

> In alterations and additions, the minimum required number is based on the total number of sleeping rooms altered or added instead of on the total number of sleeping rooms provided in a facility. As a facility is altered over time, every effort should be made to disperse accessible sleeping rooms among patient care areas such as pediatrics, cardiac care, maternity, and other units. In this way, people with disabilities can have access to the full-range of services provided by a medical care facility."
>
> 2010 ADA Standards Advisory 223.1.1

ALTERATIONS OF TRANSIENT LODGING SLEEPING ROOMS

The ADA Section 224 and 806 discusses requirements for new construction for transient lodging guest rooms. When remodeling a hotel, motel, residence hall in a place of education or similar places of lodging, some exceptions may be taken if it is not possible to bring things up to compliance. Not all places of lodging are subject to the ADA Standards. If a place of lodging is not "transient" and is owned by the person lodging in it, then it is exempted:

> **(2) Exception.** Alterations to guest rooms in places of lodging where the guest rooms are not owned or substantially controlled by the entity that owns, leases, or operates the overall facility and the physical features of the guest room interiors are controlled by their individual owners are not required to comply with § 36.402 or the alterations requirements in section ADA 224.1.1 of the 2010 Standards (2010 ADA Standards, p. 83).

Residential facilities, even if they are not permanent, such as homeless shelters, group homes, halfway houses, and other places of temporary lodging are not considered transient lodging and will not be designed like transient lodging, but residential facilities:

> **(3) Facilities with residential units and transient lodging units.** Residential dwelling units that are designed and constructed for residential use exclusively are not subject to the transient lodging standards.

In addition to those exceptions in places of lodging, if there is an addition or remodeling of existing guest rooms, only the new rooms will have to comply. Existing rooms will only have to be brought up to compliance when this is readily achievable:

> Where guest rooms are *altered* or *added*, the requirements of 224 shall apply only to the guest rooms being *altered* or *added* until the number of guest rooms complies with the minimum number required for new construction.

In alterations and additions, the minimum required number of accessible guest rooms is based on the total number of guest rooms altered or added instead of the total number of guest rooms provided in a facility. Typically, each alteration of a facility is limited to a particular portion of the facility. When accessible guest rooms are added as a result of subsequent alterations, compliance with 224.5 (dispersion) is more likely to be achieved if all of the accessible guest rooms are not provided in the same area of the facility.

ALTERATIONS OF HOLDING CELLS

Alterations to jails, prisons, and other detention and correctional facilities shall comply with the ADA 2010 Standards except that public entities shall provide accessible mobility features complying with section ADA 807.2 of the 2010 Standards for a minimum of 3%, but no fewer than one, of the total number of cells being altered until at least 3%, but no fewer than one, of the total number of cells in a facility shall provide mobility features.

Altered cells with mobility features shall be provided in each classification level. However, when alterations are made to specific cells, detention and correctional facility operators may satisfy their obligation to provide the required number of cells with mobility features by providing the required mobility features in substitute cells (cells other than those where alterations are originally planned), provided that each substitute cell—

(i.) Is located within the same prison site;

(ii.) Is integrated with other cells to the maximum extent feasible;

(iii.) Has, at a minimum, equal physical access as the altered cells to areas used by inmates or detainees for visitation, dining, recreation, educational programs, medical services, work programs, religious services, and participation in other programs that the facility offers to inmates or detainees; and

(iv.) If it is technically infeasible to locate a substitute cell within the same prison site, a substitute cell must be provided at another prison site within the corrections system.

With respect to medical and long-term care facilities in jails, prisons, and other detention and correctional facilities, public entities shall apply the ADA 2010 Standards technical and scoping requirements for those facilities irrespective of whether those facilities are licensed.

In general, alterations to cells shall not be required to comply except to the extent determined by the attorney general. Although these requirements do not specify that cells be accessible as a consequence of an alteration, Title II of the ADA requires that each service, program, or activity conducted by a public entity, when viewed in its entirety, be readily accessible to and usable by individuals with disabilities. This requirement must be met unless doing so would fundamentally alter the nature of a service, program, or activity or would result in undue financial and administrative burdens

ALTERATIONS OF RESIDENTIAL DWELLING UNITS

As it will be discussed in Chapter 9 of this book, the residential dwelling units referred to in the 2010 ADA Standards are housing that receives federal monies. They are not the housing that falls under Fair Housing and HUD Section 504. If a residential dwelling unit is being altered, Section 233.2 defers to HUD for the specification of criteria by which the technical requirements of the ADA Standards will apply to alterations of existing facilities subject to HUD's Section 504 regulations.

Where an *addition* to an existing *building* results in an increase in the number of *residential dwelling units,* the requirements of 233.3.1 shall apply only to the *residential dwelling units* that are *added* until the total number of *residential dwelling units* complies with the minimum number required by 233.3.1, and shall be on an accessible route

Where compliance with the residential sections in the 2010 Standards would be *technically infeasible*, or where it is *technically infeasible* to provide an *accessible* route to a *residential dwelling unit*, the entity shall be permitted to *alter* or construct a comparable *residential dwelling unit* to comply with 809.2 through 809.4 provided that the minimum number of *residential dwelling units* required by 233.3.1.1 and 233.3.1.2, as applicable, is satisfied.

233.3.4.1 Alterations to Vacated Buildings. Where a *building* is vacated for the purposes of *alteration*, and the *altered building* contains more than 15 *residential dwelling units*, at least 5 percent of the *residential dwelling units* shall comply with 809.2 through 809.4 and shall be on an *accessible* route as required by 206. In addition, at least 2 percent of the *residential dwelling units* shall comply with 809.5.

233.3.4.2 Alterations to Individual Residential Dwelling Units. In individual *residential dwelling units*, where a bathroom or a kitchen is substantially *altered*, and at least one other room is *altered*, the requirements of 233.3.1 shall apply to the *altered residential dwelling units* until the total number of *residential dwelling units* complies with the minimum number required by 233.3.1.1 and 233.3.1.2. *Residential dwelling units* required to comply with 233.3.1.1 shall be on an *accessible* route as required by 206.

EXCEPTION: Where *facilities* contain 15 or fewer *residential dwelling units*, the requirements of 233.3.1.1 and 233.3.1.2 shall apply to the total number of *residential dwelling units* that are *altered* under a single contract, or are developed as a whole, whether or not located on a common *site*.

Section 233.3.4.2 uses the terms "substantially altered" and "altered." A substantial alteration to a kitchen or bathroom includes, but is not limited to, alterations that are changes to or rearrangements in the plan configuration, or replacement of cabinetry. Substantial alterations do not include normal maintenance or appliance and fixture replacement, unless such maintenance or replacement requires changes to or rearrangements in the plan configuration, or replacement of cabinetry. The term "alteration" is defined both in Section 106 of these requirements and in the Department of Justice ADA regulations.

ALTERATIONS OF RESTAURANTS

If an existing restaurant is being altered, and it has dining spaces that are sunken or raised or even located in a mezzanine, the ADA allows an exception that allows the nonaccessible spaces to remain that way as long as there is a comparable space at an accessible area.

ADA 206.2.5 2. In *alterations*, an *accessible* route shall not be required to existing raised or sunken dining areas, or to all parts of existing outdoor dining areas where the same services and decor are provided in an *accessible space* usable by the public and not restricted to use by people with disabilities.

If the restaurant has a checkout stand, or service counters and the service counters are being altered, they should not decrease the number of counters. The ADA has allowed for an exception (see Figure 8.9):

> In *alterations*, when the provision of a counter complying with 904.4 would result in a reduction of the number of existing counters at work stations or a reduction of the number of existing *mail boxes*, the counter shall be permitted to have a portion which is 24 inches (610 mm) long minimum complying with 904.4.1 provided that the required clear floor or ground *space* is centered on the *accessible* length of the counter.

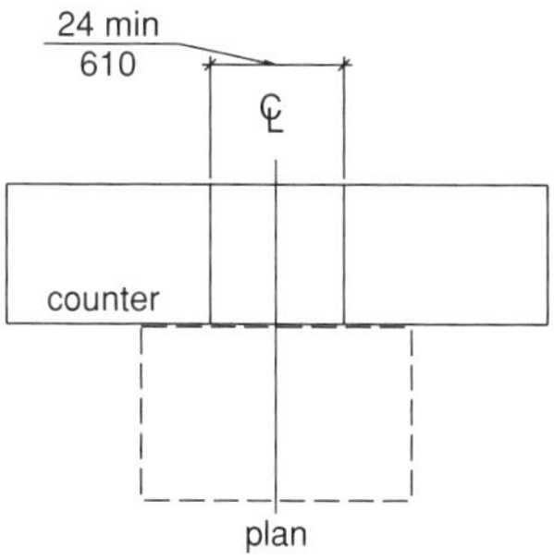

Figure 8.9: ADA Figure 904.4 (exception) shows the 24-inch counter allowed when remodeling existing counters would reduce the number of counters provided.

ALTERATIONS OF DRESSING ROOMS AND LOCKERS ROOMS

In an existing retail store, fitness center, or doctor's office that has dressing rooms or locker rooms, and those are being remodeled, there is an exception on having to bring them up to new construction compliance. If it is not technically feasible per the definition in the 2010 Standards, then a separate room that meets the requirements can be provided as an alternative solution.

> **ADA 222.1 General.** Where dressing rooms, fitting rooms, or locker rooms are provided, at least 5 percent, but no fewer than one, of each type of use in each cluster provided shall comply with 803.
>
> **EXCEPTION:** In *alterations*, where it is *technically infeasible* to provide rooms in accordance with 222.1, one room for each sex on each level shall comply with 803. Where only unisex rooms are provided, unisex rooms shall be permitted.

DISPROPORTIONALITY: THE 20% RULE

If during the alteration, it is discovered that the upgrade to the elements found along the path of travel would cost more than 20% of the total construction cost, the Department of

Justice considers it "disproportionate." Because it disproportionate, the DOJ allows a postponement to the upgrades. If the upgrades will be postponed, the DOJ requires that certain alterations be done in a certain priority order. Costs that may be counted as expenditures required to provide an accessible path of travel may include:

1. Costs associated with providing an accessible entrance and an accessible route to the altered area, for example, the cost of widening doorways or installing ramps;
2. Costs associated with making restrooms accessible, such as installing grab bars, enlarging toilet stalls, insulating pipes, or installing accessible faucet controls;
3. Costs associated with providing accessible telephones, such as relocating the telephone to an accessible height, installing amplification devices, or installing a text telephone (TTY); and
4. Costs associated with relocating an inaccessible drinking fountain.

The DOJ has established a priority list of items that are required to comply and what priority to give them. A building owner may not decide to fix the door hardware of interior doors before they fix the main entrance. In choosing which accessible elements to provide, priority should be given to those elements that will provide the greatest access, in the following order:

1. An accessible entrance;
2. An accessible route to the altered area;
3. At least one accessible restroom for each sex or a single unisex restroom;
4. Accessible telephones;
5. Accessible drinking fountains; and
6. When possible, additional accessible elements such as parking, storage, and alarms.

Sometimes the best effort finds that access cannot be accomplished because existing structural conditions would require removing or altering a load-bearing member that is an essential part of the structural frame or because other existing physical or site constraints prohibit modification. In those cases, speaking to local authorities and the DOJ to get a variance or waiver might be the proper action to take. However, even if it is not possible to provide access for wheelchair users, the building owner is still required to make sure other disabilities are accommodated. Accommodations in buildings should be provided for the visually impaired, hearing impaired, and people with other mobility issues such as walkers, crutches, and braces.

SERIES OF SMALLER ALTERATIONS

The obligation to provide an accessible path of travel may not be evaded by performing a series of small alterations to the area served by a single path of travel if those alterations could have been performed as a single undertaking. The DOJ established a rule about phases of construction:

> If an area containing a primary function has been altered without providing an accessible path of travel to that area, and subsequent alterations of that area, or a different area on the same path of travel, are undertaken within three years of the original alteration, the total cost of alterations to the primary function areas on that path of travel during the preceding three-year period shall be considered in determining whether the cost of making that path of travel accessible is disproportionate.

A facility must do its best to bring all elements up to compliance so that there will be equal treatment and access for all patrons.

SAFE HARBOR

The 1991 ADAAG and the 2010 ADA Standards have several requirements that are not similar. Some requirements are more stringent. The Department of Justice realized that it would be cost prohibitive to make all existing facilities bring their noncompliant elements to meet the new requirements. They ruled that if they met the 1991 Guidelines but not the 2010 Standards, then they would be considered a "safe harbor." This means that any element that is already compliant with the 1991 guidelines would not be required to be brought up to compliance with the 2010 Standards, until such time when the element in question would be renovated or altered (see Figure 8.10).

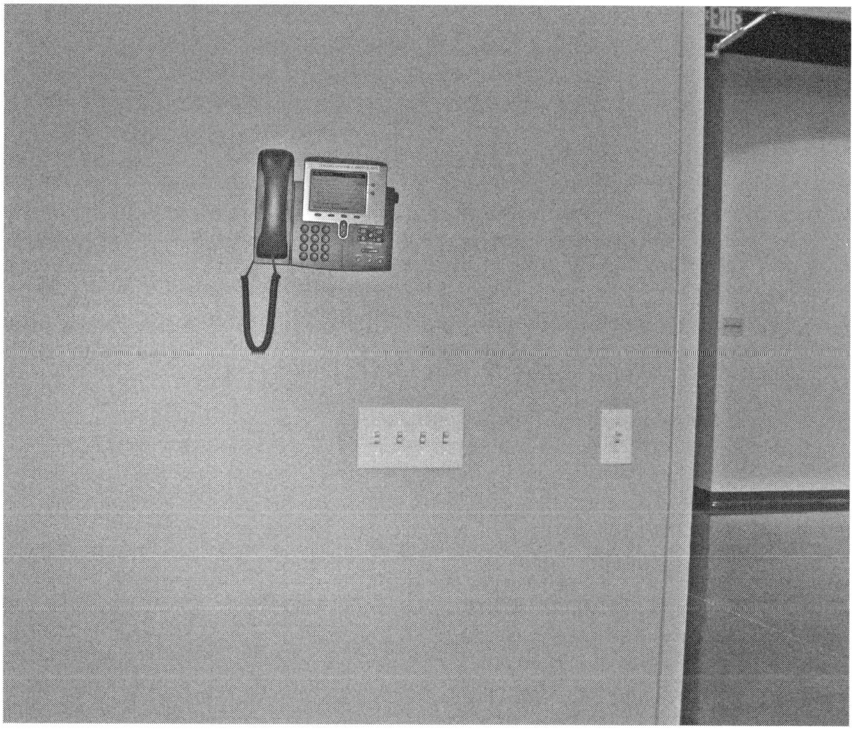

Figure 8.10: Elements like this public telephone that are mounted at 54 inches for a side approach are a safe harbor and will not be required to be lowered to 48 inches (the new requirement).

> If a public entity has constructed or altered required elements of a path of travel in accordance with the specifications in either the 1991 Standards or the Uniform Federal Accessibility Standards before March 15, 2012, the public entity is not required to retrofit such elements to reflect incremental changes in the 2010 Standards solely because of an alteration to a primary function area served by that path of travel. The compliance date is determined on the date of the final permit application or the date of construction commencement if there is no permit required.

HISTORIC FACILITIES

Facilities that are listed in the National Register of Historic Places under the National Historic Preservation Act (16 U.S.C. 470 *et seq.*), or are designated as historic under State or local law, also must comply with the ADA Standards to the best of their ability. According to the DOJ, if it is not feasible to provide physical access to a historic property in a manner that will not threaten or destroy the historic significance of the building or facility, alternative methods of access shall be provided.

ADA Section 202.5 states:

> **EXCEPTION:** Where the State Historic Preservation Officer or Advisory Council on Historic Preservation determines that compliance with the requirements for accessible routes, entrances, or toilet facilities would threaten or destroy the historic significance of the building or facility, the exceptions for alterations to qualified historic buildings or facilities for that element shall be permitted to apply.

State Historic Preservation Officers are state-appointed officials who carry out certain responsibilities under the National Historic Preservation Act. State Historic Preservation Officers consult with federal and state agencies, local governments, and private entities on providing access and protecting significant elements of qualified historic buildings and facilities.

There are exceptions for alterations to qualified historic buildings and facilities for accessible routes, entrances, and toilet facilities if adhering to the new construction requirements would endanger the historic status of the facility:

> ADA 206.2.1 EXCEPTIONS: 1. Where exceptions for alterations to qualified historic buildings or facilities are permitted by 202.5, no more than one accessible route from a site arrival point to an accessible entrance shall be required.
>
> ADA 206.2.3 EXCEPTION: 7. Where exceptions for alterations to qualified historic buildings or facilities are permitted by 202.5, an accessible route shall not be required to stories located above or below the accessible story.
>
> ADA 206.4 Exception 2. Where exceptions for alterations to qualified historic buildings or facilities are permitted by 202.5, no more than one public entrance shall be required to comply with 206.4. Where no public entrance can comply

with 206.4 under criteria established in 202.5 Exception, then either an unlocked entrance not used by the public shall comply with 206.4; or a locked entrance complying with 206.4 with a notification system or remote monitoring shall be provided.

ADA 213.2 Exception 2. Where exceptions for alterations to qualified historic buildings or facilities are permitted by 202.5, no fewer than one toilet room for each sex complying with 603 or one unisex toilet room complying with 213.2.1 shall be provided.

When an entity believes that compliance with the requirements for any of these elements would threaten or destroy the historic significance of the building or facility, the entity should consult with the State Historic Preservation Officer. If the State Historic Preservation Officer agrees that compliance with the requirements for a specific element would threaten or destroy the historic significance of the building or facility, use of the exception is permitted (see Figure 8.11).

Figure 8.11: This historic building has steps leading to the main entrance. An alternate entrance could be used if providing access at the front may threaten or destroy the historic significance.

Public entities have an additional obligation to achieve program accessibility under the Department of Justice ADA Title II regulations. These regulations require public entities that operate historic preservation programs to give priority to methods that provide physical access to individuals with disabilities. The program could be a tour of the building, or a lecture about the history of the building. If alterations to a qualified historic building or facility to achieve program accessibility would threaten or destroy the historic significance of the building or facility, fundamentally alter the program, or result in undue financial or administrative burdens, the Department of Justice ADA regulations allow alternative methods to be used to achieve program accessibility. In the case of historic preservation programs, such as an historic house museum, alternative methods include using audiovisual materials to depict portions of the house that cannot otherwise be made accessible. In the case of other qualified historic properties, such as an historic government office building, alternative methods include relocating programs and services to accessible locations. The Department of Justice ADA regulations also allow public entities to use alternative methods when altering qualified historic buildings or facilities in the rare situations where the State Historic Preservation Officer determines that it is not feasible to provide physical access using the exceptions permitted in ADA Section 202.5 without threatening or destroying the historic significance of the building will be acceptable.

If an alteration is being carried out in a historic facility, the same requirements as a regular facility must be met. In the case of an alteration of an area containing a primary function within the building or facility, the path of travel elements will also need to be brought up to compliance. As for the accessible route, only one accessible route from one site arrival to one accessible entrance will be required. The entrance to the historic facility should be accessible as well. Only one public entrance shall be required to comply. Where no public entrance can comply, then either an unlocked entrance not used by the public or a locked entrance with a notification system or remote monitoring can be provided. If the historic building has multiple stories, access will not be required to spaces above or below the accessible story. For example, if there is a multistory historic house that was converted into a museum, and the first floor is accessible, but the upper floors are not, it will not be required to provide an elevator to the upper floors if it will destroy the historic value of the house.

SUMMARY

This country was founded more than 200 years ago, and as the country developed, buildings were designed without much thought to access. Since the ADA was enacted, many existing buildings that were never designed for access are still not accessible. The disabled community were provided the opportunity to integrate as part of the rest of society by being able to work, recreate, and participate in the same activities as everyone else. In order to do that, existing buildings have to be updated to allow that to happen. Sometimes it is a simple task, but most of the time it is difficult and costly. A good faith effort on the part of the building owners to bring their facilities up to compliance is all that is required. As long as all the parties are working together for the greater good, there can be access in all existing buildings. This is beneficial to all members of society.

Reference Sections Chapter 8

The 2010 ADA Standards reference several sections for one topic. This reference table assists the designer in finding the pertinent sections pertaining to one specific area. To use the table, find the topic and below are all the different sections that the standards refer to.

DOJ CFR 35	
Section Number	**Section Title and Description**
DOJ CFR 36	
Section Number	**Section Title and Description**
ADA Chapter 1: Definitions	
Section Number	**Section Title and Description**
101.2	Effect on Removal of Barriers in Existing Facilities.
106	Definition of Alteration
106	Definition of Disproportionality
	Definition of Path of Travel
106	Definition of Primary Function
106.5.52	Qualified Historic Building or Facility
106.5.68	Technically Infeasible
ADA Chapter 2: Alterations	
Section Number	**Section Title and Description**
202	Existing Buildings and Facilities
202.3	Alterations
202.5	Alterations to Qualified Historic Buildings and Facilities
Advisory 202.5	Alterations to Qualified Historic Buildings and Facilities Exception
206.2.3.1	Stairs and Escalators in Existing Buildings
206.2.1	Site Arrival Points. EXCEPTION 1
206.2.3	Multi-Story Buildings and Facilities. Exception 7
206.4	Entrances. Exception 2
206.2.5	Restaurants and Cafeterias. Exception 2
206.4.4.1	Location. EXCEPTION
206.4.4.2	Direct Connections. EXCEPTION
206.4.4.3	Key Stations and Intercity Rail Stations
206.6.1	Existing Elevators
206.7	Platform Lifts
206.7.5	Existing Site Constraints
206.7.5	Advisory Existing Site Constraints
213.2	Toilet Rooms and Bathing Rooms. Exception 1 and 2
215	EXCEPTION Fire Alarm Systems
216.7	Elevators
216.8	Toilet Rooms and Bathing Rooms

(continued)

ADA Chapter 2: Alterations	
Section Number	**Section Title and Description**
218.3	Key Stations and Existing Intercity Rail Stations
224.1.1	(Transient Lodging Facilities) Alterations
224.1.1	Advisory Alterations
232.2	General Holding Cells and General Housing Cells. EXCEPTION
232.3	Special Holding Cells and Special Housing Cells. EXCEPTION
233.3.3	Additions
233.3.4	Alterations
233.3.4	Advisory Alterations Exception
233.3.4.1	Alterations to Vacated Buildings
233.3.4.2	Alterations to Individual Residential Dwelling Units
233.3.4.2	Advisory Alterations to Individual Residential Dwelling Units
234.4	Existing Amusement Rides
234.4	Advisory Existing Amusement Rides
234.4.1	Load and Unload Areas
238.2.1	238.2.1 Teeing Grounds. EXCEPTION
240.1	240.1 General. EXCEPTION 2
308.3.1	(Side Reach) Unobstructed. Exception 2
308.3.2	(Side Reach) Obstructed High Reach. Exception 2
404.2.3	Clear Width. Exception 1
404.2.5	Thresholds. EXCEPTION
404.2.7	Door and Gate Hardware. Exception 1
404.2.10	Door and Gate Surfaces. Exception 4
406.4	Landings. EXCEPTION
405.2	Slope. EXCEPTION
Table 405.2	Maximum Ramp Slope and Rise for Existing Sites, Buildings, and Facilities
407.2.1	Call Controls. EXCEPTION
407.2.1.1	Height. EXCEPTION
407.2.1.2	Size. EXCEPTION
407.2.1.5	Signals. EXCEPTION 2
407.2.2	Hall Signals. EXCEPTION 2
407.2.2.2	Visible Signals. EXCEPTION 2
407.2.2.3	Audible Signals. EXCEPTION 2
407.3.2	Operation. EXCEPTION
407.3.3	Reopening Device. EXCEPTION
407.3.6	Width. EXCEPTION
407.4.1	Car Dimensions. EXCEPTION

ADA Chapters 3-10: Technical	
Section Number	**Section Title and Description**
407.4.6	Elevator Car Controls. EXCEPTION
407.4.6.1	Location. EXCEPTION 2
407.4.7	Designations and Indicators of Car Controls. EXCEPTION
407.4.7.1.2	Location. EXCEPTION
408.4.1	Car Dimensions and Doors. EXCEPTION 2
505.10	Handrail Extensions. Exception 3
608.7	Thresholds. EXCEPTION
810.5.1	Slope. EXCEPTION
810.9	Escalators. EXCEPTION
808.3	Clear Floor Space. Exception
904.4	Sales and Service Counters. EXCEPTION
Figure 904.4	(Exception) Alteration of Sales and Service Counters
1003.2.1	Boat Slips. Exception 1
1003.3.1	Boat Slip Clearance. Exception 3
1003.3.1	Advisory Boat Slip Clearance Exception 3

Residential Projects

9

by Jeromy Murphy, AIA RAS

INTRODUCTION

The lack of accessible or adaptable housing is a growing concern as our population ages. State and city governments are often tasked with providing affordable housing, group homes, or retirement communities, filling a need not supported by the private market. Providing accessible residences has been complicated by overlapping and sometimes conflicting requirements. The 2010 ADA standards attempts to harmonize the requirements for residential dwelling units.

Residential versus Transient Lodging

The primary difference between residential facilities and transient lodging is the length of stay. Residential dwelling units are provided primarily for long-term occupancy, and transient lodging is primarily for short-term occupancy.

> 106.5.54 Residential Dwelling Unit. A unit intended to be used as a residence that is primarily long-term in nature. Residential dwelling units do not include transient lodging, inpatient medical care, licensed long-term care, and detention or correctional facilities.
>
> 106.5.71 Transient Lodging. A building or facility containing one or more guest room(s) for sleeping that provides accommodations that are primarily short-term in nature. Transient lodging does not include residential dwelling units intended to be used as a residence, inpatient medical care facilities, licensed long-term care facilities, detention or correctional facilities, or private buildings or facilities that contain not more than five rooms for rent or hire and that are actually occupied by the proprietor as the residence of such proprietor.

There are no specific durations provided in the standards to define "long term" and "short term." Hotels and other transient lodging facilities are required to provide a high-level of accessibility within a limited number of rooms, while the focus for residential facilities is more on adaptability. It is not practical for visitors to a hotel to modify their room for access if they are staying just a few days, so it is essential that rooms with mobility features and communication features be made ready for their use. Because residential facilities are occupied for a longer term, it is possible to make alterations to accommodate a person with a disability at the time it is needed; this also permits a dwelling unit to be occupied by a person who may not need or desire grab bars, shower seats, high toilet seats, or low sinks.

Applicability

A common misunderstanding is how the ADA standards apply to residential facilities. Overlapping requirements from Section 504 of the Rehabilitation Act, Fair Housing Act, and the ADA have created confusion and sometimes contradictory requirements for certain facilities.

The 1991 ADA standards did not include requirements for residential facilities; social service establishments were grouped with transient lodging. In order to harmonize requirements for federally funded housing, the 2010 ADA standards adds requirements for residential facilities. Previously, housing subject to Section 504 of the Rehabilitation Act was required to comply with the Uniform Federal Accessibility standards (UFAS).

State and local governments are subject to Title II of the ADA. This requires that state and local governments provide access to all programs they offer, including housing. Publicly funded group homes, halfway houses and shelters, and dormitories at publicly funded universities are required to provide dwelling units that include mobility features and communication features. The following sections are excerpted from Chapter 28 of the Code of Federal Register and apply specifically to housing provided by state and local governments:

28 CFR 35.151(e) Social service center establishments. Group homes, halfway houses, shelters, or similar social service center establishments that provide either temporary sleeping accommodations or residential dwelling units that are subject to this section shall comply with the provisions of the 2010 standards applicable to residential facilities, including, but not limited to, the provisions in Sections 233 and 809.

1. In sleeping rooms with more than 25 beds covered by this section, a minimum of 5% of the beds shall have clear floor space complying with Section 806.2.3 of the 2010 standards.

2. Facilities with more than 50 beds covered by this section that provide common use bathing facilities, shall provide at least one roll-in shower with a seat that complies with the relevant provisions of Section 608 of the 2010 standards. Transfer-type showers are not permitted in lieu of a roll-in shower with a seat, and the exceptions in Sections 608.3 and 608.4 for residential dwelling units are not permitted. When separate shower facilities are provided for men and for women, at least one roll-in shower shall be provided for each group.

28 CFR 35.151(f) Housing at a place of education. Housing at a place of education that is subject to this section shall comply with the provisions of the 2010 standards applicable to transient lodging, including, but not limited to, the requirements for transient lodging guest rooms in Sections 224 and 806 subject to the following exceptions. For the purposes of the application of this section, the term "sleeping room" is intended to be used interchangeably with the term "guest room" as it is used in the transient lodging standards.

1. Kitchens within housing units containing accessible sleeping rooms with mobility features (including suites and clustered sleeping rooms) or on floors containing accessible sleeping rooms with mobility features shall provide turning spaces that comply with Section 809.2.2 of the 2010 standards and kitchen work surfaces that comply with Section 804.3 of the 2010 standards.
2. Multi-bedroom housing units containing accessible sleeping rooms with mobility features shall have an accessible route throughout the unit in accordance with Section 809.2 of the 2010 standards.
3. Apartments or townhouse facilities that are provided by or on behalf of a place of education, which are leased on a year-round basis exclusively to graduate students or faculty and do not contain any public use or common use areas available for educational programming, are not subject to the transient lodging standards and shall comply with the requirements for residential facilities in Sections 233 and 809 of the 2010 standards.

28 CFR 35.151(j) Facilities with residential dwelling units for sale to individual owners.

1. Residential dwelling units designed and constructed or altered by public entities that will be offered for sale to individuals shall comply with the requirements for residential facilities in the 2010 standards including Sections 233 and 809.
2. The requirements of paragraph (1) also apply to housing programs that are operated by public entities where design and construction of particular residential dwelling units take place only after a specific buyer has been identified. In such programs, the covered entity must provide the units that comply with the requirements for accessible features to those pre-identified buyers with disabilities who have requested such a unit.

Dormitories at a public or private university or other places of education, must meet the requirements for transient lodging, but often dormitories will include apartments for resident assistants or other faculty. These apartments are subject to the residential requirements instead of the transient lodging requirements if they are leased on a year-round basis. When 15 or fewer residential units are provided in a building, the exception in 233.3.1, permits the required number of accessible dwelling units to be determined by the total units developed under one contract rather than on a building-by-building basis. This is particularly advantageous when each dormitory building may contain only a few apartment units.

Although it might not seem logical, crew quarters provided within publicly funded fire stations or for other emergency responders are required to meet the same requirements as other residential facilities and include rooms with mobility features and communications features. The ADA does not make assumptions about the physical requirements for a specific job and offers no unique exceptions for facilities such as fire stations.

Privately funded housing is not subject to the residential dwelling unit requirements in the ADA standards, including all types of privately funded housing, single-family, duplexes, or multi-family facilities such as apartments or condominiums. Multi-family buildings that include four or more dwelling units are subject to the design requirements of the Fair Housing Act (FHA). Refer to The U.S. Department of Housing and Urban Development (HUD) for information regarding compliance with the FHA design requirements.

Privately funded shelters and dormitories are subject to the same requirements as publicly funded social service establishments. Sections 36.406(d) and (e) of the ADA law provides the scoping requirements for privately funded social service establishments and housing at places of education.

Because religious organizations are exempt from the ADA, housing provided as part of a religious facility or institution is not subject to the design requirements for accessible dwelling units. Some state and local municipalities impose construction standards that exceed the requirements of the ADA and may require accessible dwelling units within religious institutions. Always check local requirements for accessibility. The ADA does not "supercede" local or state building codes; in all cases, the most restrictive requirement should apply.

The following sections are excerpted from Chapter 28 of the Code of Federal Register and apply specifically to housing provided by private organizations:

§36.406(d) Social service center establishments. Group homes, halfway houses, shelters, or similar social service center establishments that provide either temporary sleeping accommodations or residential dwelling units that are subject to this part shall comply with the provisions of the 2010 standards applicable to residential facilities, including, but not limited to, the provisions in Sections 233 and 809.

1. In sleeping rooms with more than 25 beds covered by this part, a minimum of 5% of the beds shall have clear floor space complying with Section 806.2.3 of the 2010 standards.
2. Facilities with more than 50 beds covered by this part that provide common use bathing facilities shall provide at least one roll-in shower with a seat that complies with the relevant provisions of Section 608 of the 2010 standards. Transfer-type showers are not permitted in lieu of a roll-in shower with a seat, and the exceptions in Sections 608.3 and 608.4 for residential dwelling units are not permitted. When separate shower facilities are provided for men and for women, at least one roll-in shower shall be provided for each group.

§36.406(e) Housing at a place of education. Housing at a place of education that is subject to this part shall comply with the provisions of the 2010 standards applicable to transient lodging, including, but not limited to, the requirements for transient lodging guest rooms in Sections 224 and 806, subject to the following exceptions. For the purposes of the application of this section, the term "sleeping room" is intended to be used interchangeably with the term "guest room" as it is used in the transient lodging standards.

1. Kitchens within housing units containing accessible sleeping rooms with mobility features (including suites and clustered sleeping rooms) or on floors containing accessible sleeping rooms with mobility features shall provide turning spaces that comply with Section 809.2.2 of the 2010 standards and kitchen work surfaces that comply with Section 804.3 of the 2010 standards.

2. Multi-bedroom housing units containing accessible sleeping rooms with mobility features shall have an accessible route throughout the unit in accordance with Section 809.2 of the 2010 standards.

3. Apartments or townhouse facilities that are provided by or on behalf of a place of education, which are leased on a year-round basis exclusively to graduate students or faculty and do not contain any public use or common use areas available for educational programming, are not subject to the transient lodging standards and shall comply with the requirements for residential facilities in Sections 233 and 809 of the 2010 standards.

Public and Common Use Spaces

All public spaces are required to be accessible and meet the same requirements as any other public space. Common-use spaces that serve residential dwelling units required to have mobility features are also required to be accessible. Those common-use elements that do not serve units with mobility features are not required to be accessible. For instance, if common-use laundry rooms are provided on each floor of a building, the laundry room on the floor that does not include accessible dwelling units is not required to meet the requirements in Section 214 for washing machines and dryers.

203.8 Residential Facilities. In residential facilities, common use areas that do not serve residential dwelling units required to provide mobility features complying with Sections 809.2 through 809.4 shall not be required to comply with these requirements or to be on an accessible route.

An elevator is not required in multi-story residential facilities where all of the dwelling units required to have mobility features and all public spaces are located on an accessible route. For example, a three-story apartment building with the management office and all accessible apartments located on the first floor does not require an elevator.

Leasing Office

The leasing office is always required to be accessible. Even in the case of private apartment complexes that are not subject to any other section of the standards. The leasing office is regarded as an area of public accommodation and must comply with all of the requirements for a business, including accessible parking, entrances, and restrooms (see Figure 9.1).

Exterior Routes

If a public sidewalk and/or public transportation stops are provided within the perimeter of the site, an accessible pedestrian route is required between the public sidewalk and the accessible buildings.

Parking

Where separate parking areas are provided for visitors to a leasing office and for resident parking, accessible parking is required to be provided in each parking area and is calculated separately. At least one van accessible parking space is required at the leasing office. If four or fewer parking spaces are provided at the leasing office, the accessible parking space is not required to be reserved, but still must meet all other requirements for accessible parking.

Figure 9.1: Visitor parking at a leasing office/clubhouse.

If parking is provided for residents, at least one accessible parking space is required for each residential dwelling unit required to provide mobility features. This accessible parking is required to be on the shortest route to the residential dwelling unit it serves. It is not necessary to identify accessible parking spaces as reserved if the parking spaces are assigned to specific residential dwelling units.

If more than one parking space is provided per dwelling unit, 2% of the total parking is required to be accessible, and 1:6 of the required accessible spaces shall be van accessible. Accessible parking is required to be dispersed or otherwise configured to ensure equivalent user convenience.

Mail Boxes

Five percent of mail boxes are required to be provided within the accessible reach ranges, 15 inches minimum to 48 inches maximum, and located on an accessible route. If mail boxes are provided for each dwelling unit, at a minimum, the mail boxes for each of the units with mobility features shall be accessible.

Dumpsters/Recycling Areas

When dumpsters, trash bins, trash chutes, or recycling centers are provided for use by the residents, they shall be located on an accessible route. Openings to receptacles are required to be within the accessible reach ranges, 15 inches minimum and 48 inches maximum. Some facilities offer door-to-door trash pick-up and the dumpsters are only accessed by employees; in this case, the dumpsters are not required to be accessible to people with disabilities.

Play Areas, Grills, Picnic Areas, and Fitness Areas

Playgrounds that are provided as part of a residential facility, subject to the ADA standards, are required to include accessible play components and be located on an accessible route. Other amenities such as picnic tables, grills, and sport courts are required to be located on accessible routes. Five percent of picnic tables should provide wheelchair seating. A general rule of thumb is that if an amenity is provided, access is required. Avoid making assumptions about which activities people with disabilities can and cannot participate in.

Swimming Pools

Swimming pools that are provided as part of a residential facility subject to the ADA standards are required to include accessible means of entry. Accessible means of entry include ramps, lifts, transfer systems, and stairs. Smaller pools with less than 300 linear feet of perimeter are required to have either a ramp or a lift. Larger pools with 300 linear feet or greater of perimeter, shall have two means of accessible entry. One of which must be either a lift or ramp.

Existing swimming pools will require access if they are altered. Existing swimming pools provided by a state or local government are only required to be provided with accessible means of entry to satisfy the requirement for "program access" as described in Title II of the ADA. It is not necessary for all existing swimming pools operated by a state or local government to be made accessible if all pool-related programs offered are available at a pool with accessible means of entry.

Residential Dwelling Units

Alterations to existing dwelling units are not required to comply with standards unless the unit being altered is required to be accessible by the ADA or Section 504 of the Rehabilitation Act. In most cases, an alteration that affects the usability of or access to an area containing a primary function will require that the existing "path of travel," including accessible routes, restrooms, drinking fountains, and public telephones serving the altered area, be made accessible. Alterations to only the dwelling units do not impose this "path of travel" obligation.

In order to encourage visitors, all dwelling units, even those not required to have mobility features, shall have an accessible door at the primary entry.

Residential Dwelling Units with Mobility Features or Communication Features

Because the term "accessible" is a broad term that is often applied generically, more accurate and specific language is used to describe accessible residential dwelling units. Rooms with mobility features include accessible doors and routes, clear floor space at fixtures, and other clearances to accommodate people with physical disabilities, especially wheelchair users. Rooms with communication features include visual alarms and other devices to assist people with hearing or vision impairments.

Five percent of the total residential dwelling units shall include mobility features and 2% of the units shall include communication features. These units shall be dispersed among the various unit types to afford people with disabilities the same or equivalent range of options available to everyone. It is not necessary to provide one of each type of dwelling unit if the total number of unit types exceeds the total number of required units with mobility or communication features. Multi-story units are not required to include mobility features if single-story units of similar size and with similar amenities are provided. These units should be integrated with other dwelling units and not segregated or set apart from the larger community.

Residential Units with Mobility Features

An accessible entrance and accessible route throughout the unit is required, including access to patios, garages, and storage. The accessible route should not pass through bathrooms, closets, or similar spaces. Unfinished attics and basements are not required to be on an accessible route.

A 5 ft. 0 in. diameter turning space or T-turn is required within all rooms, including bathrooms served by an accessible route. Narrow balconies, less than 30 inches deep or wide, and shallow closets that do not require user passage to access the storage are not required to have turning space.

Operable parts including light switches, thermostats, and power or communication outlets are required to be provided within the accessible reach ranges (15 inches minimum to 48 inches maximum) and located on an accessible route. Controls that residents would not typically use such as circuit breakers or water heater controls are not required to be accessible. Operable windows are not required to be accessible.

Kitchens: The standards identify two general types of kitchens, pass-through and U-shaped. This is not intended to limit or prohibit other kitchen layouts, but all kitchen layouts shall conform to one of these layouts.

Pass-through kitchens are required to have 40-inch minimum clear space between all opposing base cabinets, countertops, appliances, or walls and at least two entries. Galley kitchens or small kitchenettes without opposing walls are examples of pass-through kitchens (see Figure 9.2).

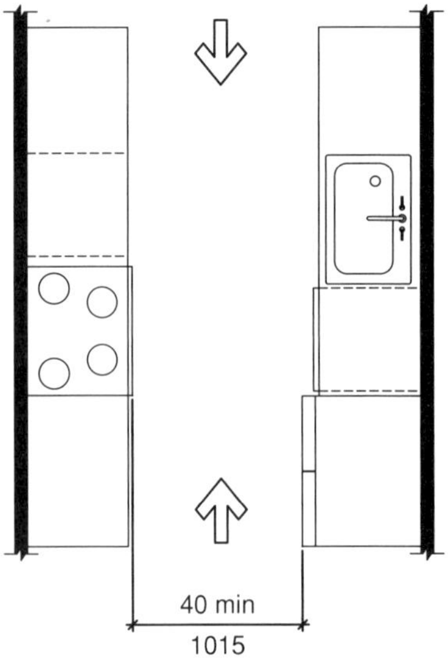

Figure 9.2: Pass through kitchen. (ADA standards Figure 804.2.1).

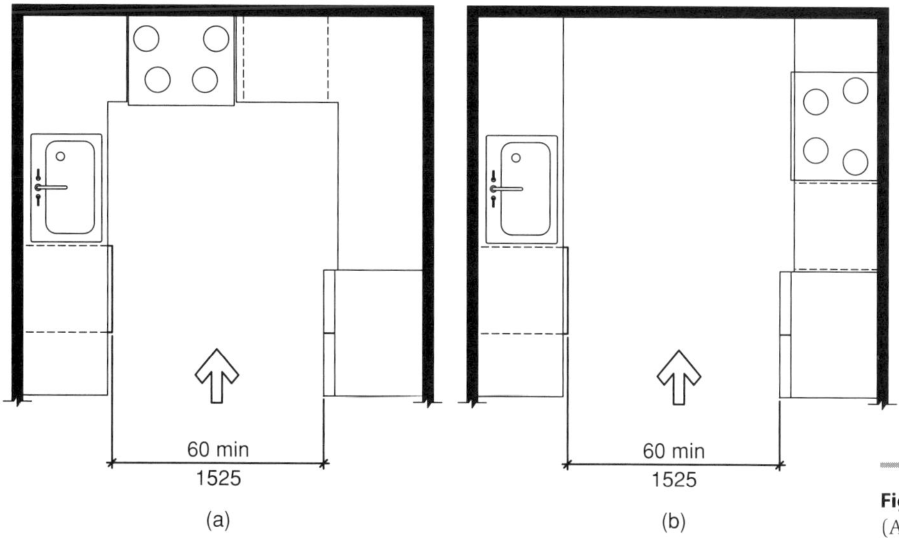

Figure 9.3: U-Shaped kitchen. (ADA standards Figure 804.2.2).

U-Shaped kitchens require a minimum of 60 inches between all opposing base cabinets, countertops, appliances, and walls (see Figure 9.3). A kitchen with only one entry or where turning is required to maneuver to access the appliances are considered U-Shaped.

An accessible sink and kitchen work surface shall be provided with a maximum height of 34 inches and a 30–inch-wide clear floor space that allows a front approach with knee and toe clearance. Base cabinets may be provided under the work surface and sink, if the flooring and wall finishes are extended under the work surface and the cabinetry can be removed without replacing the countertop.

At multibowl sinks, knee and toe clearance is only required at one bowl. In kitchenettes that do not have a cook top or conventional range, knee and toe clearance is not required at the sink.

Storage: At least 50% of shelf space shall be accessed from a 30 inch x 48 inch wide clear floor space and shall be within the accessible reach ranges (15 inches minimum and 48 inches maximum). Shelf space is measured in linear feet. The use of upper cabinets may be limited because of this 50% requirement. The amount of shelving provided within the accessible dwelling units should have shelf space equivalent to shelf space provided in other units (see Figure 9.4).

At each appliance, a 30 inch x 48 inch clear floor space shall be provided. Clear floor or ground spaces are permitted to overlap. Appliance controls shall be within accessible reach ranges and easy to use. Bottom-hinged appliance doors are permitted to be lower than 15 inches when in the open position.

The clear floor space shall be positioned according to appliance type as noted in the following list:

- *Dishwasher*: The required clear floor space shall be adjacent to the dishwasher door when it is in the open position. The dishwasher door may not obstruct the clear floor space at the sink but is permitted to obstruct the clear floor space at other appliances.

Figure 9.4: Accessible kitchen counter with work surface and lower upper cabinets.

- *Range or cooktop*: A side approach is permitted to a cooktop, but in layouts where knee and toe clearance is provided, the underside of the appliance must be insulated. Controls shall be located so that users are not required to reach over burners. The height of cooktops is not specified.
- *Oven*: The accessible kitchen work surface is required to be located adjacent to the oven. If the door to the oven is side-hinged, the work surface must be on the latch side of the oven.

- *Refrigerator/freezer*: A clear floor space shall be provided for a side approach to the space dedicated for a refrigerator. Unique to refrigerators, this clear floor space must be centered. Therefore, the refrigerator space shall be at least 24 inches on center from adjacent walls or obstructions. Fifty percent of freezer space shall be 54 inches maximum above the finish floor.

Bathrooms: When bathrooms are provided within a dwelling unit, at least one shall be accessible and include at least one of each type of accessible fixture. The accessible toilet fixtures are required to be within the same toilet or bathing area. For example, it is not acceptable to have the accessible lavatory and water closet located in the master bathroom and the accessible bathtub located in a separate bathroom. In congregate housing or group homes where common-use toilet or bathing facilities are provided, all common use bathrooms are required to be accessible.

The standard clear floor space for an accessible water closet is 60 inches wide and 56 inches deep. In residential dwelling units only, the lavatory is permitted to overlap the required clear floor space if the depth of the clear floor space is increased to 66 inches minimum (see Figure 9.5). This allows sufficient space in front of the water closet for a wheelchair to make diagonal approach.

The walls to the rear and side of the water closet shall be reinforced to permit future installation of the required grab bars.

The lavatory shall either be accessible with clear floor space and knee and toe clearance or may have removable base cabinets and adjustable height. When removable base cabinets are installed, the flooring and walls behind the fixture must be finished; removal of the base cabinet may not require extensive work or replacement of the fixture. It is recommended that the vanity countertop within the accessible bathroom be equivalent to the

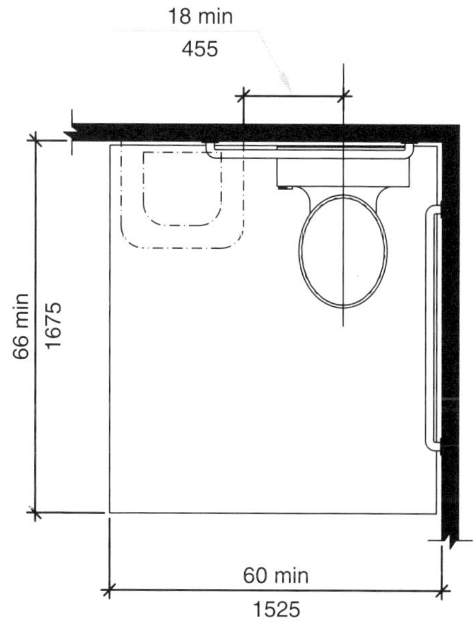

Figure 9.5: Overlap of water closet clearance in residential dwelling units. (ADA standards Figure 604.3.2).

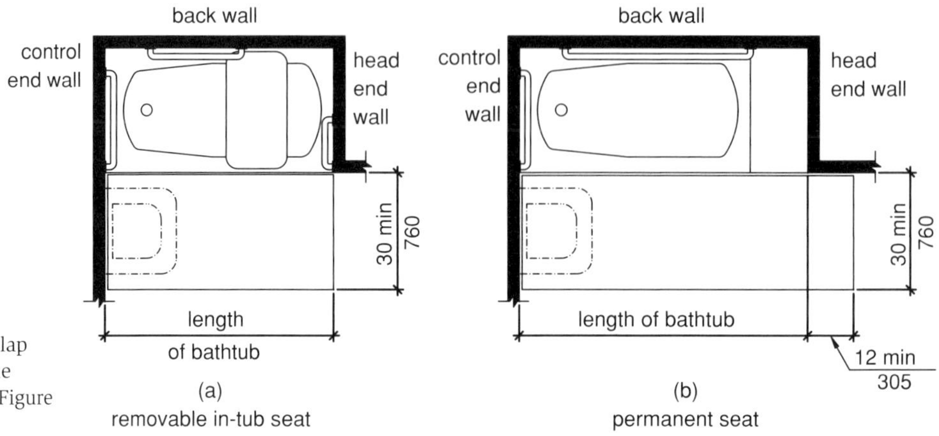

Figure 9.6: Permitted overlap of lavatory at an accessible bathtub. (ADA standards Figure 607.2).

counter space provided in other units, but unlike transient lodging facilities, this is not a mandatory requirement.

At least one bathtub or shower is required to be accessible. If both a bathtub and shower are provided, only one is required to be accessible. Grab bars are not required if blocking is provided within the surrounding walls to permit future installation of the grab bars (see Figure 9.6).

Residential Units with Communication Features

Units with communication features will be mostly indistinguishable from other units, except for the addition of some equipment. The primary focus of this requirement is to notify an occupant with either a hearing or vision impairment of fire or smoke detection.

When provided, fire alarm systems shall include visual alarms (strobes) and comply with NFPA 72. These visible alarms may be used for fire and smoke notification only and may not be used for any other purpose such as doorbell notification.

A hardwired doorbell with audible and visual signals is required at the primary entrance. If visible signals are located within sleeping areas, controls shall be provided to deactivate the signal.

A peephole or other system that allows a 180-degree range of view shall be provided at the primary entrance. The resident shall not be required to open the door to visually identify visitors. If call boxes or closed circuit telephones are provided for communication between a visitor and the resident, the system shall accommodate TTY.

SUMMARY

Shelter is a basic need that is denied to so many people with disabilities. Finding affordable housing that will accommodate their specific needs and is located within a safe neighborhood close to needed services is sometimes impossible. Although the need for accessible housing is expected to increase, the 2010 ADA Standards along with the Fair Housing Act will help to ensure a stock of housing for our aging population.

Reference Sections Chapter 9

The 2010 ADA Standards reference several sections for one topic. This reference table assists the designer in finding the pertinent sections pertaining to one specific area. To use the table, find the topic and below are all the different sections that the standards refer to.

§ 35.151 New Construction and Alterations	
(e)	Social service center establishments
(e)(2)	Facilities with more than 50 beds
(f)(3)	Housing at a Place of Education
(j)	Facilities with residential dwelling units for sale to individual owners.
(j)(1)	Designed and constructed or altered by public entities
(j)(2)	Operated by public entities
§ 36.401 New Construction	
(b)(1)	**Commercial facilities located in private residences**
§ 36.406 Standards for New Construction and Alterations	
(c)(3)	Facilities with residential units and transient lodging units
(d)	**Social Service Center Establishments**
(d)(2)	**Social Service Center Establishments**
(e)(3)	**Housing at a Place of Education**
Chapter 1: Application	
106.5.54	Residential Dwelling Unit
106.5.54	Transient Lodging
202.3	Alterations. EXCEPTION 2
202.3	Alterations. EXCEPTION 3
202.4	Alterations Affecting Primary Function Areas. EXCEPTION
203.8	Residential Facilities
206.2.3	Multi-Story Buildings and Facilities. Exception 4
206.4.6	Residential Dwelling Unit Primary Entrance
206.5.4	Residential Dwelling Units
206.6	Elevators. EXCEPTION 2
206.7.6	Guest Rooms and Residential Dwelling Units
208.2.3	Residential Facilities
208.2.3.1	Parking for Residents
208.2.3.2	Additional Parking Spaces for Residents
208.2.3.3	Parking for Guests, Employees, and Other Non-Residents
208.3.2	Residential Facilities
Advisory 208.3.2	Residential Facilities Exception
215.5	Residential Facilities
216.5	Parking. EXCEPTION 2

(continued)

Chapter 2: Scoping: Residential Facility	
Advisory 224.1	Transient Lodging Guest Rooms: General.
228.2	Mail Boxes
229	Windows. General. Exception 1
233	Residential Facilities (entire section)
Technical Standards	
409	Private Residence Elevators
409.1	Private Residence Elevators: General
604.3.2	Overlap. EXCEPTION
Figure 604.3.2 (Exception)	Overlap of Water Closet Clearance in Residential Dwelling Units
604.4	Seats. EXCEPTION 2
604.5	Grab Bars. EXCEPTION 2
606.2	Clear Floor Space. EXCEPTIONS 3
606.3	Height. EXCEPTION 2
607.4	Grab Bars. EXCEPTION 2
608.3	Grab Bars. EXCEPTION 2
608.4	Seats. EXCEPTION
608.6	Shower Spray Unit and Water. EXCEPTION
708.4	Residential Dwelling Unit Communication Systems
708.4.1	Common Use or Public Use System Interface
708.4.2	Residential Dwelling Unit Interface
804.3	Kitchen Work Surface
809	Residential Dwelling Units (entire section)

Universal Design beyond the ADA

10

by Marcela Abadi Rhoads, AIA RAS

The ADA has opened up doors to the disabled community in so many ways. It has made them free to gain employment, participate in society, and be productive members of our community. It has given them freedom, autonomy, and dignity. It achieves this by eliminating barriers, both physical and cultural, but the rules that the ADA sets down are the minimum requirements that one can do. Universal Design is the next step. To make everything so that anyone can use it, regardless of age, size, ability, or disability, architect Ron Mace from the University of North Carolina School of Design, in 1985, coined the term "Universal Design."

> *"Universal design is the design of products and environments to be usable by all people, to the greatest extent possible, without the need for adaptation or specialized design."*
>
> *1 Excerpted from Universal Design: Housing for the Lifespan of all People, by Ron Mace for the U.S. Department of Housing and Urban Development, 1998*

Universal design is an approach to design that incorporates products, as well as building features and elements, which to the greatest extent possible, can be used by everyone. His idea was that barriers existed for everyone and that eliminating them could benefit everyone. His concept became a reality when the Center for Universal Design was established. The Center became a research think tank to assist the public in rethinking design. The design principles were not only for building access, but for products as well.

There are seven principles of Universal Design and each come with design guidelines to achieve them. The building designer can apply these principles and guidelines together with the ADA in order to achieve a Universal design strategy and solutions.

PRINCIPLE ONE: EQUITABLE USE

"The design should be useful and marketable to people with diverse abilities."

Principle One Design Guidelines

1a. Provide the same means of use for all users: identical whenever possible and equivalent when not.

The first guideline for Universal Design suggests that the design should be useful to not only people with disabilities but also a person with full abilities. One example of the design principle is an automatic sliding door. This type of door is used in supermarkets, shopping centers, and even hotels. People carrying packages or people who are unable to open doors easily will be able to use this door, and building owners can benefit from more traffic because of it. So, in essence this door is useful and marketable to everyone (see Figure 10.1).

Figure 10.1: An automatic door is a good example of the first principle of Universal Design. It is useful to persons with disabilities, but marketable for everyone else.

Figure 10.2: A stair with different-height handrails allows people with different requirements to use the same stair.

Just as the Universal Design guidelines suggest that the same means be used by all, the ADA requires equal treatment for everyone. This is one example of the way that the ADA and Universal Design guidelines work in tandem (see Figure 10.2).

1b. Avoid segregating or stigmatizing any users.

This guideline is also similar to the ADA, where equal treatment for all means that the design will be available to everyone in the same locations. A person with a disability should not be made to feel like a second-class citizen. One way that would happen is if a person is directed to a secondary location to use the space. For example, making a person use a different entrance from everyone else or go to a different location to fill out a form or use the telephone would be segregating them or even stigmatize them (see Figures 10.3 and 10.4).

1c. Provisions for privacy, security, and safety should be equally available to all users.

This design guideline is suggesting that everyone deserves the same privacy and security. A person with disabilities should be able to have the same safe, private, and secure space as everyone else. One example is a dressing room that is large enough for a person who uses a wheelchair (see Figure 10.5).

Figure 10.3: A registration desk at an office, which does not have a lower counter for a person with disability would be an example of segregating someone.

Figure 10.4: This is the solution to create an equitable counter.

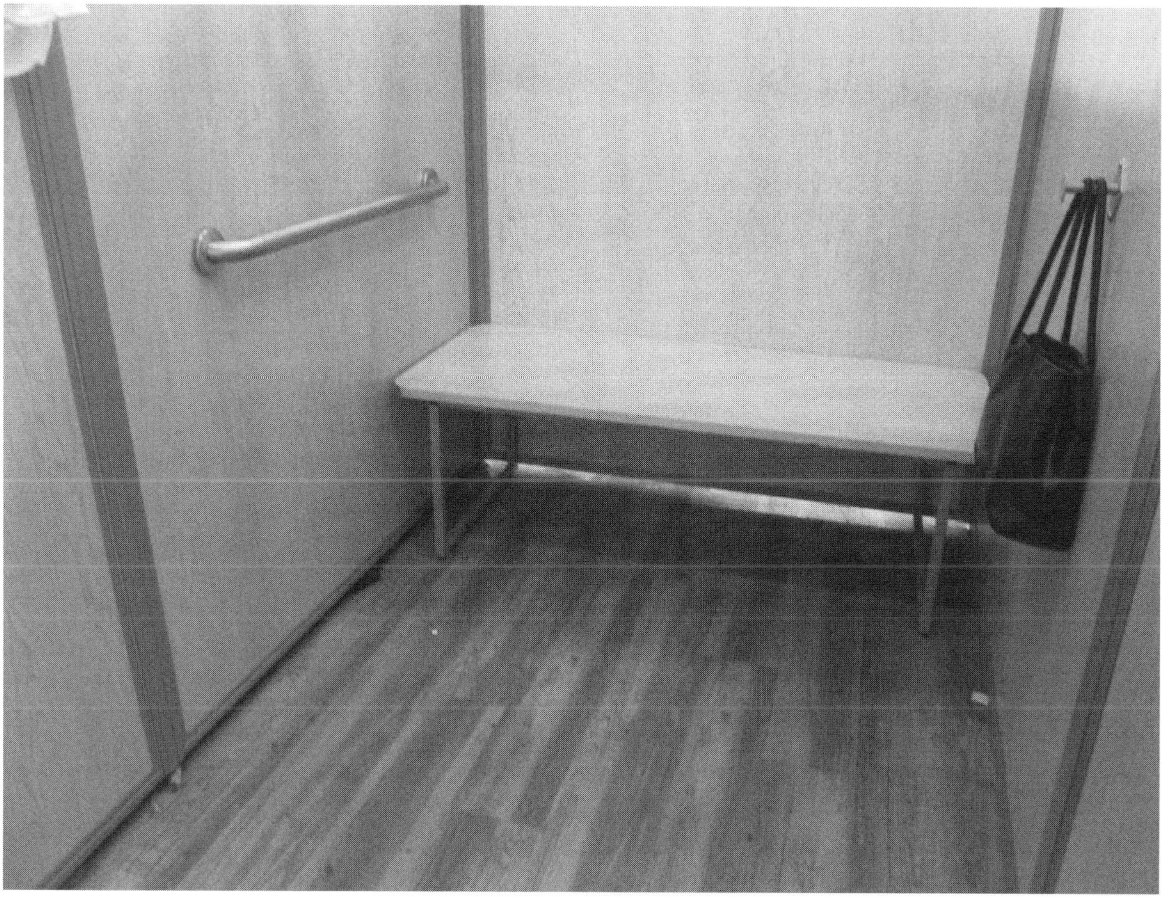

Figure 10.5: This dressing room is large enough for a wheelchair user, but also someone with a stroller or someone who wants to feel comfortable changing.

1d. Make the design appealing to all users.

A Universal Design element does not have to be utilitarian or industrial looking. A universally designed concept should look thought through and intentional, not like an afterthought (see Figure 10.6).

PRINCIPLE TWO: FLEXIBILITY IN USE

> "The design should accommodate a wide range of individual preferences and abilities. The design should be flexible in the way that it will be utilized and accommodate different users and their needs."

Figure 10.6: A sloped sidewalk that is part of the landscape is an example of a design that is appealing to all.

Principle Two Design Guidelines

2a. Provide a choice in methods of use.

Because the universal design guidelines are for products as well, an example of this guideline is flexible-height furniture or even having flexible heights for counters. This ensures the choice for people of lower stature to use the desk at their comfort level (see Figure 10.7).

2b. Accommodate right- or left-handed access and use.

A flexible environment allows for different ways of using elements. When a space allows for flexibility, it allows for persons with different abilities to use the space. A person might be left handed trying to use a credit card station at a grocery store, but the machine is only set up for right-handed access. This is not a universal design feature. An element that allows for either right-handed or left-handed use is a much better solution for everyone (see Figure 10.8).

Figure 10.7: This office furniture has adjustable legs, which allow a choice of height for different people.

2c. Facilitate the user's accuracy and precision.

A universally designed element does not require precision or accuracy. To be designed for everyone, It should be an easy operation. One example of this design guideline is door hardware that is easy to open and does not require exertion (see Figure 10.9).

Another way this guideline can be implemented is when a pedestrian is walking along a path that has pavers with large gaps in between the joints. A person walking will have to be precise and land on the pavers in order to not lose his or her balance and fall (see Figure 10.10).

2d. Provide adaptability to the user's pace.

Different people have different paces when they maneuver, walk, or wheel through an element. A universal design will allow for differences in the speed that someone may have. An example of this would be the amount of time someone will take to go through a door with a closer. The ADA requires that a door close in no less than five seconds (see Figure 10.11).

Figure 10.8: A ramp that has two handrails is not only acceptable under the ADA guidelines, but also allows a person to use either side, depending on the direction of travel.

Figure 10.9: A lever door hardware is a universally designed element that does not require accuracy to operate and can be used by people with different abilities.

Figure 10.10: Pavers along this path could be a hazard, since it requires the pedestrian to accurately land on the pavers so as not to lose his or her balance.

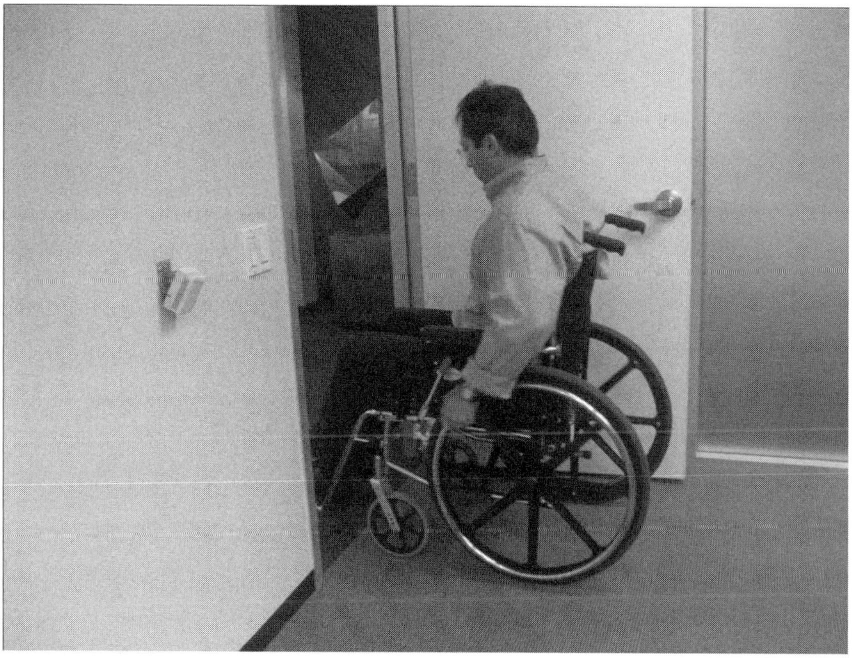

Figure 10.11: A universal design for a doorway will not take less than 5 seconds to close.

PRINCIPLE THREE: SIMPLE AND INTUITIVE USE

"The use of the design is easy to understand, regardless of the user's experience, knowledge, language skills, or current concentration level."

Principle Three Design Guidelines

3a. Eliminate unnecessary complexity.

The universal designed element will be simple to use. It should not be complicated, and it should be easy to figure out. Some designers make the elements of products ambiguous to keep the artistic feel, but in creating a beautiful abstract piece, the designer makes it more complex and harder to figure out. Many times the designer will try to hide the operating mechanism in order to beautify the product, but in doing that he or she makes it difficult to comprehend how to use it. Keeping things simple and minimal is good design, but at times it eliminates cues for users on how to use the element or product (see Figure 10.12).

Figure 10.12: This faucet would be considered a universal faucet because it is simple to use and not hard to figure out.

3b. Be consistent with user expectations and intuition.

When a user encounters an element, is it suggested that the design follow the way it is always used and in the same location that it is usually found. An example of this is placing the elevator signal on the wall next to the elevator, which is where typically found and where most people would expect to find it (see Figure 10.13).

3c. Accommodate people with a wide range of literacy and language skills.

There are many people who are unable to read in our society and being sensitive to that fact can greatly affect the way different people experience their built environment. If signage has redundancy, which allows different people to understand the sign, it allows more people to use the space (see Figure 10.14).

3d. Arrange information consistent with its importance.

An example of this design guideline is a sign that shows the important information in an easy way so that people can easily find what they are looking for. A person who is in a hurry or may not have the cognitive skills to decipher difficult situations, will benefit from easy-to-understand and easy-to-see signage or symbols (see Figure 10.15).

Figure 10.13: An elevator hall button is typically found on the wall adjacent to the elevator. This one was located in the ceiling, which is not a universal location.

Figure 10.14: Symbols instead of words are a good way to keep things universal for persons who cannot read.

Figure 10.15: This sign has the word "Emergency" larger than the other words, which allows a person looking for the emergency room find it easily

Figure 10.16: An elevator call button will prompt the user that the cab has arrived.

3e. Provide effective prompting and feedback during and after task completion.

Prompting does not always occur in the built environment, except in limited areas. Elevators have prompting when the cab has arrived or when the doors are about to open. ATM machines also have the ability to prompt the user in different ways. Prompting also occurs in computers and other devices. This allows many people with different abilities to understand that a task has been completed and that they should expect a certain outcome (see Figure 10.16).

PRINCIPLE FOUR: PERCEPTIBLE INFORMATION

> "The design communicates necessary information effectively to the user, regardless of ambient conditions or the user's sensory abilities."

Principle Four Design Guidelines

4a. Use different modes (pictorial, verbal, tactile) for redundant presentation of essential information.

The ADA requires that a sign have redundancy of information so that persons who is visually impaired, as well as those who are not literate, can understand the same information as a person who is able to read the sign. A sign that has both written text, Braille, and pictures is considered universal (see Figure 10.17).

4b. Provide adequate contrast between essential information and its surroundings.

When you have contrast between the element and its background it helps persons with disabilities as well as persons who might be distracted or might need landmarks to find their way around. Signage with contrast between the words and the background is a good example. Another example is painting the door trim a different color than the surrounding walls so that anyone can find the openings (see Figure 10.18).

Figure 10.17: Signage with text, Braille, and pictograms allows different people with different reading abilities to understand it.

Figure 10.18: Door trims that are painted a contrasting color help with wayfinding.

4c. Maximize "legibility" of essential information.

The ADA requires that fonts be only Sans Serif (see Figure 10.19). This allows a person with low vision or even learning disabilities to be able to read the information on the sign without difficulty. A Universal Design principle also suggests that the information be "legible." This guideline follows right in line with the ADA. When important information is organized in a clear way, it helps a person with disabilities decipher what the message wants to be.

4d. Differentiate elements in ways that can be described (i.e., make it easy to give instructions or directions).

When giving or receiving directions to a location, a great way to do it is to describe a nearby landmark. In the built environment, approaches like using different colors on elements allow a person to find their way around by describing the element that might be a different color (see Figure 10.20). Another example is a fountain in a lobby or a different texture on the floor, which allows persons who are visually impaired to find their way around.

Figure 10.19: Fonts that are not san serif are harder to read, making it more difficult to understand the words.

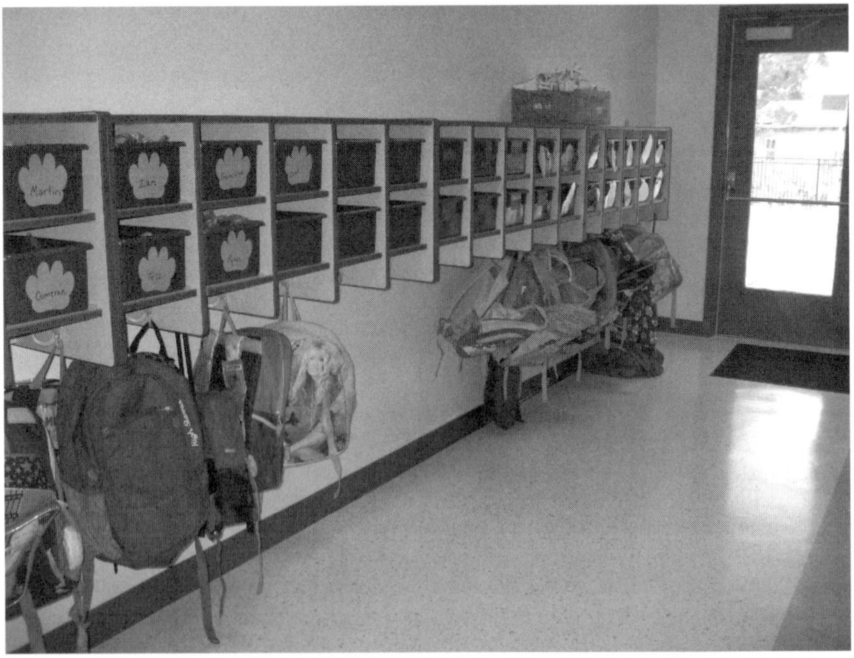

Figure 10.20: These purple cubbies in a preschool allow persons who are trying to find a classroom to know that their location is near the cubbies just by describing them.

4e. Provide compatibility with a variety of techniques or devices used by people with sensory limitations.

A person who is deaf, blind, or autistic will have different limitations in perceiving their environment. Providing a variety of techniques to communicate will make it easier for everyone. A public phone with a TYY will allow deaf people to use the phone, as well as if the computer had a way to enlarge the text so that people with low vision could read it better (see Figure 10.21).

PRINCIPLE FIVE: TOLERANCE FOR ERROR

> "The design minimizes hazards and the adverse consequences of accidental or unintended actions."

Principle Five Design Guidelines

5a. Arrange elements to minimize hazards and errors: most used elements, most accessible, hazardous elements eliminated, isolated, or shielded.

Many elements inside or outside of a building could be a hazard to pedestrians as well as wheelchair users. The ADA has a rule that an object should not be mounted higher than 27 inches a.f.f. and lower than 80 inches a.f.f. to the bottom so that it will not be a hazard to the blind. A universal designed element will be mounted so that it is not a hazard to the blind or to anyone who might be distracted. Also, there are hazards along the travel path for wheelchairs, such as ramps that are freestanding and might have a drop-off. The ADA requires that edge protection be provided in order for the wheelchair not to slip off the ramp. Many Universal Design suggestions in these principles correlate to the ADA's guidelines as well.

The first guideline suggests that you eliminate, isolate, or shield a hazardous element. This is exactly in line with what the ADA requires with the protruding object rule. Many times, there are elements mounted on the wall such as paper towel dispensers, drinking fountains, or emergency elements like fire extinguishers. For persons who are blind or even distracted, they may be a potential hazard. There are times when grand stairs in lobbies are left open all the way around to create a sense of elegance. However, the open stair could be a hazard for persons if they are not aware that they are open. Those elements should be either shielded so that people don't harm themselves or removed altogether (see Figures 10.22 and 10.23).

5b. Provide warnings of hazards and errors.

Another way to apply this guideline is to create a warning system to alert people to hazards. Blind persons are taught that when they reach a different texture along the path of travel, it might be a hazard. This gives them a warning to be careful and see what might be found on the other side of the textured area. The ADA requires "detectable warnings" at platform edges of train stations. These detectable warnings will inform the person that a potential hazard is up ahead (see Figures 10.24 and 10.25).

5c. Provide fail-safe features.

In life there are always things that will fail. The Universal Design guidelines suggest that since we know things will fail, we should make sure failure results in a safe outcome. In other words, if there will be failure, the outcome should not be a hazard. An elevator is a great example

Figure 10.21: This telephone is equipped with TYY so that a deaf person can use it.

of this. Because the automatic doors close after a certain number of seconds, and there is a possibility that a person will try to enter or exit before that time is up, a fail-safe mechanism has been incorporated on those doors. Once the elevator door begins to close and a laser detects a person in the way, the doors will reopen. Since the door closing before a person gets through it would be considered a "failure," the reopening mechanism guarantees a safe outcome (see Figures 10.26 and 10.27).

Figure 10.22: This is a high drinking fountain that is being shielded by a rail. This allows a person to either feel or see the rail without hitting themselves with the edge of the drinking fountain.

Figure 10.23: An open stair would require a way to stop a person from hitting their head with the treads behind the stair. In this case, a planter was used to enhance the space as well as to shield the hazard.

Figure 10.24: Having detectable warnings at train station platforms is a Universal Design guideline, which helps more than blind persons to stay away from hazards, such as a train track.

Figure 10.25: The rail at the base of the open stair is used as a warning for persons who are visually impaired so they will not walk into the stair.

Figure 10.26: A GFI electrical outlet reduces the risk of shock in restrooms.

5d. Discourage unconscious action in tasks that require vigilance.

This guideline goes beyond the ADA requirements. The ADA can't control people's actions, but by using Universal Design guidelines, we can make sure people are more vigilant. Texting while walking or even driving is a distraction when vigilance should be at the utmost. Some Universal Design features that discourage unconscious acts include a handle on power lawn mowers that automatically locks in place and keeps them running rather than requiring the user to squeeze the lever to keep the engine running. This ensures that the person is paying attention instead of concentrating on making the lawn mower run (see Figure 10.28).

Figure 10.27: This path does not have a fail-safe feature. If people do not land on the flagstone, they will land on the mulch, which is not a stable surface and they could lose their balance trying to get across.

PRINCIPLE SIX: LOW PHYSICAL EFFORT

"The design can be used efficiently and comfortably and with a minimum of fatigue."

Principle Six Design Guidelines

6a. Allow user to maintain a neutral body position.

Many of the ADA requirements fall in line with this design guideline. There are requirements for drinking fountains so that a person in a wheelchair can use it, as well as a tall person who many not be able to bend down easily. Other ADA requirements are for reach ranges and counter heights that allow the people to operate and use elements without straining their body (see Figure 10.29).

Figure 10.28: People who are distracted while walking may find themselves in a dangerous predicament when approaching a hazard such as this.

Figure 10.29: Drinking fountains that are high and low in the same area will allow for the use of the drinking fountain without straining the body.

6b. Use reasonable operating forces.

The ADA also requires that operating forces be less than 5 lbs., a bit more in some cases, which fall under the same principle and Universal Design guidelines (see Figure 10.30).

6c. Minimize repetitive actions.

There aren't so many repetitive actions in the built environment, but there are in the equipment and elements used by the public. If these actions could be minimized, fewer accidents would occur and there would be less strain on the body as well (see Figure 10.31).

6d. Minimize sustained physical effort.

This guideline can be applied to the built environment as well as for products. When used in the design of products, it allows a person to operate certain mechanisms with less strain and effort, which reduces the risk of injury and maximizes the enjoyment of the activity (see Figures 10.32 and 10.33).

Figure 10.30: A dual flush valve is used for saving energy. However, the amount of force required to flush with this type of valve is greater than 5 lbs. which is not recommended for many older or younger people who may not have strong upper bodies.

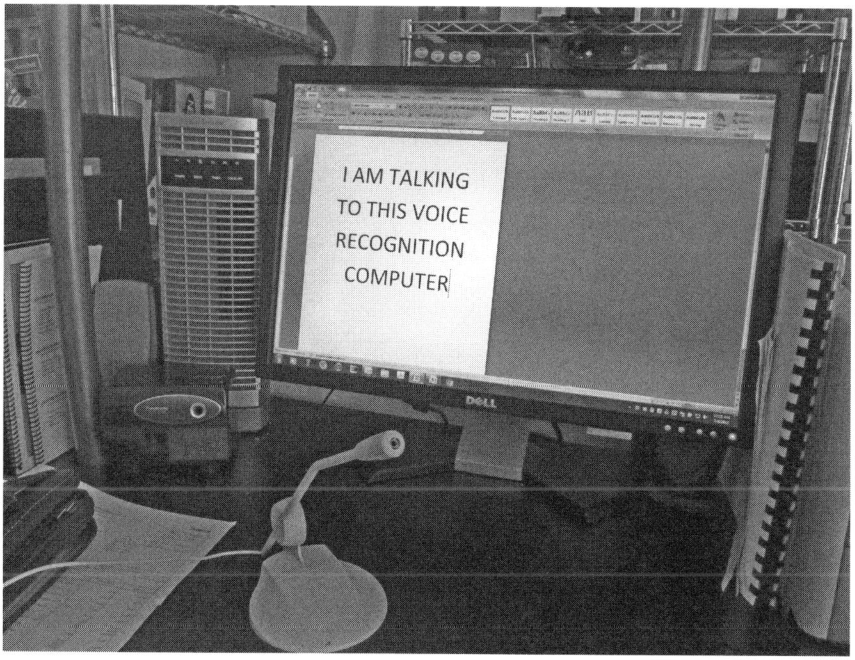

Figure 10.31: A computer with voice recognition technology eliminates the need for highly repetitive keystrokes.

Figure 10.32: A thumb latch for pocket doors is not a good Universal solution since it takes more effort to open the door with this type of mechanism.

Figure 10.33: A curb ramp is a good example of an element which minimizes physical effort. It is easier to use than lifting objects over the curb.

PRINCIPLE SEVEN: SIZE AND SPACE FOR APPROACH AND USE

"Appropriate size and space is provided for approach, reach, manipulation, and use regardless of user's body size, posture, or mobility."

Principle Seven Design Guidelines

7a. Provide a clear line of sight to important elements for any seated or standing user.

In the Universal Design world, this design guideline is probably one of the hardest to apply (see Figure 10.34). There are so many different types of users with different needs that it would be impossible to provide different heights for everyone. In general, making things lower and also have options for other heights is good practice.

Figure 10.34: A mirror mounted higher than 40 inches a.f.f. is not accessible per the ADA, but also not universal. A line of sight for seated patrons as well as standing ones should be taken into consideration.

7b. Make reach to all components comfortable for any seated or standing user.

A person who uses a wheelchair or even a person with lower stature cannot reach items that are located very high. This design guideline suggests that we keep this in mind when we mount things for reaching (see Figure 10.35).

7c. Accommodate variations in hand and grip size.

The ADA understands that the members of the disabled community have different challenges with gripping and grasping. The standards have options for gripping surfaces to be anywhere

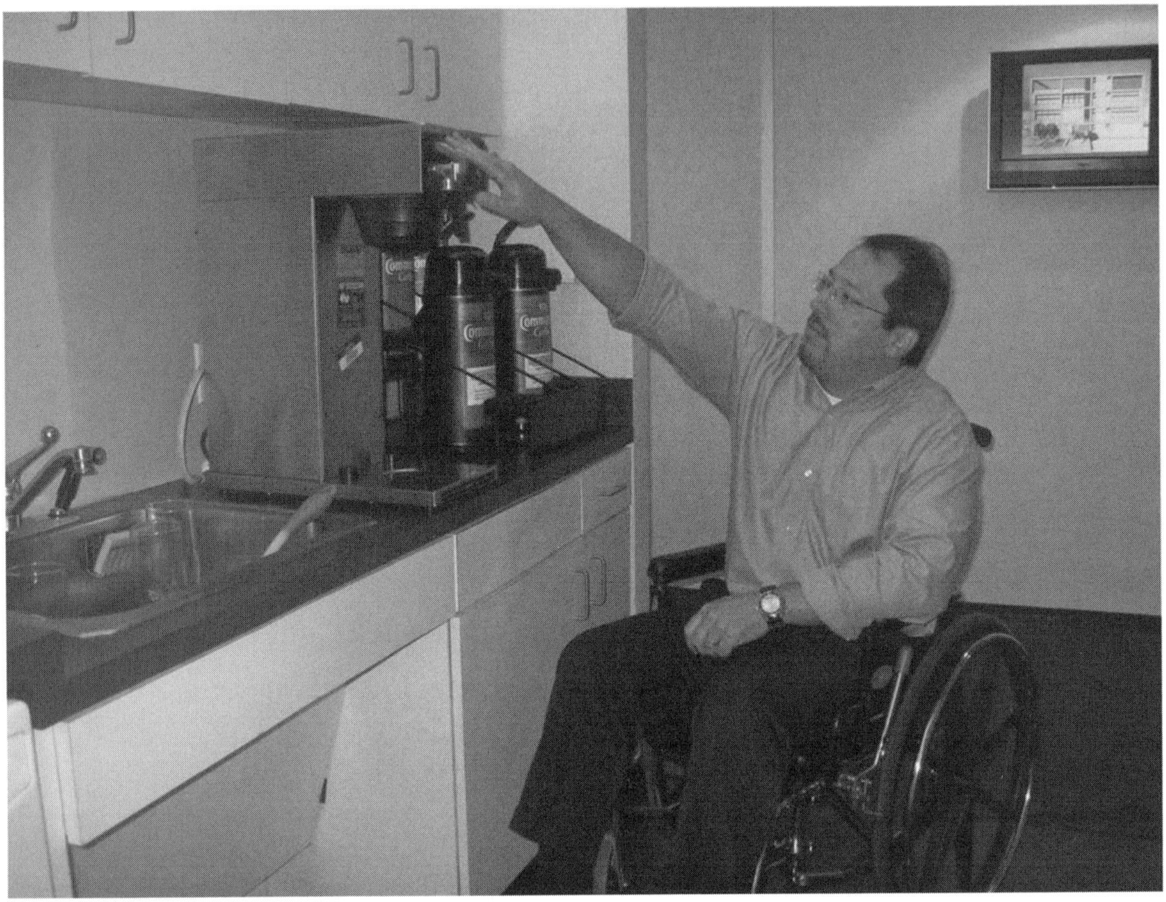

Figure 10.35: A break room has many items that both wheelchair users and able-bodied people will use. Locating things within a wheelchair reach range is also useful for other people.

from circular and no smaller than 1¼ inch in diameter to oval or square, which can even go up to 6¼ inches in width. Beyond the disabled community, we also have children, adults, and adults of lower stature who might need different gripping surfaces (see Figure 10.36).

7d. Provide adequate space for the use of assistive devices or personal assistance.

The ADA sizes were designed with ergonomics in mind and knowing the sizes of assistive devices such as wheelchairs, walkers, service animals, and the like. Most of the requirements in the ADA take into consideration the space required for these assistive devices. This is useful not only for persons with disabilities, but also for many people who are temporarily using such aids (see Figure 10.37). Persons pushing strollers will also benefit greatly from having enough room to place their baby stroller while they do shopping or even while they use the restroom.

Figure 10.36: A handrail that is not too large or hard to grasp will be able to be used by many people with different grip and hand sizes.

Figure 10.37: Allowing a 30 inch × 48 inch space for wheelchairs near certain elements makes a space universal for others to enjoy.

SUMMARY

Accessible design as well as Universal Design concepts and guidelines are more important than ever. As our population ages, their abilities will diminish and they will require more assistance. Disability and difficulty with everyday tasks increase dramatically with age, and products that accommodate a wide range of abilities will be ever more in demand. The ADA and Universal Design work together to eliminate discrimination, empower people with different abilities, advance human dignity, and enhance and enlarge markets, which ensure equal treatment for all.

APPENDIX A: Reference Tables

The 2010 ADA Standards reference several sections for one topic. The reference tables in this Appendix assist the designer in finding the pertinent sections pertaining to one specific area. To use the table, find the topic and following it are all the different sections that the standards refer to.

CHAPTER 2 RETAIL AND MIXED-USE FACILITIES

Reference Sections Chapter 2 Retail and Mixed-Use Facilities.

SHOPPING CENTER	
DOJ § 36.401 New construction	
Section Number	**Section title and description**
(d)(1)(ii)	Definition-Shopping Center
(d)(1)(ii)(B)	Definition
(d)(2)(i)	Regarding elevators
(d)(3)	Elevator exemption
DOJ 36.404 Alterations: Elevator exemption.	
(a)	Elevator exemption
(a)(2)	Definition
(a)(2)(iii)	Definition
ADA Chapter2: Scoping	
206.2.3	EXCEPTIONS (1) In *private buildings or facilities* that are less than three *stories* or that have less than 3000 square feet (279 m2) per *story*
206.2.1	ADVISORY: Site Arrival Points Exception 2.
PLAY AREAS	
ADA Chapter 1: Definitions	
Definitions	**Play area**

ADA Chapter 2: Scoping	
105.2.3	ADVISORY
204.1	EXCEPTIONS (2)
206.2.17	Play Areas
206.2.17.1	Ground Level and Elevated Play Components
206.7.8	Platform Lifts
233.1	ADVISORY: General
240	Play Areas
240.1	General
240.1	EXCEPTIONS (1)
240.1	EXCEPTIONS (2)
240.1.1	Additions
240.1	ADVISORY: General
240.1.1	ADVISORY: Additions
240.2.1	Ground Level Play Components
240.2.1	ADVISORY: Ground Level Play Components (continued)
240.2.1.2	Additional Numbers and Types EXCEPTION
240.2.1.2	ADVISORY: Additional Numbers and Types
ADA Chapter 3-10: Technical	
1008	Play Area
1008.1	General
1008.2	Accessible routes
1008.2.4.1	Ground Level EXCEPTIONS (1)
1008.2.5	Ramps
1008.2.6	ADVISORY: Ground Surfaces
1008.4.2	ADVISORY: Clear floor or ground space

CHAPTER 3 PRIMARY EDUCATION

Reference Sections Chapter 3 Primary Education

Children's Requirements	
ADA Chapter 1: Definitions	
Section Number	**Section Title and Description**
106.5.18	Children's Use.

ADA Chapter 2: Scoping	
Section Number	**Section Title and Description**
234.3	Amusement Rides Minimum Number Exception 2
Advisory 234.3	Minimum Number Exceptions 1 through 3.
Advisory 234.3	Minimum Number Exception 2.
240	Play Areas
240.1	General
Advisory 240.1	General
ADA Chapter 3-10 Technical Standards	
Section Number	**Section Title and Description**
308	Reach Ranges
Advisory	Children's Reach Ranges
Advisory 505.4	Height.
	Chapter 6 Plumbing Fixtures
602.2	Clear Floor Space. EXCEPTION
Advisory 603.3	Mirrors.
604.1	General. EXCEPTION
604.8.1.1	Size.
604.8.1.4	Toe Clearance.
604.8.1.4	EXCEPTION:
604.9	Water Closets and Toilet Compartments for Children's Use.
Advisory 604.9	Water Closets and Toilet Compartments for Children's Use.
Advisory	Specifications for Water Closets Serving Children Ages 3 through 12
606.2	Clear Floor Space. EXCEPTION 4
609.4	Position of Grab Bars.
Advisory 803.1	General.
902.1	General. EXCEPTION
902.4	Dining Surfaces and Work Surfaces for Children's Use.
902.4	Dining Surfaces and Work Surfaces for Children's Use. EXCEPTION
Advisory 1008.3	Transfer Systems.
Advisory 1008.3.2.3	Transfer Supports.
1008	Children's Reach Ranges
Advisory 1008.4.2	Clear Floor or Ground Space.
1008.4.3	Play Tables. EXCEPTION

CHAPTER 4 SECONDARY AND POSTSECONDARY EDUCATION

Reference Sections Chapter 4 Secondary and Postsecondary Education

DOJ § 35.151 New construction and alterations	
Section Number	**Section Title and Description**
(g)	Assembly areas
(g)(2)	Wheelchair space
DOJ § 36.406 Standards for new construction and alterations	
Section Number	**Section Title and Description**
(f)	Assembly Areas
(f)(2)	Wheelchair space
ADA Chapter 1: Definitions	
Section Number	**Section Title and Description**
Definition	Assembly Area
Definition	Space
ADA Chapter 2: Scoping	
Section Number	**Section Title and Description**
206.2.4	EXCEPTIONS: (2)
206.2.7	Press Boxes
206.2.7	ADVISORY: Press Boxes Exception 2
210.1	General: EXCEPTIONS: (3)
216.1	General: EXCEPTIONS: (1)
216.10	Assistive Listening Systems
216.10	Assistive Listening systems: EXCEPTION: ticket windows
219.2	Required Systems
219.3	Receivers
219.3	Receivers: EXCEPTIONS: (1)
219.3	Receivers: EXCEPTIONS: (2)
Table 219.3	Receivers for Assisted Listening Systems
221	Assembly Areas
221.1	General
221.2	Wheelchair spaces
Table 221.2.1.1	Number of Wheelchair Spaces in Assembly Areas
221.2.2	ADVISORY: Integration
221.2.3.1	Horizontal Dispersion: EXCEPTIONS: (1)
221.2.3.2	Vertical Dispersion: EXCEPTIONS: (1)
221.4	ADVISORY: Designated Isle Seats

ADA Chapters 3-10: Technical	
Section Number	**Section Title and Description**
405.1	Ramps: General: EXCEPTION
505.2	Handrails: Where Required: EXCEPTION
505.3	Handrails: Continuity: EXCEPTION
505.10	Handrail Extensions: EXCEPTIONS: (2)
706.1	Assistive Listening Systems: General
Chapter 2: Scoping	
209.2.2	**Bus Loading Zones**
209.2.2	ADVISORY: Bus Loading Zones
§ 35.151 New construction and alterations	
(g)(2)	**Assembly Areas and Wheelchair spaces**
§ 36.406 Standards for new construction and alterations	
(f)(2)	**Assembly Areas and Wheelchair spaces**
Chapter 2: Scoping	
206.2.6	Performance Areas
206.7.1	**Platform Lifts**
221.2.3.2	Vertical Dispersion (Wheelchair Spaces)
221.2.3.1	ADVISORY: Horizontal Dispersion (wheelchair spaces)
Chapter 3-10: Technical Standards	
802.2	Lines of sight

CHAPTER 5 HOSPITALITY

Reference Sections Chapter 5 Hospitality

Chapter 5 Section References	
ADA Chapter 1: Definitions	
Section Number	**Section Title and Description**
106.5	Residential Dwelling Unit
106.5	Transient Lodging
DOJ 35.151 New construction and alterations.	
Section Number	**Section Title and Description**
(f)	Housing at a place of education.
(f)(3)	Apartments or townhouse facilities

DOJ 36.406 Standards for new construction and alterations	
Section Number	**Section Title and Description**
(c)	**Places of lodging**
(c)(1)	Guest Rooms
(c)(3)	Facilities with residential units and transient lodging units.
(e)	Housing at a place of education.
(e)(3)	Apartments or townhouse facilities
ADA Chapter 2: Scoping: Transient Lodging	
Section Number	**Section Title and Description**
106	Definition
206.2.3	Accessible Route in multi-story buildings Exception (5)
206.5.3	Transient Lodging Facilities
206.2.5	Entrances and doorway to non-mobility rooms
206.7.6	Platform lifts
215.4	Fire Alarms
224	Transient Lodging Facilities and Guest Rooms
224.1	EXCEPTIONS: 1. Facilities with Residential Units and Transient Lodging Units.
Advisory 224.1	General
224.2	Guest Rooms with Mobility Features.
224.4	Guest Rooms with Communication Features
224.6	Housing at a Place of Education
224.6	EXCEPTION 3
241	Saunas and Steam Rooms
242	Swimming Pools, Wading Pools, and Spas
Advisory 242.2	Swimming Pools.
Advisory 242.2	Swimming Pools Exception 1.
242.3	Wading Pools.
242.4	Spas.
ADA Chapters 3-10 Technical Standards	
Section Number	**Section Title and Description**
608.4	Shower Seats
612	Saunas and Steam Rooms
608.6	EXCEPTION: fixed shower head
Advisory 801.1	Scope
806	Transient Lodging Guest Rooms
806.1	General
	1009 Swimming Pools, Wading Pools, and Spas

CHAPTER 6 HEALTHCARE AND SENIOR LIVING COMMUNITIES

Reference Sections Chapter 6 Healthcare and Senior Living Communities

CHAPTER 6 REFERENCE SECTIONS	
DOJ § 35.151 New construction and alterations.	
Section Number	**Section Title and Description**
(h)	Medical care facilities.
(k)(2)(iii)	Alterations to detention and correctional facilities.
(k)(3)	medical and long-term care facilities in jails, prisons, and other detention and correctional facilities
DOJ § 36.406 Standards for new construction and alterations.	
Section Number	**Section Title and Description**
(g)	Medical Care Facilities
ADA Chapter 2: Scoping	
Section Number	**Section Title and Description**
Advisory 201.1	Scope.
208.2.1	Hospital Outpatient Facilities.
Advisory 208.2.1	Hospital Outpatient Facilities.
209.3	Medical Care and Long-Term Care Facilities.
217.4.6	Hospitals.
223	Medical Care and Long-Term Care Facilities
223.2	Hospitals, Rehabilitation Facilities, Psychiatric Facilities and Detoxification Facilities.
232.3	Special Holding Cells and Special Housing Cells.
ADA Chapters 3-10:Technical Standards	
Section Number	**Section Title and Description**
608.6	Shower Spray Unit and Water. EXCEPTION
702	Fire Alarm Systems EXCEPTION
805	Medical Care and Long-Term Care Facilities

CHAPTER 7 AMUSEMENT PARKS AND PLAY AREAS

Reference Sections Chapter 7 Amusement Parks and Play Areas

ADA Chapter 1: Definitions	
Section Number	**Section Title and Description**
106.5	Defined Terms: Amusement Attraction
106.5	Defined Terms: Amusement Ride
106.5	Defined Terms: Amusement Ride Seat
106.5	Defined Terms: Transfer Device
ADA Chapter 2: Scoping	
Section Number	**Section Title and Description**
206.2.9	Amusement Rides
206.2.9.2	Wheelchair Spaces, Ride Seats Designed for Transfer, and Transfer Devices.
206.7.7	Platform Lifts
216.12	Signs
216.12	Signs**: ADVISORY:** Amusement rides
234	Amusement Rides (entire section)
240.1	Play Areas: General: EXCEPTIONS (3)
ADA Chapters 3-10: Technical	
Section Number	**Section Title and Description**
1002	Amusement Rides (entire section)

Amusement (Rides) and Play Areas

ADA Chapter 2: Scoping	
Section Number	**Section Title and Description**
105.2.3 ASTM.	**ADVISORY**
204.1	EXCEPTIONS (2)
206.2.17	Play Areas
206.2.17.1	Ground Level and Elevated Play Components
206.7.8	Platform Lifts
233.1	**ADVISORY:** General
240	Play Areas
240.1	General
240.1	EXCEPTIONS (1)
240.1	EXCEPTIONS (2)
240.1.1	Additions

240.1	**ADVISORY:** General
240.1.1	**ADVISORY:** Additions
240.2.1	Ground Level Play Components
240.2.1	**ADVISORY:** Ground Level Play Components (continued)
240.2.1.2	Additional Numbers and Types EXCEPTION
240.2.1.2	**ADVISORY:** Additional Numbers and Types
ADA Chapter 1: Definitions	
Section Number	**Section Title and Description**
Definitions	Play area
ADA Chapter 3-10: Technical	
Section Number	**Section Title and Description**
1008	Play Area
1008.1	General
1008.2	Accessible routes
1008.2.4.1	Ground Level EXCEPTIONS (1)
1008.2.5	Ramps
1008.2.6	**ADVISORY:** Ground Surfaces
1008.4.2	**ADVISORY:** Clear floor or ground space

CHAPTER 8 HISTORIC PRESERVATION AND REMODELS

Reference Sections Chapter 8 Historic Preservation and Remodels

DOJ CFR 35	
Section Number	**Section Title and Description**
DOJ CFR 36	
Section Number	**Section Title and Description**
ADA Chapter 1: Definitions	
Section Number	**Section Title and Description**
101.2	Effect on Removal of Barriers in Existing Facilities.
106	Definition of Alteration
106	Definition of Disproportionality
	Definition of Path of Travel
106	Definition of Primary Function
106.5.52	Qualified Historic Building or Facility.
	106.5.68 Technically Infeasible.

ADA Chapter 2: Alterations	
Section Number	**Section Title and Description**
202	Existing Buildings and Facilities
202.3	Alterations
	202.5 Alterations to Qualified Historic Buildings and Facilities.
Advisory 202.5	Alterations to Qualified Historic Buildings and Facilities Exception.
206.2.3.1	Stairs and Escalators in Existing Buildings.
206.2.1	Site Arrival Points. EXCEPTION 1
206.2.3	Multi-Story Buildings and Facilities. Exception 7
206.4	Entrances. Exception 2
206.2.5	Restaurants and Cafeterias. Exception 2
206.4.4.1	Location. EXCEPTION
206.4.4.2	Direct Connections. EXCEPTION
206.4.4.3	Key Stations and Intercity Rail Stations.
206.6.1	Existing Elevators.
206.7	Platform Lifts.
206.7.5	Existing Site Constraints.
206.7.5	Advisory Existing Site Constraints.
213.2	Toilet Rooms and Bathing Rooms. Exception 1 and 2
215	EXCEPTION Fire Alarm Systems
216.7	Elevators.
216.8	Toilet Rooms and Bathing Rooms.
218.3	Key Stations and Existing Intercity Rail Stations.
224.1.1	(Transient Lodging Facilities) Alterations.
224.1.1	Advisory Alterations.
232.2	General Holding Cells and General Housing Cells. EXCEPTION
232.3	Special Holding Cells and Special Housing Cells. EXCEPTION
233.3.3	Additions.
233.3.4	Alterations.
233.3.4	Advisory Alterations Exception.
233.3.4.1	Alterations to Vacated Buildings.
233.3.4.2	Alterations to Individual Residential Dwelling Units.
233.3.4.2	Advisory Alterations to Individual Residential Dwelling Units.
234.4	Existing Amusement Rides.
234.4	Advisory Existing Amusement Rides.
234.4.1	Load and Unload Areas.
238.2.1	238.2.1 Teeing Grounds. EXCEPTION
240.1	240.1 General. EXCEPTION 2

ADA Chapters 3-10: Technical	
Section Number	**Section Title and Description**
308.3.1	(Side Reach) Unobstructed. Exception 2
308.3.2	(Side Reach) Obstructed High Reach. Exception 2
404.2.3	Clear Width. Exception 1
404.2.5	Thresholds. EXCEPTION
404.2.7	Door and Gate Hardware. Exception 1
404.2.10	Door and Gate Surfaces. Exception 4
406.4	Landings. EXCEPTION
405.2	Slope. EXCEPTION
Table 405.2	Maximum Ramp Slope and Rise for Existing Sites, Buildings, and Facilities
407.2.1	Call Controls. EXCEPTION
407.2.1.1	Height. EXCEPTION
407.2.1.2	Size. EXCEPTION
407.2.1.5	Signals. EXCEPTION 2
407.2.2	Hall Signals. EXCEPTION 2
407.2.2.2	Visible Signals. EXCEPTION 2
407.2.2.3	Audible Signals. EXCEPTION 2
407.3.2	Operation. EXCEPTION
407.3.3	Reopening Device. EXCEPTION
407.3.6	Width. EXCEPTION
407.4.1	Car Dimensions. EXCEPTION
407.4.6	Elevator Car Controls. EXCEPTION
407.4.6.1	Location. EXCEPTION 2
407.4.7	Designations and Indicators of Car Controls. EXCEPTION
407.4.7.1.2	Location. EXCEPTION
408.4.1	Car Dimensions and Doors. EXCEPTION 2
505.10	Handrail Extensions. Exception 3
608.7	Thresholds. EXCEPTION
810.5.1	Slope. EXCEPTION
810.9	Escalators. EXCEPTION
808.3	Clear Floor Space. Exception
904.4	Sales and Service Counters. EXCEPTION
Figure 904.4	(Exception) Alteration of Sales and Service Counters
1003.2.1	Boat Slips. Exception 1
1003.3.1	Boat Slip Clearance. Exception 3
1003.3.1	Advisory Boat Slip Clearance Exception 3.

CHAPTER 9 RESIDENTIAL PROJECTS

Reference Sections Chapter 9 Residential Projects

§ 35.151 New Construction and Alterations	
(e)	Social service center establishments
(e)(2)	Facilities with more than 50 beds
(f)(3)	Housing at a Place of Education
(j)	Facilities with residential dwelling units for sale to individual owners.
(j)(1)	designed and constructed or altered by public entities
(j)(2)	operated by public entities
§ 36.401 New Construction	
(b)(1)	**Commercial facilities located in private residences**
§ 36.406 Standards for New Construction and Alterations	
(c)(3)	Facilities with residential units and transient lodging units.
(d)	**Social Service Center Establishments**
(d)(2)	**Social Service Center Establishments**
(e)(3)	**Housing at a Place of Education**
Chapter 1: Application	
106.5.54	Residential Dwelling Unit.
106.5.54	Transient Lodging.
Chapter 2: Scoping: Residential Facility	
202.3	Alterations. EXCEPTION 2
202.3	Alterations. EXCEPTION 3
202.4	Alterations Affecting Primary Function Areas. EXCEPTION
203.8	Residential Facilities.
206.2.3	Multi-Story Buildings and Facilities. Exception 4
206.4.6	Residential Dwelling Unit Primary Entrance.
206.5.4	Residential Dwelling Units.
206.6	Elevators. EXCEPTION 2
206.7.6	Guest Rooms and Residential Dwelling Units.
208.2.3	Residential Facilities.
208.2.3.1	Parking for Residents.
208.2.3.2	Additional Parking Spaces for Residents.
208.2.3.3	Parking for Guests, Employees, and Other Non-Residents.
208.3.2	Residential Facilities.
Advisory 208.3.2	Residential Facilities Exception.
215.5	Residential Facilities.
216.5	Parking. EXCEPTION 2
Advisory 224.1	Transient Lodging Guest Rooms: General.
228.2	Mail Boxes.
229	Windows. General. Exception 1
233	Residential Facilities (entire section)

Technical Standards	
409	Private Residence Elevators
409.1	Private Residence Elevators: General
604.3.2	Overlap. EXCEPTION
Figure 604.3.2 (Exception)	Overlap of Water Closet Clearance in Residential Dwelling Units
604.4	Seats. EXCEPTION 2
604.5	Grab Bars. EXCEPTION 2
606.2	Clear Floor Space. EXCEPTIONS 3
606.3	Height. EXCEPTION 2
607.4	Grab Bars. EXCEPTION 2
608.3	Grab Bars. EXCEPTION 2
608.4	Seats. EXCEPTION
608.6	Shower Spray Unit and Water. EXCEPTION
708.4	Residential Dwelling Unit Communication Systems.
708.4.1	Common Use or Public Use System Interface.
708.4.2	Residential Dwelling Unit Interface.
804.3	Kitchen Work Surface
809	Residential Dwelling Units (entire section)

APPENDIX B:
Resources

U.S. Access Board
Summary of Accessibility Guidelines for Play Areas
Guidance on the 2010 ADA Standards for Accessible Design
(800) 872-2253 (voice)
(800) 993-2822 (TTY)
fax: (202) 272-0081
e-mail: ta@access-board.gov
www.access-board.gov

The U.S. Department of Justice
(800) 514-0301 (voice)
(800) 414-0383 (TTY)
www.usdoj.gov
www.ada.gov

The U.S. Department of Transportation
(202) 366-1656 (voice)
(202) 366-4567 (TTY)
www.dot.gov U.S. Access Board

Marcela Abadi Rhoads, AIA RAS
Abadi Accessibility
www.abadiaccess.com
e-mail: marhoads@abadiaccess.com

Wally Tirado, ICC RAS
NORTEX Code, LLC
Building Codes Consultant
www.nortexcode.com
e-mail: wally@nortexcode.com

National Clearinghouse for Educational Facilities
www.ncef.org/

Greg Hunteman, AIA RAS
Pi Architects Inc.
www.piarch.com

Jeromy Murphy, AIA RAS
www.acico.com
e-mail: jmurphy@acico.com

AIA Academy of Architecture for Health
www.aia.org/AAH

SAGE Federation
Society for Advanced Gerontological Environments
www.sagefederation.org

Index

A
ABA (Architectural Barriers Act), xiii, xiv
Accessible Means Egress. *See* Means Egress
Accessible Routes, 9, 13, 28, 32, 66, 120, 129, 135, 186, 210, 216
ADA (Americans with Disabilities Act), xiv, 27, 179, 183
Addition(s), 247, 248
Aisle Seats, 162, 165, 176,177. *See* Designated Aisle Seats
Alteration(s), 164, 171, 179, 184, 185, 236–250
Amusement Ride(s), 217, 219, 221, 225, 226
ANSI/BHMA, xiv
Apartments, 261–263
Area Sport Activity, 123, 126–128
ASME, 18
Assembly Area(s), 108–109, 122–123, 129–130, 140–142
Assisted Living, 184, 191, 198
Assistive Listening System(s), 141
ASTM, 216–217
Attics, 266
ATMs, 285. *See* Automatic Teller Machines

B
Balconies, 266
Bar, 58, 168
Barrier Removal, 171, 179
Basements, 266
Bathing Facilities, 269
Bathing Rooms, 269
Bathtub, 173, 177, 270
Beds, 173, 174, 176, 178
Benches, 104, 146, 189. *See* also Judges' Benches
Boat Slips, 257, 313
Bus Shelters/Stops, 64, 112, 118
Business Center, 161

C
Cafeterias, 110–111, 151. *See* Restaurants and Cafeterias
Changes in Level, 16
Children, Provisions for, 89
Clear Floor or Ground Space, 3
Clearances, 3, 4, 5
Closets, 9, 51, 266
Clothes Dryers, 171, 188, 263
Coat Hooks, 46, 196
College, 117, 123, 135, 142, 148, 150, 154. *See also* Higher Education, University
Common Use, 52
Common Use Circulation Paths, 5
Communication Features, 23, 173, 174, 175, 176
Communication Systems. *See* Two-Way Communication Systems
Companion Seats, 122, 125, 129, 130, 240
Condominiums, 262
Cooktop, 154, 155, 268

Correctional Facilities. *See* Detention and Correctional Facilities
Counters, Sales and Service, 44, 76, 88, 90, 123, 142–144, 153–154, 167
Countertops, 266, 267
Court Sport, 123, 126–128
Cross Slope, 9, 36
Curb Ramp, 35, 36

D
Detectable Warnings, 289, 292
Detention and Correctional Facilities, 247, 259
Dimensions, 1
Dining Areas, 56, 89, 151, 168, 249
Dining Surfaces, 56, 150, 151, 168, 189
Dishwasher, 267
Door Swing, 21, 44
Doors, Doorways, and Gates, 10, 16–17, 38, 39, 47, 66, 79, 126, 128, 194, 242, 297
Doorbells, 173, 270
Dormitories, 163–164, 260–262
Dressing, Fitting, and Locker Rooms, 44–46, 104, 106, 146–147, 188–189, 249, 277
Drinking Fountains, 41–42, 56, 98, 114, 185, 244, 294
Dryers. *See* Washing Machines and Clothes Dryers
Dumpsters (Trash Enclosures), 264
Duplexes, 261
Dwelling Units, 248, 259, 265

E
Edge Protection, 9, 16, 229, 289
Elevators, 17–19, 40, 74, 75, 175, 242, 254, 283, 285, 289–290
Employee Work Area, 46, 50, 86, 87, 88, 150, 154, 171, 190
Entrances, 16, 28, 29, 32, 38, 66, 186, 242
Equivalent Facilitation, 274
Exam rooms, 185, 190–191
Exercise Machine, 143, 145, 168, 169
Existing Facilities, 164, 235–236, 251
Exits. *See* Means Egress

F
Fair Housing Act, 75, 159, 164, 248, 260, 262, 270
Figures
– ADA Figure 305.3, 3
– ADA Figure 307.2, 5
– ADA Figure 308.2.1, 7
– ADA Figure 308.3.1, 7
– ADA Figure 308.2.2, 8
– ADA Figure 308.3.2, 8
– ADA Figure 402.5.1, 9
– ADA Figure 406.4, 10
– ADA Figure 302.3, 15
– ADA Figure 604.8.1.1, 20
– ADA Figure 604.8.2, 20
– ADA Figure 608.3.1, 22
– ADA Figure 608.3.2, 23
– ADA Figure 406.4, 35
– ADA Figure 903.4, 46
– ADA Figure 802.2.1, 138
– ADA Figure 802.2.2, 138
– ADA Figure 608.2.2, 174
– ADA Figure 608.5.3, 197
– ADA Figure 1008.3.1, 214
– ADA Figure 1008.3.2, 215
– ADA Figure 1002.4.4.3, .226
– ADA Figure 1005.3.2, 230
– ADA Figure 904.4, 249
Fire Alarm Systems, 173, 176, 188, 270
Fire Stations, 261
Fishing Piers and Platforms, 229, 230
Floor or Ground Surfaces, 216, 217, 228
Food Service Lines, 56, 58, 60, 168, 190
Forward Reach. *See* Reach Ranges
Fitness, 168, 169, 170, 249, 265

G
Garages, 10, 12, 29, 30, 72, 74, 188, 266
Gates, 126, 128. *See* Doors, Doorways, and Gates
General Exceptions, 161, 232, 306, 310
Grandfather(ing), 178, 179, 235. *See* F203.2 Existing Elements
Ground Level Play Components, 60, 82, 204, 206, 210, 211, 213, 233, 304, 311. *See* Play Areas
Ground Surfaces, 83, 111, 216, 217, 233, 304, 311. *See* Floor or Ground Surfaces
Group Homes, 246, 259, 260, 262, 269
Guest Rooms 156, 163, 164, 173, 174, 175, 179, 180, 181, 246, 247, 259, 261, 262, 271, 272, 308, 314. *See* Transient Lodging

H
Halfway Houses, 246, 260, 262
Handrails, 9, 16, 106, 107, 108, 162, 214, 243, 257, 275, 280, 301, 307, 313
Higher Education, 117, 148
Historic Buildings and Facilities, 244, 252, 253, 254, 255, 311, 312
Historic Preservation, 235, 244, 252, 253, 254, 311. *See* Historic Buildings and Facilities
Holding Cells, 154, 156, 199, 244, 247, 256, 309, 312. *See* Cells
Hospitals, 12, 183, 184, 186, 194, 198, 199, 246, 309. *See* Medical Care Facilities
Hospitality, 148, 163, 179, 307
Hotels, 163, 164, 165, 167, 171, 173, 174, 175, 177, 178, 179, 246, 260, 274. *See* Transient Lodging
Housing Cells, 199, 256, 309, 312. *See* Cells

I
Intercity Rail, 255, 256, 312

K
Kitchens and Kitchenettes, 19, 60, 87, 150, 151, 154, 155, 159, 171, 173, 190, 192, 248, 261, 262, 266, 267, 268, 315
Knee and Toe Clearance, 50, 89, 96, 102, 111, 165, 168, 267, 268, 269

L
Laundry Rooms, 171, 263
Lavatories, 54, 78, 97, 102, 103, 105, 114, 188, 196, 198, 236
Lavatory, 21, 50, 52, 80, 97, 192, 195 196, 197, 269, 270
Leases, 75, 121, 136, 159, 202, 246, 261, 263
Leasing Office, 75, 263, 264
Light Rail, 223
Light Switches, 173, 266
Limited-Use/Limited-Application Elevators, 18
Lines of Sight, 138, 162, 298, 299, 307
Lockers, 95, 106, 156, 157, 170, 171. *See also* Storage
Locker Rooms, 46, 122, 129, 146, 147, 151, 164, 173, 177, 185, 186, 189, 236, 249. *See* Dressing, Fitting, and Locker Rooms
Long-Term Care Facilities, 164, 183, 184, 186, 188, 189, 191, 193, 194, 198, 199, 247, 259, 309

M
Mail Boxes, 249, 264, 272, 314
Maneuvering Clearances, 10, 17, 46, 47, 71, 87, 177, 194, 195, 196, 197, 225
Means Egress, 91,242
Medical Care Facilities, 164,199, 244, 245, 259, 309
Meeting Rooms, 164, 167, 168
Mezzanine, 143,168, 249
Mirrors, 50, 102, 114, 115, 196, 299, 305
Mobility Features, 158, 159, 173, 174, 175, 176, 180, 210, 247, 260, 261, 262, 263, 264, 265, 266, 309
Motels, 163, 173, 179, 246. *See* Transient Lodging
Multi-Story Buildings and Facilities, 180

N
NFPA, 188, 270

O
Occupational Therapy, 190, 192
Openings, 15, 153, 223, 264, 286
Operable Parts, 168, 190, 266
Outlets, 173, 195, 236, 266, 293

P
Parking, xiv, 9, 10, 12, 13, 14, 28, 29, 30, 31, 32, 33, 34, 63, 66, 67, 68, 72, 73, 74, 112, 118, 120, 121, 122, 127, 164, 165, 186, 187, 188, 202, 240, 241, 250, 263, 264, 271, 314
Passenger Loading Zones, 112, 113, 164, 165, 186
Path travel, 6, 15, 17, 37, 40, 52, 53, 164, 179, 185, 239, 240, 241, 242, 243, 244, 249, 250, 251, 252, 255, 265, 289, 311
Patios, 36, 66, 71, 163, 173, 176, 266
Peephole, 270
Performance Areas, 108, 135
Physical Therapy, 187, 188
Picnic Areas, 265

Platform Lifts, 82, 162, 180, 232, 255, 304, 307, 308, 310, 312
Play Areas, 28, 52, 60, 61, 62, 82, 83, 86, 111, 115, 171, 201, 204, 205, 206, 207, 210, 217, 232, 233, 265, 303, 304, 305, 310, 311
Player Seating, 122, 123, 125
Plumbing Fixtures, 6, 18, 115, 188, 190, 195, 305
Pools, 148, 149, 170, 171, 180, 181, 184, 201, 265, 308. *See also* Wading Pools
Press Boxes, 123, 126, 161, 306
Primary Function, 164, 184, 185, 186, 236, 238, 239, 240, 251, 252, 254, 255, 265, 271, 311, 314
Prisons, 163, 199, 247, 309
Privately Funded Housing, 261
Private Residence Elevators, 272, 315
Protruding Objects, 5, 6, 52, 78, 81, 98, 99, 237, 241
Psychiatric Facilities, 183, 199, 309
Public Entrance, 252, 254. *See also* Entrances
Public Spaces, 46, 52, 153, 263
Public Transportation, 112, 118, 164, 263
Public Use, 112, 129, 159, 186, 188, 261, 263, 272, 315

Q
Qualified Historic Building or Facility, 252, 253, 254, 255, 311, 312

R
Ramp(s), 9, 10, 14, 16, 36, 73, 106, 114, 165, 171, 203, 211 - 214, 216, 250, 265, 289
Range, 88, 267, 268
Reach Ranges, 7–8, 18, 46, 48, 50, 52, 54, 92, 93, 105, 143 150, 156, 167, 168, 166, 176, 194, 196, 197, 207, 209, 221, 237, 264, 266, 267, 294
Readily Achievable, 164, 166, 170, 171, 176, 178, 179, 235, 242, 244, 246
Recreation Facilities. *See* Amusement Rides, Boating Facilities, Exercise Machines, Fishing Piers and Platforms, Golf, Miniature Golf, Saunas and Steam Rooms, Shooting Facilities, Swimming Pools, Wading Pools, or Spas
Recreational Boating Facilities. *See* Boating Facilities
Recycling Areas, 164
Refrigerators, 151, 261
Registration Counter, 153, 166, 167
Rehabilitation Facilities. *See* Medical Care Facilities
Religious Facilities, 262
Resident Room Bathrooms, 194, 196
- dispensers 195, 196
- mirrors 196
- shelves 196
- sinks 196

Residential, 28, 72, 75, 159, 163, 164, 192, 244, 246, 248, 259–70
Residential Dwelling Unit, 164, 244, 246, 248, 259–65, 269
Residential Facilities, 75, 159, 163, 246, 259–63, 271
Restaurants, 56, 249
Restaurants and Cafeterias, 108, 110, 151
Restrooms, 6, 7, 18, 19, 21, 28, 40, 46, 48, 50, 52, 53, 54, 75, 78, 80, 81, 94, 151, 154, 164, 173, 177, 179, 185, 186, 188, 190, 201, 203, 236–38, 243, 244, 250, 263, 265, 293
Retail, 27, 28, 38, 40, 41, 43, 44, 46, 61, 72, 72, 81, 163, 166, 167, 249
Roll-in showers. *See* showers – roll in
Running Slope, 9, 36, 70

S
Safe Harbor, xiv, 169, 170, 178, 244, 245, 251
Sales and Service, .257, 313
Saunas, 170, 171, 180, 181, 308
Seats, Tub and Shower, 181, 197, 260, 270, 308
Section 504 Rehabilitation Act, 159, 260, 265
Security Barriers, 128, 129
Service Counter, 44, 56, 76, 88, 89, 90, 123, 142, 143, 144, 153, 154, 166, 168, 189, 249, 257, 313
Shelters, 118, 246, 260, 262

Shelves, 41, 46, 56, 58, 95, 142, 159, 166, 168, 194, 196
Shopping Center, 12, 18, 19, 27, 28, 29, 30, 39, 40, 54, 60, 61, 63, 64, 65, 66, 67, 68, 72, 82, 210, 274, 303
Shower, 21, 22, 23, 122, 146, 147, 148, 164, 170, 171, 173, 174, 175, 178, 181, 189, 190, 192, 193, 196, 197, 198, 199, 260, 262, 270, 272, 308, 309, 315
- clearance, 196, 197, 198
- compartments, 147
- controls, 197
- roll in, 22, 23, 146, 173, 174, 175, 178, 193, 196, 197, 260, 262
- rooms, 146, 147, 164, 170, 190, 192
- seats, 181, 197, 260, 308
- transfer, 21, 22, 173, 196, 197
- threshold, 197

Sidewalk, 9, 14, 15, 16, 28, 34, 35, 36, 37, 63, 64, 66, 68, 164, 240, 263, 278
Signs (or sinage), 16, 21, 23, 24, 25, 38, 39, 54, 104, 107, 154, 236, 283, 286
Single Family, 261
Sinks, 10, 50, 87, 97, 102, 103, 104, 105, 114, 132, 133, 134, 154, 155, 185, 190, 196, 236, 260, 267
Site Access, 122, 164
Site Arrival Points, 9, 28, 29, 63, 82, 118, 202, 240, 241, 252, 254, 255, 303, 312
Sleeping Rooms, 159, 163, 183, 185, 191, 193, 194, 244, 245, 246, 260, 261, 262, 263
- closets, 159, 194, 266
- doors, 173, 194
- windows, 173, 194

Slope. *See* Running Slope or Cross Slope
Snack Bars, 168
Social Service Center, 260, 262, 271, 314
Spas, 170, 171, 174, 180, 181, 308
Sport Areas, 118, 123, 126, 128, 150, 265
Stairs and Escalators in Existing Buildings, 255, 312
Steam Rooms, 171, 180, 181, 308
Storage, 6, 48, 50, 51, 78, 86, 92, 142, 146, 151, 154, 157, 159, 173, 185, 186, 190, 191, 196, 236, 250, 266, 267
Strip Shopping Center, 28, 61, 63, 64, 66, 67, 68, 72
Swimming Pools, 148, 170, 171, 180, 181, 201, 265, 308

T

Team or Player Seating, 122, 123, 125
Teeing Grounds, 256, 312
Telephones, 23, 52, 54, 55, 76, 78, 156, 158, 164, 167, 173, 179, 185, 239, 243, 244, 250, 251, 265, 270, 275, 290
Temporary Facilities, 129, 168, 172, 219, 236, 246, 260, 262
Tenant Spaces, 66, 71
Thermostats, 173, 176, 266
Thresholds, 176, 197, 256, 257, 313
Title II ADA, 159, 247, 260, 265
Toe Clearance, 50, 89, 96, 99, 102, 111, 115, 165, 168, 267, 268, 269, 305. *See also* Knee and Toe Clearance
Toilet Compartments, 97, 99, 100, 115, 244, 305
Townhouses, 158, 159, 180, 261, 263, 307, 308
Transient Lodging, 156, 158, 159, 163, 164, 173, 179, 180, 181, 244, 246, 256, 259, 260, 261, 262, 263, 270, 271, 272, 307, 308, 312, 314
Transportation Facilities, 86, 112, 185
TTY, 54, 173, 250, 270
Turning Space, 44, 60, 87, 154, 159, 171, 173, 176, 190, 194, 207, 210, 217, 221, 229, 261, 262, 266
Two-Way Communication Systems, 88

U

Uniform Federal Accessibility Standards (UFAS), 260
Unisex, 53, 78, 185, 188, 244, 249, 250, 253
University, 132, 148, 156, 163, 261. *See also* Higher Education
Urinals, 19, 21, 188

V

Valet Parking, 165
Van Parking Spaces, 13, 14, 31, 74, 120, 263, 264

Vending Machines, 150, 171, 190, 237
Vertical Clearance, 3, 165, 186

W
Wading Pools, 180, 181, 308
Waivers, 250. *See also* Modifications and Waivers
Walking Surfaces, 106
Washing Machines, 188, 263
Water Closet, 7, 19, 21, 50, 51, 52, 78, 97, 99, 101, 102, 114, 115, 188, 195, 269, 272, 305, 315
Wheelchair Spaces, 109, 123, 124, 126, 129, 130, 132, 135, 140, 141, 150, 151, 152, 161, 162, 225, 226, 232, 306, 307, 310
Whirlpool Tubs, 190, 192
Windows, 77, 88, 161, 173, 176, 194, 236, 266, 272, 306, 314
Work Surfaces, 54, 92, 97, 114, 115, 142, 145, 153, 159, 189, 261, 262, 267, 268, 272, 305, 315